This book is due for return on or before the last date shown below.

EXPERIENTIAL MARKETING

A practical guide to interactive
brand experiences

SHAZ SMILANSKY

KoganPage

LONDON PHILADELPHIA NEW DELHI

First published in Great Britain and the United States in 2009 by
Kogan Page Limited
Reprinted 2010, 2012, 2013

120 Pentonville Road	1518 Walnut Street, Suite 1100	4737/23 Ansari Road
London N1 9JN	Philladelphia PA 19102	Daryaganj
United Kingdom	USA	New Delhi 110002
www.koganpage.com		India

© Shaz Smilansky, 2009

ISBN 978 0 7494 5275 9

British Library Cataloguing-in-Publication Data

A CIP record for this book is available from the British Library.

Library of Congress Cataloging-in-Publication Data

Smilansky, Shaz.
   Experiential marketing : a practical guide to interactive brand experiences / Shaz Smilansky.
      p. cm.
   ISBN 978-0-7494-5275-9
   1. Branding (Marketing) 2. Target marketing. I. Title.
   HF5415.1255.S55 2008
   658.8'27--dc22
                                                      2008039199

Typeset by JS Typesetting Ltd, Porthcawl, Mid Glamorgan
Print production managed by Jellyfish
Printed and bound by CPI Group (UK) Ltd, Croydon, CR0 4YY

Contents

Foreword

In an age of information clutter and privacy theft, today's time-poor and cash-rich customers are erecting barriers to many of the traditional communications tools. Experiential Marketing (ExM) breaks through these barriers and nurtures brand relationships amongst potential advocates.

This book explains how ExM's added value, multi-sensory, interactive, engaging brand experiences go beyond boosting brand awareness and embed an emotional brand connection deep in the minds of the target market. This emotional connection is the link between the brand personality and values and the customer's feelings. This requires an engaging experience relevant to both the customer's desires and, of course, the brand's personality. ExM creates 'dazzling sensory and interactive experiences delivering memorable brand moments'.

Although this is a highly creative area, it is underpinned by a thorough management process. Shaz Smilansky reveals how ExM is 'a process of identifying, satisfying customer needs and aspirations, profitably, by engaging them through two-way communications that bring brand personalities to life and add value to the target audience's experience'. The key is to involve the audience intellectually, physically and emotionally. This book shows how.

It also triggers new questions in an era of rapid change for marketing. Is CEM (Customer Experience Management) part of CRM or should CRM be part of CMR (Customer Managed Relationships), particularly since the web invites customers to take more control and create, in classic marketing parlance, customer-driven marketing?

As consumers aspire to the lifestyles that their favourite brands portray, ExM helps consumers be a part of the brand and its associations. Companies like Disney, PlayStation, Red Bull, Sony, Nike, Ben & Jerrys and Innocent place ExM at the heart of their marketing strategies.

Instead of being perceived as an expensive peripheral tactical tool, ExM can be part of the core strategy to bond with customers, develop advocates and accelerate word-of-mouth. This is not just integrated marketing communications, but integrated marketing.

Although deemed expensive on a cost per thousand (CPT) basis, ExM can be more effective on a CPTBA (cost per thousand brand advocates) basis. ExM has an exponential component, as consumers are encouraged to spread the word by mouth and mouse.

This is a creative book, yet thorough in its approach to risk reduction with risk assessment, careful planning and constant measurement. It demonstrates systems and processes for brainstorming, developing ideas, pitching and reducing risk to razor-sharp execution and, ultimately, gauging effectiveness to continually improve ExM's return on investment. Read on.

P R Smith

P R Smith is author of the best-selling book Marketing Communications, *also published by Kogan Page, and creator of the SOSTAC® Marketing Planning System.*

Acknowledgements

I would like to thank the following people for the support, contributions, inspiration and encouragement that they gave to me while writing this book: Marvin Foster, Eva Fedderly, Olga Ilyasova, Jonathan and Alex Smilansky, Errica Moustaki, Boo and Racoon, P R Smith, Annika Knight and her team at Kogan Page, the team at Blazinstar Experiential and Staff Warehouse, the 7Wonders & Cantaladies, David Polinchock CXO, Richard and Kirsten, Live Marketing USA, Erik Hauser, EMF, Kevin Jackson, Jack Morton Worldwide, Justin Singh, Spero Patricios, Ian Whiteling, Events Review, Paul Ephremsen, ID brand experience, Sarah, Lambert and Bloch, Matt Shoard, and also everyone at Experiential News, VIP Ideas, 5Senses, OOTB, EMF, Onepartners Brand Experience Group, Brand Experience Lab, Adscreens, DHC, Palm, Akvinta Vodka, MediaCom, and Launch Factory.

Introduction

Consumers are constantly inundated with repetitive traditional advertising messages, bombarding their lives, interrupting their TV shows and generally getting in the way. It is true that if you see an ad enough times, it is likely that at some point when you are ready to purchase, it will come to mind. That is not to say that consumers are buying because they have a real emotional connection with the brand; usually it is simply because the brand that shouted the loudest got their attention. This outdated approach to marketing communications is dying, and fast.

Brands are realizing that to secure the lifetime value of their customers by gaining true customer loyalty, they must give back. The relationships between brands and their target audiences are being revolutionized. The new marketing era, the experiential marketing era, focuses on giving target audiences a fabulous brand-relevant customer experience that adds value to their lives, and ultimately makes the consumer remember the brand's marketing – not because it shouted the loudest, but because it gave them an unforgettable experience.

People talk about experiences every day because life is ultimately an amalgamation of daily experiences. Experiences are real. They are true life. If someone is going about their daily lives as usual, and within their normal routine they engage in a positive brand experience, then that consumer will be likely to discuss or mention it to most of the people that they interact with for the rest of the day or even week. By giving something positive back to the people who spend their hard-earned cash purchasing your products and services, you are strengthening and building a real relationship between your customers and brands.

Experiential marketing is a methodology that is fast revolutionizing the face of marketing as we know it. This book is a practical guide to experiential marketing, and by applying the experiential methodology to their marketing communications, readers will find that their consumers will become brand advocates and even brand evangelists, who give personal recommendations, ultimately doing the most important marketing for them.

This book strives to clarify how experiential marketing fits within the current marketing climate, and how to go about planning, activating and evaluating it for best results. By providing many examples (both real and generic) focused on customer interactions, it illustrates how experiential marketing can be applied to every sector, with every target audience, and can best utilize every marketing communications channel. It addresses many myths and criticisms about the cost, reach and measurement capacities of experiential marketing, also distinguishing between the terms 'experiential marketing' and 'live brand experience'.

Live brand experiences, that is, brand-relevant, two-way communications between consumers and brands, can be delivered face to face or remotely. These live experiences, designed to bring brand personalities to life while adding value to the consumer, are at the core of the experiential marketing approach detailed in this book. The philosophy is simple. The other, non-live (both traditional and innovative) marketing communication channels are then inspired by the live brand experience, and integrated around it to amplify the impact of the big idea.

The content of this book is weaved around tried-and-tested creative, planning and activation models that facilitate best practice and generate successful experiential marketing campaigns. Suitable for readers from client, agency or business backgrounds alike, the book aims to demonstrate to the reader an experiential marketing philosophy and planning framework that can be applied to every consumer touch point, and to all marketing communications.

This book aims to serve as a blueprint for the new marketer: the experiential marketer.

1 Why experiential?

The context: marketing communication

Marketing communication messages, through media or other marketing channels, exist to communicate with different consumers or business sectors. Marketing communication channels traditionally include advertising, direct mail, packaging and sales promotion, along with the relatively more recent prominence of sponsorship, public relations, digital and live brand experiences. The selected channels need to be integrated to maximize the impact of a campaign and more effectively achieve marketing communication objectives.

This book focuses on experiential marketing as a key approach for achieving marketing objectives. The experiential approach is focused on a two-way interaction in real-time, a live brand experience and thereby a significantly deeper consumer bonding process. Live brand experiences usually manifest in the form of live events that allow the consumer to live, breathe and feel the brand through interactive sensory connections and activities. The activities are usually designed to add value to target audiences in their own environments, during their natural existence. However, live brand experiences are simply live, two-way branded experiences, and can be equally successful across many interactive technologies and platforms that facilitate communication between consumers and brands in real time. For example, consumers can participate in live brand experiences on TV where the shows' content is fluid, and they participate in it and contribute to it in real time. Likewise, a live brand experience can be activated online in a virtual world such as second life. It is the recommendation of this book that marketers place live brand experiences at the core of their marketing communications strategies.

But live brand experiences are rarely done alone and the sophisticated marketing executive will integrate them with the rest of their marketing efforts utilizing a broad array of channels. Marketers go to each channel to achieve different goals and objectives. Advertising is usually implemented to achieve brand awareness and to gain recognition of the brand or product within mass markets. Advertising has high 'reach' and is typically effective at raising awareness but is expensive to implement on an effective scale. When used on a large scale, advertising can have a low CPT (cost per thousand), but overall it is an expensive tool and can normally only be used to great effect by market-leading brands that can afford to run large-scale campaigns.

Direct mail, which can involve posting marketing materials directly to people's homes, can be used as part of CRM (customer relationship management) programmes, in order to engage consumers for a direct response or sale at home. Packaging is important to every brand as it communicates a brand identity to the consumer through the colours, shape and overall look and feel of the product.

Sales promotion involves driving sales in the retail environment through special offers, discounts, rewards and vouchers. Field marketing activities (such as in-store promotional staff, field sales, auditing, mystery shopping, merchandising and sampling) are generally classified within the sales promotion channel.

Sponsorship is a great tool for brands that target niche audiences; it can earn credibility and communicate with an audience in their preferred environment. Traditionally, sponsorship is a practice that involves branding at sporting and cultural events, and others at which there is a desired association with the event or people at hand. Sponsorship aligns the brand directly with people's current perceptions of the company or event in question.

Public relations (PR) is the process of managing the flow of information between an organization and its public. Its activities include award ceremonies, celebrity endorsements, press and media relations, and events that aim to project a positive image of an organization to its key stakeholders.

Digital is one of the fastest growing marketing channels in a fluid technological age. Consumers are connecting with brands online more than ever before, and digital can be a cost-effective channel for generating word-of-mouth online (otherwise known as word-of-web). Viral marketing is also an emerging discipline, which is part of the digital spectrum: a successful viral campaign creates word-of-web at exponential rates, allowing a message to travel as fast as a virus, hence the name.

These marketing channels traditionally work together, currently delivering successful campaigns worldwide for global brands and small businesses alike. Although brands and companies benefit from using these channels, marketers worldwide are looking for new ways to utilize these channels to their full potential in order to engage their target audiences on a deeper level, and build relationships that create loyalty and brand advocacy. Experiential marketers are converting their consumers from shoppers (who can be disloyal at times and promiscuous with their choice of brands) into brand evangelists who preach the brand, its personality and core message or features to their friends, families, colleagues and communities.

These brand evangelists are building brands at the speed of light. They are not only communicating messages that traditional marketing could likewise do, but are creating something unique: a personal recommendation. This golden brand bond is priceless. Think back to the last time you went to eat in a restaurant. Did you go there because you heard it was good, or because you saw an advert in a magazine saying it was? Or when a friend rants and raves about a new miracle cleaning product that removed seven stains from her white tablecloths, and you pass that same cleaning product in the aisle on your next supermarket visit – do you think you'll give it a try? The answer is *yes!*

Word-of-mouth is priceless, and leads us to the all-important question: which marketing communication channel or approach drives consumers to spread word-of-mouth? Today's consumers are bored of being inundated with endless invasive adverts and messages urging them to buy products that drown in a sea of noise. They want brands to engage with them, to add value to their lives, to give something back. Consumers aspire to lifestyles that their favourite brands portray; they want to be a part of the brand and what is associated with it, and they want to immerse themselves in the brands they love. Once they become loyal, they start to do your marketing for you. This is why the marketing world of today, and leading brands, are competing in a new era: the era of experiential marketing.

What is experiential marketing?

Experiential marketing is the process of identifying and satisfying customer needs and aspirations profitably, engaging them through two-way communications that bring brand personalities to life and add value to the target audience:

- Experiential marketing is an integrated methodology, always engaging target audiences at their will through brand-relevant communications that add value.
- The experiential marketing campaign is built around one big idea that should involve two-way communication between the brand and the target audience in real time, therefore featuring a live brand experience at its core.
- The other marketing communications channels that are selected and integrated are the amplification channels, which amplify the impact of the big idea (the live brand experience) – see Figure 1.1.

The purpose of this book is to ensure that the next time you read about which marketing approaches are most effective, there will be no doubt that experiential marketing will be at the top of the list. This is the future strategy behind successful marketing communication. It is experiential marketing, the two-way experience-oriented strategy.

AIDA is an acronym used in marketing. It describes a process that marketers aim to take the consumer through when marketing a product:

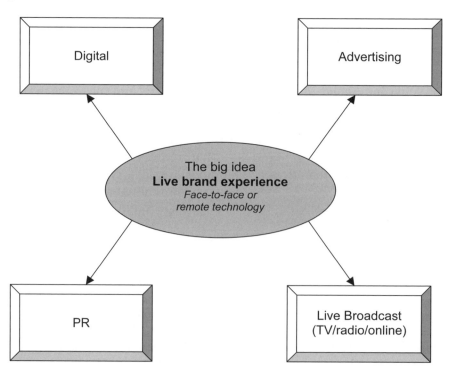

Figure 1.1 Amplification channels

Awareness: the attention or awareness of the customer (advertising would be a favourite for this stage).
Interest: we traditionally raise consumer interest by creating public conversation or demonstrating features and benefits (PR is a favourite for this).
Desire: convince customers that they want the product or service and that it will satisfy their needs.
Action: the all-important stage leading customers towards a purchase (face-to-face sales or sales promotions are mostly used here).

There have been other additions to the AIDA model, such as S for Satisfaction. Satisfy the customer so he or she becomes a repeat customer and recommends the product. This shift is in line with the emerging focus and emphasis on word-of-mouth and personal recommendation.

Live brand experiences, especially when integrated into a broader experiential marketing campaign, can be effective for achieving each of the AIDA stages. Take the A for Awareness. Live brand experiences are sometimes accused of being ineffective at reaching large numbers of consumers, but this is far from the truth. In some situations, the live brand experience, which is at the core of the experiential campaign (in many cases the live brand experience is delivered face to face), may only have a reach of, say, 500,000 people. This figure should not be taken at face value, because it has been shown that consumers who engage in a live brand experience are likely to tell 17 people.[1] Therefore, that 500,000 quickly grows into millions when factoring in the word-of-mouth reach. Research shows that each of those people who heard about the live brand experience is likely to tell an additional one-and-a-half people, skyrocketing the reach of the campaign even further. Word-of-mouth truly is the most effective marketing tool of all.

Live brand experiences can certainly be used in the I stage of AIDA, to create Interest by engaging consumers, not only demonstrating features, advantages and benefits of a product, but more importantly interacting with the target audience through brand-relevant engagement. In fact, what better way to stimulate interest and convey a brand personality or message than to allow consumers to immerse themselves in the essence of the brand as well as to try the product, play around with it, eat it, drink it, touch it or press it? It does not matter what the product is; if you can get its core brand values into the everyday lives of your target audience through pleasant interaction, and at the same time engage them and let them try it, then you can truly demonstrate your brand positioning, and your USPs, converting a customer into an advocate.

Likewise, you can also use live brand experiences at the D stage in AIDA, to provoke Desire by creating experiences that communicate the aspirations of the target audience, creating the subconscious sense that using the product or service will bring them the lifestyle that they desire.

Sales promotion is traditionally a tool that is effective at driving people to action and leading the consumer towards taking a final purchase decision (when that decision to purchase is primarily influenced by cost). Statistics prove that live brand experiences (which should be placed at the core of the experiential marketing strategy) are more likely to drive purchase decisions than almost any marketing channel.[2]

When planning your marketing channels around the AIDA or AIDAS model, it is important to approach every channel with an experiential marketing ethos. If you embrace two-way, experiential marketing communication and place the live brand experience (delivered face-to-face or remotely) at a core part of your broader marketing communications strategy, the results will speak for themselves.

Traditional approaches are losing effectiveness

Marketers are finding through extensive research that traditional media channels and one-way communications are losing their effectiveness. This can be attributed to many different factors, such as Generation X and Y, media fragmentation, noise/clutter and the emergence of interactive technologies. The internet generation (aka Generation Y: those born between 1980 and 1995), are a media-savvy generation adverse to obvious marketing and advertising ploys. This is the iPod generation. While mass media and traditional advertising are being shunned by this demographic, online social networking media such as Facebook and MySpace are growing exponentially and demonstrate the power of word-of-mouth via word-of-web.

Technology is another factor that is leading to the decline in the success of traditional media channels. TV advertising still boasts the biggest budget slices in the marketing cake, but consumers are using technology to actively avoid the very adverts that cost millions to produce and air. TiVo in the United States, Sky Plus in the United Kingdom, plus countless other brands with copycat technology, allow consumers to fast-forward and rewind past adverts.

The fragmentation of TV channels is another familiar challenge for marketing and advertising professionals, with hundreds or even thousands of TV channels allowing consumers endless choice. It is hard to decide how to plan a TV advertising budget effectively without having to water it down across countless TV channels, or spend a big budget that generates low ROI.

Pop-up blockers allow web surfers to block annoying adverts that invade their screens and spam filters eradicate many of the online e-marketing attempts. Soon, technology will allow consumers to pick and choose which messages they consume across the board, and this creates a further challenge.

As marketers, we must think creatively and engage with consumers in ways that make them want brand communication. We want them to choose not only to receive messages, but to communicate back with the brand and their immediate peers and publics. This raised level of business consciousness we are experiencing around the world is elevating us to a new marketing era: that of experiential marketing. In the experiential marketing era, the consumer and the employees of a company are equally part of its marketing as its ad agencies and marketing department.

Experiential marketing: a differentiator

In the business world, commoditization is a process where unique brands and products compete. As a result, standards are raised and equalized, forcing brands into undifferentiated price competition. In the early days of marketing and advertising, companies used to focus on differentiation based on the product features and benefits. As competition forced rival brands to create competitive products, price wars began lowering the cost of products and driving consumers to make cost-based purchase decisions. Thanks to innovators in the mid-20th century such as Ogilvy, advertising was revolutionized and brands evolved, taking on unique personalities. Through customer-focused marketing communications, they encouraged consumers to aspire to a lifestyle that the brand represented. Thus began the shift from a product-focused era to the customer-focused, brand and lifestyle inspired advertising era. This marked a shift from a rational message to an emotional message, or a combination of both.

As competitive brands were positioned similarly to each other, and differentiation became difficult again, consumers started to demand more. Successful companies realized that high-quality service was an excellent way to add value and differentiate from their competitors; for example, adding free delivery to a video chain or picking up customers from their home to take them to the car rental shop. As time went on, fierce competition snowballed with competitors all offering relatively similar added-value services with their products, or by adding relatively similar added-value products to their services. Lifestyle branding and differentiation through service became the norm. Again, once there are no clear points of differentiation, price becomes a primary differentiating factor. Clearly, this is not desirable from a marketing perspective.

The growing popularity during the late 20th century of relationship marketing, which focuses on long-term relationships with customers and customer retention, saw a rise in the investment in CRM (customer relationship management) programmes that aim to drive customer loyalty through frequent communication and reward programmes.

The next level of thinking on the subject of maintaining customer loyalty is CEM (customer experience management), defined as 'the process of strategically managing a customer's entire experience with a product or a company'.[3] CEM is at the frontier of successful loyalty-driven programmes, taking companies into an era where the primary and most valuable way they can differentiate themselves is through a brand immersive experience at every customer touch point. Successful CEM programmes build the consumer's experience with an organization, ensuring that every step of his or her journey (from the retail environment to the customer services phone attendants) is brand relevant, differentiated and positive.

Experiential marketing allows brands to engage with their target audiences through initiatives and engagements that aim to achieve marketing communication objectives, and add value to consumers' lives. When CEM is partnered with experiential marketing (the innovative methodology that facilitates positive brand-relevant two-way communications with target audiences); astonishing business results can be achieved. By successfully implementing a CEM orientation throughout every department of an organization, and then reaching out and communicating with target audiences through experiential marketing campaigns, organizations can successfully convert consumers into brand advocates.

Today, products that are trying to differentiate through additional free services, or services that are trying to differentiate by additional free products, along with traditional CRM programmes, are all beginning to look like commodities. This is largely due to the full circle that business and marketing have made on their way back to human interaction and two-way engagement. Experience is the new currency of the modern marketing landscape, because experiences are life, and people talk about experiences every day.

Sam is the marketing director at a petrol company that had recently opened a coffee shop in each of its larger outlets but was struggling to differentiate without competing on price. Service was originally its key differentiator and is what allowed it to charge a higher premium for its services in the past. Its competitors had become wise to this, and improved their service, providing little room for differentiation and lack of justification for the higher price. By adding a positive added value and brand-relevant experience, Sam hoped that he could appeal to the commuter who spends long hours on the road and wants to stop for a refreshing, high-quality cup of coffee on his way home. Sam knew he would have to position the brand as a quality choice for premium coffee and sandwiches, as well as petrol; three things that traditionally do not go hand-in-hand. He knew from the market research that their agency conducted, that when consumers refuelled, they often sought a little caffeine to help them stay awake on the road. Nevertheless, the research also uncovered that consumers wouldn't trust the quality of the coffee and have been less likely to purchase it from a petrol station. Therefore, they visited the petrol station with the cheapest petrol rather than the best coffee. The agency creative team came up with the suggestion of creating a live brand experience that could be rolled out across most of the stations. Sam had overlooked the importance of the fact that the coffee beans they used were purchased from fair-trade sources. The experiential campaign would position the coffee brand as being one that cares for people and the environment, with the credibility stemming from the fact that they only used fair trade organic coffee beans and ground each coffee freshly. As an environmentally friendly brand that gives back to the community, the coffee bar was redesigned to show photos of the rainforest farmers who harvest the coffee beans, and gave consumers the chance to win trips to visit the rainforest coffee plants, by answering questions about fair trade coffee and endangered regions. The consumers were also provided with a free sample of coffee when they purchased their fuel, and were encouraged to sign up to a 'care and share' loyalty card that donated money to relevant charities every time they filled their tanks. The broader media campaign was also designed to reflect this initiative, focusing on the fact that the brand and its customers were working hard to counteract the negative effect that the petroleum industry has on the environment and labour. The petrol stations were also fitted with scent machines that emitted the smell of freshly ground coffee beans, further strengthening the front-of-mind affiliation between fair trade quality coffee and the petrol outlet.

Following this integrated campaign there was a dramatic uplift in the number of customers who bought coffee as well as fuel when visiting this chain of gas stations. At this point, the premium rate they were paying became less significant and the competitive pressure and commoditization eased. The reason that this petrol station company wanted to position itself as a caring, environmentally oriented brand was to try to counteract the perceptions that consumers have of the negative effects that petrol and oil cause to the environment and also the affiliation with lack of quality food. By using the experiential marketing concept as part of a creative integrated campaign designed to bring the consumers closer to the brand personality of its coffee shop, it also managed to reposition the brand as a whole. This brought it one step closer to succeeding in its corporate goal of increasing sales and differentiating itself from the competition.

Some companies have implemented experiential marketing strategies for years and confidently differentiated themselves from the competition, forming long-lasting relationships with their target audience and maintaining customer loyalty. They have tantalized the five senses through live brand experience events, and amplified that through their other marketing communication channels. This process adds value to the consumer, and gives something back, paving the way for innovating, market-leading brands. Consumers have gone to amusement parks such as Disneyland, Sea World and Universal Studios for decades, revelling in the universe of their favourite characters and brands. By allowing consumers to touch, smell, taste, see and hear, Disney has created immersive experiential environments that generate an emotive response. For years, this has propelled guests to talk and rave about those memorable events to loved ones and acquaintances alike.

It is no surprise that while the experiential revolution is occurring and marketers are shifting focus from one-way to two-way communication, the same thing is happening in education. World-class educational experts (from kindergarten teachers to quantum physicists) are concluding in unison that when learning, the best way to truly understand and absorb information is through experiencing the problem, the process and the solution. Teachers have always taken kids on field trips to lakes, to help them understand natural biology through engaging with the real thing. They regularly facilitate experiments as a key part of learning. However, it is not only schools and teachers that believe engagement is the key to successfully educating and informing students. London, along with many other cities worldwide, is home to a fascinating science museum, which allows visitors to touch, hear, see and taste, taking them through a journey of staged experiences and interactive tools, all the while communicating key messages. They succeed in educating, informing and achieving their objectives within a creative exploratory environment. Similarly, MOMI (the Museum of the Moving Image) has captured the attention and wonder of film fans for years, allowing them to immerse themselves in a movie-themed environment, which is at once interactive, entertaining, informative and educational. This is how establishments like these spend so little of their budgets on traditional marketing. They know that the consumers who provide their revenue execute their most effective word-of-mouth marketing. When you apply the same principles to a business and marketing context, not only will you increase consumer loyalty and achieve commercial results, but you will also truly add value to your consumers' everyday lives.

Experiential marketing is the process of identifying and satisfying customer needs and aspirations, profitably, engaging them through two-way communications that bring brand personalities to life and adding value to the target audience. Two-way communication and interactive engagement is the key to creating memorable experiences that drive word-of-mouth, and transform consumers into brand advocates and brand evangelists. The power of a personal recommendation is unbeatable. We can all agree that if a consumer feels strongly about your brand, strongly enough to personally recommend it, you have succeeded. The trust between your brand and your consumer is an indicator that a real relationship has been established.

For example, if you went to a dinner date and were not able to 'get a word in', you would assume the person you were with was not interested in you. Likewise, from a consumer perspective, brands that only talk at people, not with them, are not going to develop long-term relationships with their consumers or drive brand loyalty. There is a sense that the brand doesn't care. Two-way engagement is the key to establishing loyal consumers who trust and recommend brands to their peers.

An international survey of senior marketers, conducted by MICE Group, predicts that experiential marketing is set to be a major growth area in the next few years, as senior marketers shift increasing proportions of their marketing budgets to this emerging form. Even though spending in this area has already grown, it is projected that growth will continue at a much higher rate. Marketing communications budgets traditionally have not allocated specific portions to experiential marketing, though it is often perceived to be an independent channel, rather than a methodology. Experiential marketing spend often comes from other allocated budgets such as the PR or below-the-line budget, or the sales promotion budget. Now, many decision makers are realizing that experiential marketing offers considerable advantages compared to the other approaches. They find experiential marketing to be especially useful in achieving objectives that the others find hard to accomplish, such as building brand loyalty, encouraging word-of-mouth, and bringing the brand personality to life. When MICE conducted the survey internationally, it found a majority of respondents (80 per cent) described experience-based activities as being highly important within their marketing mix, accounting for around a third of their entire marketing budget (a percentage that is set to rise in the future).[4]

A lack of suitable and consistent methods for evaluating experiential marketing has been a major criticism faced by the industry. This means experiential marketing is often measured using similar metrics to traditional marketing and advertising (such as opportunity to see) – methods that are far from suitable in measuring the success of the campaign.

At first glance, and after failing to impress in this respect, some people perceive experiential marketing as a tactical tool, rather than as a strategic approach that marketers should consider central to their integrated marketing communications plan. In fact, word-of-mouth reach is so valuable and can expand the campaign's reach to such a massive scale that if experiential marketing were to be measured according to its unique benefits, marketers would find that it is hugely successful in impacting large numbers of people. As with all marketing, this is not always the case if only last-minute tactical activities are implemented. To gain maximum benefits, customer experience management and experiential marketing should be central to the long-term marketing strategy of any brand.

Other key findings that emerged from the research were that nearly all respondents viewed experiential marketing as an effective part of their marketing. There was a general feeling among marketers that experiential marketing provides better ROI than other marketing activities in use, and over three-quarters of the respondents would welcome more effective measurement tools.[5] This book outlines several methods for measurement and evaluation that provide a clear format for analysing results.

Jack Morton Worldwide has found that 75 per cent of marketers surveyed in the United States, the United Kingdom, Europe, China and Australia planned to spend more on experiential marketing in 2008 than in previous years. Half of the 75 per cent planned to spend between 5 and 10 per cent more than previously, 12 per cent said they would increase their spend by 11–25 per cent and almost one in 10 said they would increase their spend by over 25 per cent. The Jack Morton global survey spoke to almost 300 senior marketers and revealed the level of trust that marketers are placing in experiential marketing: 70 per cent said that experiential marketing is extremely or very important to their organization and 71 per cent reported that experiential marketing will become increasingly important in that years to come. Ninety-three per cent of the respondents agreed that experiential marketing generates advocacy on word-of-mouth recommendations and 92 per cent agreed that experiential marketing builds both brand awareness and brand relationships; 77 per cent also stated that it generates sales.[6]

Traditional channels aim to increase brand awareness, market share and sales. Experiential marketing can achieve these objectives, but the live brand experience must be at the core of the integrated marketing communications strategy in order to gain maximum results. Experiential marketing brings a great deal more than brand awareness to the table. It also brings more than a quick sale from a promiscuous customer. To gain maximum benefits from implementing experiential marketing we should look at the more sophisticated results that it can achieve.

The benefits

Experiential marketing is a fabulous approach for bringing a brand personality to life. For example, if you have an energy drink that targets sporty, energetic people and the brand personality is active and bubbly, then the interactive experience will be focused on a similarly energetic, active and bubbly interactive activity, such as a game that involves jumping on a branded trampoline whilst surrounded by blown bubbles. The product would be featured as part of the experience through product trial and the brand imagery would be represented through the colour scheme, look and feel of the experiential set. However, the actual interaction is inspired by the brand personality. Therefore, once a consumer has engaged with the brand, he or she is left with a memorable understanding of complex brand values and will automatically affiliate the product with that personality. If this experience were targeted effectively and reached its target audience, it would connect with the aspirational and lifestyle aims of the consumer (to be energetic and active) and result in a genuine connection, strengthening the relationship between the brand and the purchaser. This live brand experience, which is focused on an interactive game, can also be amplified through all the marketing communications channels, for example digital gaming and ads.

Experiential marketing also creates brand advocacy. It drives word-of-mouth through personal recommendations that are the result of consumers feeling that the brand experience added value and connected with them through relevant interaction. The obvious results are strengthened brand relationships, an increase in customer loyalty, and therefore a more long-term strategic approach to gaining and maintaining market share. Sometimes the product itself is truly superior to its competitors, with innovative features and benefits that can only be communicated through experience, which is why experiential marketing campaigns often have the objective of driving product trial.

When you choose a restaurant, it is often a direct result of a personal recommendation or word-of-mouth. Word-of-mouth increases sales more effectively than advertising, and experiential marketing drives word-of-mouth better than a traditional approach to marketing can hope to.

When coming up with the big idea for an experiential campaign, to get maximum value the brand personality and brand values should be at the core of the concept, along with the inspiration from the aspirations and lifestyle of the target audience. This is not to say that the product's features and benefits are not important. In fact, live brand experiences, when executed face to face, can provide an ideal platform for demonstrating a product's features and benefits – because the product is trialled by the consumer in real life.

By bringing a brand personality to life, an experiential marketing campaign conveys sophisticated messages that traditional approaches cannot easily achieve, and it is especially effective at communicating complex brand personalities and values. This can connect with the aspirational lifestyle of the customer.

Picture a financial services brand with a funky, jazzy brand personality. Its ads show its workers dancing and singing its virtues. In this case, when creating experiential ideas, experiential thinking would bring to life the fun, dancing, singing brand personality rather than the boring, sober elements traditionally associated with a financial services product. On the other hand, a popular pure fruit drink with a healthy and organic brand personality would need an experience that brings to life healthy and organic values through engaging two-way communication, such as a live health-themed experience, tying the product back into the experience through taste, smell and branding. Experiences bring to life brand personalities by creating situations in which the consumer participates in interactive experiences, automatically affiliating those emotional values with the product and its brand. By doing this, serious benefits are gained, one of which is clear differentiation.

There are some products that have to compete in a saturated sector, where differentiating through product features is difficult. By creating a brand experience, which makes an emotional connection with its target consumers, those consumers are more likely to develop brand loyalty to that product, allowing the company to stabilize market share and avoid relying on sales promotions.

For example, in the beauty sector there are many products that focus a brand personality on values such as attractiveness, freshness or glamour. There are some beauty products that have a more complex brand personality. There is one in this sector whose brand values are inspired by the concept of beauty secrets being passed from generation to generation. It may be hard to convey this personality through, for example, traditional billboard or print advertising. Experiential marketing provides the perfect platform for bringing it to life in an integrated experiential campaign, including a live brand experience. Consumers who participate in the live brand experience write down their beauty secrets – secrets that have been passed on from previous generations, then place them into a competition box to win a beauty secrets makeover by a world expert.

Regardless of what the activity is, the important fact is that beauty secrets are at the core of the experience, and it is nearly impossible for the consumer to interact with this brand through an added-value, brand-relevant experience without learning on an intrinsic level that beauty secrets are a key part of what the product represents. Even if consumers do not think about it in terms of a brand personality, they will understand the concept subliminally or subconsciously. Either way, the next time they come across that product, they will automatically associate it with the brand personality: beauty secrets that can be learnt from wise forebears

Brand personality and target audience are the inspirations, not the sector

Experiential marketing in the same sector could lead to very different ideas if the creative process is executed correctly. This may seem obvious in the drinks sector, for example, but not so much in areas that are more formal. Experiential marketing can be implemented across all sectors, from financial services to FMCG, from drinks to music, from technology to leisure. No one sector (whether product or service) is more or less appropriate for experiential marketing, because the inspiration for experiential marketing ideas comes from the brand personalities and the target audiences. The emotional connection that can be reached through brand-relevant experiences transcends the selling points of the product, its features and benefits. This is not to suggest that the product and its features and benefits do not play a role in the experience; they do, as the consumer usually has the opportunity to trial the product, especially in the live brand experience when executed face to face. It really does not matter which sector or industry the product belongs to; as long as you understand the brand values and the target audience, you have what is needed to generate spectacular concepts for brand experiences.

For example, there is a brand of cream liquor, which originated in South Africa and which uses traditional African symbols in its packaging.

It has an African, indulgent and traditional brand personality, inspired by its roots and heritage. The brand gained market share quickly after its launch by building an emotional connection with the target audience and engaging them through live brand experiences and interactive PR competitions. The African themed branded set featuring a life-size model of an elephant and traditional indulgent African hut has visited luxury events for several years. The experience features costumed, dancing Brand ambassadors and traditional African craft-making sessions. Consumers find out about the upcoming live brand experience tour dates through articles in the press, which invite consumers to send photos of themselves 'being indulgent', for a chance to win a premium safari trip. While brainstorming the creative, the marketing agency behind this campaign remembered to take the target audience and their lifestyle into consideration and create an interactive two-way experience, which adds value to them, and reflects African indulgence and traditional themes at the same time.

A completely different cream liquor brand with a young, urban brand personality used an integrated experiential marketing approach. Their above-the-line advertising campaign showed city people holding house parties in loft-style apartments, and gave cocktail tips, provided by viewers. The advert invited the target audience to text back with cocktail ideas in order to receive a free 'cocktail party experience' in their own homes, complete with a bartender and drinks. Hence, the experiential idea was brand personality-specific and different every time, even though both products are very similar.

There is a power tools brand, whose brand personality and values reflect powerful, intelligent men; its target audience is affluent men who fancy themselves capable of a bit of DIY at the weekends. To bring the brand personality to life, the agency designed an experiential marketing campaign with a live brand experience that is two-way and interactive, engaging the consumer through sensory activities that represent power and intelligence, allowing the values to be communicated through relationship-building activities that generate word-of-mouth and achieve objectives. In this case, the experiential marketing campaign involved a series of face-to-face live brand experiences with online amplification. The live brand experience was held at a series of car shows (frequented by the target demographic), where the target audience had the opportunity to participate in a drilling challenge that acts as an IQ test. Every participant had the opportunity to win prizes such as super-powerful and intelligent state-of-the-art computers, and free Mensa membership, thus engaging the target audience and bringing to life the intelligent and capable brand personality of the power tools.

A different brand of tools has a reliable, trustworthy, 'family values' brand personality, and a key communication message that focuses on the fact that you can always rely on its tools to last for years. Experiential marketing is the approach behind this brand's marketing communications strategy, and the big idea, forming the live brand experience, is amplified throughout all its marketing channels. This brand targets workmen who use tools for a living. When the brand wanted to bring its trade adverts to life, it held an experiential road-show, which involved visiting building sites and allowing workmen to have a quick break inside a branded air-conditioned trailer. While they were relaxing in the seating zone, they had a free refreshing drink and watched the plasma screens which aired the TV adverts. While they waited, the Brand ambassadors ran a family-tree search for them at the computer bar. They received a print out of their family-tree, which also featured a sales discount code for use when purchasing tools, and came with a five-year warranty. The TV adverts showed the tools being passed from father to son; the adverts showed real consumers that actually used the tools and submitted photos of themselves using the tools, in response to a press initiative. The TV ads, which were aired on local interest stations, also featured a list of upcoming dates when the family search experience would be visiting the respective building sites.

When comparing the two campaigns, it is clear to see how the two power tool brands use different experiential concepts in their campaigns, even though there is little variation in the actual product itself. One is targeted at a more affluent DIY man, concentrating on intelligence and challenge, while the other targets a niche demographic and focuses on the longevity, trust and family values.

This same approach to formulating experiential marketing concepts can be applied across every sector and target audience, from FMCG to luxury, to B2B, to highflying executives, to housewives, to niche individuals and opinion formers. The principle here is that no matter what the industry is, be sure that you are clear on what your brand represents, how your target audience lives their lives and what is important to them. Then you can begin brainstorming about how you or your agency can bring these values to life through sensory and interactive activities. The brand personality, and this emotional connection that will be created with your target audience, will be the core inspiration behind your experiential idea.

Brand personalities do not have to be exciting and over-the-top for them to become the inspiration for experiential ideas. You can have a serious and intelligent brand personality, an intellectual brand personality, a regal and luxurious brand personality; in fact, the brand personality can be anything, just like a human being. Some people are fun, some are serious, some are active, some are relaxed, and some are loud and extravagant, while others are subtle and sophisticated. No matter which sector you are in, and no matter what your brand personality is, you can bring it to life through experiential marketing.

A mobile phone that targets the business traveller has an intuitive and intelligent brand personality. Marcia, a creative planner at an experiential marketing agency, was responsible for launching the phone and bringing to life these brand values, as well as demonstrating the phone's unique features. After careful research into the target audience and the length of interaction that would be required to demonstrate the phone's features, she concluded that airport lounges would be ideal. The target audience frequently visited these areas while making business trips and it would be easy to engage them there because they had spare time on their hands. She devised a plan to give away a free phone every 15 minutes and had the business travellers play a news quiz where Brand ambassadors wearing 'Adscreens' (17-inch plasma backpacks) on their backs would show half the morning's headlines, and the travellers would be required to guess the story. This required them to use their intelligence and intuition. The incentive of a free phone and the intellectual cachet of guessing correctly was enough to entice them into participation. They enjoyed playing the game, and in between each quiz question they would participate in demo tutorials on the Adscreen. In the demo, the Brand ambassadors would show off the phone's features, tailoring the demonstration to the lifestyle of the business traveller. Because the phones were secured to the Adscreens, the target audience had the opportunity to hold the phones, play around with them and use their special computer-like intuitive features while watching what they were doing on the Adscreen. This live brand experience was also successfully integrated with in-flight advertising and a press competition that promoted the live brand experience.

Whenever creating an experiential marketing concept, it is important to tie the product itself into the live brand experience, allowing consumers to engage with it and discover its features and benefits. But the core concept and inspiration for the experiential idea should be sourced from the brand personality.

In summary, it doesn't make a difference to your idea if your sector or industry is perceived to be exciting, dull or sophisticated; what really counts are the brand personality and the target audience. No matter what values that brand personality consists of, if you follow the planning guidelines in this book, then experiential marketing will be a methodology that will work for you. When the big idea (brand-relevant two-way communication) is integrated into your existing marketing communications, with a live brand experience at the core, it will offer results and benefits that will revolutionize your business and marketing strategies.

Experiential marketing, appropriate for B2B

Experiential marketing can be effective for products and services in the B2B sector, not only those in the B2C sector. For example, when Blazinstar Experiential, an experiential marketing agency, wanted to bring its unique approach to life, it sponsored a branding conference in the UK. At the conference, delegates would visit the break room in between lectures for light refreshments. Blazinstar Experiential created an experience that reflected its brand personality, which is focused on 'creative and fresh ideas'. The objective was to bring to life the brand personality of the agency and communicate the key message – that experiential marketing can be implemented successfully with fresh ideas and fruity concepts. The agency decided to create a fruity, fresh experience that encouraged the target audience (the marketing industry and, in this case, the delegates of the conference) to engage with them by coming up with fresh, fruity ideas themselves. First, they built an interactive set, which was a light-up smoothie bar. The smoothie bar was built from clear acrylic boxes to form a wall filled with real fresh fruit. The bar itself was branded grey and pink to reflect the brand identity and was lit up with flowing liquid. The raised platform that the delegates stepped onto to pick their fruit was also lit up. In fact, the whole front of the set shone with light through the different tropical fruit: mangoes, strawberries, oranges, papayas, bananas and grapes. This highly attractive set represented the bright side of the ideas and communicated that the agency's creative strategies are fresh and fruity.

As the delegates entered the raised platform area in front of the bar, they were greeted by three Brand ambassadors (carefully trained about the agency), one of whom invited them to take a basket and pick the real fruit from the open part of the low wall themselves. By choosing their own fruit, they were invited to create their own smoothie recipe. Once they selected a choice of three fruits, delegates were instructed to bring their selection basket to the bar and name their smoothie. They were then escorted to the branded Hummer golf buggy and chill-out area, where they would be given a brochure to read. Here, they could watch Blazinstar's agency show reel on a plasma screen and wait no longer than two minutes to receive an agency goody bag including their own smoothie in a branded bottle. The smoothie brand inventions were entered into a competition for the best brand concept. To enter, delegates had to supply their business card. The Brand ambassadors wrote the delegates' smoothie brand name on the back of their card, with all the cards going into a box, ready to be judged by the conference organizers (publishers of leading trade magazines). The prizes (which brought to life the aspirations of the target audience) of a ride home in a Hummer limo and an article about their smoothie creation in the next issue of a *Brand X* magazine, as well as the delicious fruit smoothies and exciting, fresh-looking set, were the talk of the conference.

The agency also had cards made with their 'fresh and fruity experiential concepts' motto emblazoned on the front. This reinforced the message and the positive experience that the marketing professionals found when they created their own smoothies and brands. In this case, the objectives were to bring to life the agency's brand personality while adding value to the delegates' experience of the conference, as well as capturing valuable data that would allow them to continue in strengthening their relationship with the target audience. By allowing them to engage creatively with fruity elements on the bright and engaging set, as well as giving them an experiential incentive, the agency succeeded in achieving its experiential objectives.

Two other experiential agencies sponsored this conference, and both provided interesting alternatives to the first approach. One agency had its logo on the conference website and a banner stand in the hallway, while the other had a table with a white tablecloth and two Brand ambassadors wearing branded T-shirts, giving away chocolate. This chocolate had little resemblance to that experiential agency (the chocolates were not branded), and in retrospect, the smoothie experience was significantly more impressive without a massive increase in cost. When you combine the cost of building the set, providing the fruit and implementing the experience as a whole (the Hummers and press prizes were free, because of a partnership agreement), there is not much difference from the cost of the banner stand, sponsorship package and Brand ambassadors that the second agency had in place. In fact, it remains an issue of genuine surprise to many experiential marketers that when so many agencies choose traditional marketing tactics to promote their own company, such as advertising and direct mail, they leave out experiential marketing because its effectiveness in B2B is apparently not clear to them.

When B2B businesses use traditional approaches to marketing and advertising, they often find low returns on investment. In a market where it is unlikely that B2B competitors are going to be using experiential marketing, it can be an ideal way to differentiate and create a memorable experience in the eyes of your target audience, even if they are hard-to-reach decision makers or senior people within an organization. It is always possible to find your target audience and relate to them appropriately as long as the proper research is conducted. If you want to be an innovative marketer, and you work in a B2B business, consider using experiential marketing as a differentiator that will add value for your audience and build a strong relationship. Even in industries where the target audience is small, and you're reaching senior people who are busy decision makers, you can still create experiential marketing campaigns that will grab their attention, entice them to try your product or service and make them remember your organization.

Criticisms: fact and fiction

Some people confuse experiential marketing with field marketing. Field marketing involves traditional face-to-face promotional and sales promotion tactics. Field marketing activities usually involve the use of promotional staff on a tactical basis. The promotional staff are deployed to distribute leaflets, samples, merchandise displays and in-store promotions, audit compliance of promotions (as communicated by regular store staff), mystery shop and capture data. Large portions of these services are part of sales promotion, which is why, typically, field marketing budgets are taken from the sales budgets and not from the marketing budget. The distribution of samples or leaflets is not two-way and interactive. It does not create a brand-relevant interactive and engaging experience; therefore, it is not in its own right experiential marketing.

There is also the mistaken belief that experiential marketing is interchangeable with event marketing. The simplest way to see it is that field marketing is normally the application of field staff to support sales promotions, market research or advertising. Events are face-to-face meetings that can be, but are not exclusively experiential in nature, while experiential marketing is a methodology that utilizes a live brand experience (involving either face-to-face or remote two-way communication) at its core, and then amplifies that 'big idea' with a selection of communications that are integrated to promote the two-way communication concept. It brings brand personalities to life, creating sensory experiences that engage consumers through two-way com-munications that involve input from the consumer. The benefits that can be gained from the effective execution of experiential marketing campaigns are different to the benefits of a field marketing activity.

Field marketing is appropriate and effective in supporting existing promotions or activities. For example, if you had a two-for-one offer on a drink and you felt that the offer needed additional reinforcement, then maybe it would be valuable to position promotional staff near the point of sale, encouraging consumers to purchase the product or giving out samples. Or, if you had recently established a new distribution channel in a major supermarket and part of this contract gives your products a top-shelf position and a poster displayed in the window, you might find it useful to have field marketing staff visiting these supermarkets and auditing, to check that the supermarkets comply with the agreement. The potential benefits of experiential marketing are broader than the traditional objectives that are affiliated with most marketing communication approaches.

Some people have negative perceptions about experiential marketing. Some say that live brand experiences can be expensive when compared to advertising campaigns, using the same metrics that are used to compare the success of an ad campaign between one media channel and another; for example, the cost per thousand (CPT) in terms of how many people from the target audience will have the opportunity to see (OTS) an advert or brand message. Obviously, the CPT people who see or hear an advert may be less than the CPT people who see or hear a live brand experience.

The important words in this phrase are 'see and hear'. Seeing and hearing are only two of the five senses, and without a level of two-way interaction, the value of those thousand exposures to a media message is different from the value of an experience that is immersive, multi-sensory and involves brand-relevant two-way interaction.

To understand the value of experiential marketing, it is important to look at exactly what it can achieve in terms of experiential objectives, such as word-of-mouth generated because of brand advocacy and brand evangelism, or the strengthening of deeper relationships with the target audience resulting in brand loyalty. Experiential marketing is key when your brand aims to have its target audience on the same side as the brand, working with you to increase your sales and spread your key messages. Traditional marketing approaches and their one-way exposure of messages to consumers have their purpose, but cannot achieve these benefits on their own. When an experiential marketing strategy is integrated into existing marketing channels as part of the overall marketing communications strategy, rather than simply implementing live experiential events as a tactical afterthought, it can make an excellent impact on sales, and also begin to create a dynamic where your customers do the most successful part of the marketing of your organization.

Experiential marketing is in fact a very cost-effective approach. If you compare the cost of achieving the aforementioned objectives through a traditional approach, to the cost of achieving those objectives through an experiential strategy, then you will find that the LROI (long-term return on investment) is likely to be greater when live brand experiences are at the core of the campaign.

In addition, the success of traditional channels when they are designed to amplify that live (two-way) brand experience is also likely to be much greater. It does not matter which country you look at, the billings of the big media agencies worldwide are huge. Consider how positive the ROI could be, when you take into account what consumers really think about the interruptions (adverts) in their lives that cost so much to roll out on a scale that will make any impact. Consumers rarely choose to watch traditional adverts and, as we have seen, technology is rapidly empowering consumers and giving them choices about which (if any) adverts they watch.

As well as the cost criticism, some people think that experiential marketing, specifically live brand experiences, do not reach a high enough volume of people in comparison to traditional marketing. When you take on board the impact that quality brand-relevant interaction or engagement can make on your target audience, and when you factor in the word-of-mouth reach (each person who interacts with a live brand experience is likely to tell 17 people), then you realize why experiential marketing is successful at building long-term brand equity and reaching large volumes of people. The cost of generating positive word-of-mouth amongst your target audience, if measured as a cost per thousand brand advocates (CPTBA) is low if compared to the extremely high CPTBA generated from a media campaign or a direct mail campaign. Therefore, the quality of the initial (seeding) reach of the live brand experience part of the experiential marketing campaign, compared with the quality of the reach of a traditional media campaign, is very high.

Another common myth is that experiential marketing is hard to measure. Again, this claim is erroneous. Experiential marketing is measurable, but to measure the success of a campaign effectively, there need to be systems and mechanisms for measurement that are tailored to the experiential objectives during the planning of an experiential campaign. The difference between measuring live brand experiences and measuring traditional advertising media is that traditional media has existing metrics, such as OTS or CPT. While there are some methods of evaluation that can be applied across all live brand experiences (such as number of interactions), overall, it requires a more tailored approach. It is true that if a marketer is used to measuring the success of a campaign by benchmarking based on advertising metrics, and tries to measure the live brand experience part of the experiential marketing campaign using the same metrics, he or she may be misled into thinking that the brand experience is lacking. To measure experiential marketing successfully, one needs to shift the approach to evaluation and understand how to tailor systems and mechanisms for measurement into the plan, correlating the mechanisms with the experiential objectives of each campaign. Such an approach, as well as other ways to evaluate experiential marketing and live brand experiences, will be detailed in several chapters later in this book.

Experiential marketing can be implemented on a small or a large scale to target many different types of people. It has been proven that experiential marketing is effective at targeting all demographics and target audiences. Both niche groups and mass-market audiences respond well because it can add value to all types of consumers. Experiential marketing campaigns should always have the live brand experience at their core (whether delivered in person or remotely).

Some examples of a small-scale approach include targeting students at a university, business people in their offices, or health-conscious women at gyms. It can equally be implemented to target larger audiences, such as commuters at rail stations, mass audiences at large-scale sporting or racing events, millions of spectators at the Olympics, or hundreds of thousands of young people at music festivals. The most important thing to remember in this respect is to plan the right experience for the right people, not prioritizing the initial reach of the live brand experience over the suitability of the location. In fact, regardless of how many people you reach, whether you have 15 experiences running simultaneously in different towns and areas around the country, or whether you have one experience per month or year, experiential marketing and live brand experiences can be adapted and tailored to suit your brand, target audience, objectives, timescale and budget.

What level of resources?

Look at the level of resources that you invest in your traditional marketing. The scale on which you implement traditional marketing should be similar to the scale on which you begin to implement experiential marketing. This is because the channels that worked for you in the past can still be used as part of your experiential marketing strategy. In reading this book and shifting your perception of experiential marketing, hopefully you will begin or continue to integrate live brand experiences into your overall marketing communications mix, and eventually to place them at the core of your marketing communications strategy. You will begin to see your other existing marketing communications channels as opportunities to amplify the core two-way interaction; the live brand experience. Customer experience management is becoming one of the highest priorities in customer-focused organizations, where an experiential strategy is leading the way. Therefore, when you think about the amount of resources that you will want to invest in CEM and in experiential marketing, you should think of allocating on the same scale that your organization is running as a whole.

There is a global organization whose ad agency has won several industry awards for the advertising campaigns that it created for the brand, ads that used to be generically broadcast on a mass scale across more than 10 countries. Since appointing a new CEO and shifting the marketing communications strategy to an experiential one, this organization's live brand experience programme is implemented worldwide across 10 countries, and its adverts now feature footage of the local live brand experiences. Since changing the approach, the brand has benefited from a significant increase in market share.

Likewise, an experiential marketing campaign for a local restaurant chain, which is a family-owned business, whose brand values are inspired by the fact that the restaurant only uses natural, locally sourced ingredients, can effectively bring the company's brand personality to life through a long-running series of locally targeted live experiential events. These events can engage the target audience and differentiate this restaurant chain from others in the area. The chain in question started off as a local Italian restaurant that prided itself on its food, and began to implement an experiential campaign that featured a mobile Italian roadshow. Its branded bus visited town centres near each of its restaurants and had a team of Italian Brand ambassadors giving out free samples of the pasta to passers-by, while engaging them with a 'make your own calzone' themed experience, allowing consumers to choose their own flavours and ingredients. Consumers were also entered into a competition with the chance to win a three-course meal for their family. The restaurant chain provided a sales promotion voucher for use on specials, enticing consumers to visit the restaurant and increase sales. The owner of the business invited the local press to a photocall at one of the experiential events, and convinced them to run a story following the locals who participated in the 'make your own calzone' experience. This small-scale integrated experiential marketing campaign succeeded in bringing the restaurant chain's brand to life and achieve its objectives of driving product trial (allowing the strength of a product to speak for itself), and increasing sales.

The moral of these stories is that the scale of the experiential marketing initiatives should be equal to the scale of all the marketing initiatives of the organization, because where possible a live brand experience should be used to generate the big idea for the overall marketing communications strategy. Therefore, the resources that already go into the traditional marketing channels can remain the same. The shift is in the approach to them, carefully building them around the live brand experience, as amplification of the big idea.

A shift in awareness

Historically, a lot of experiential marketing, specifically live brand experiences, have been implemented on a tactical basis, when marketing and brand managers had left-over budgets and wanted to reinforce an above-the-line campaign with some face-to-face events. In recent years, there has been a shift away from the perception of experiential marketing as a tactical, field marketing-style afterthought, with an increasing number of marketers understanding the benefits and seeing the evidence themselves. As the live brand experience sector starts to take a large part of the marketing budget cake and the spend is increasing, we can see that experiential marketing is moving away from its image as a tactical short-term solution, and brands are realizing that long-term investment is needed in order to achieve long-term experiential objectives. Shifting customer perceptions of a brand, developing consumer loyalty and driving word-of-mouth on a large scale are important to many organizations, and all are being achieved with experiential marketing.

When live brand experience budgets are planned at an early stage, at the same time as the other communication channels' budgets, the long-term benefits increase dramatically, because you can utilize the other tools to amplify the effect. Then, not only will you gain amazing benefits from engaging with your consumers through exciting and dazzling sensory experiences, but you can also broadcast the experiences, and therefore dramatically increase the reach of the live brand experiences at the same time. This provides the benefits of the traditional channels, enjoying vast numbers and volumes, along with the in-depth quality engagement that comes with strategically planned live brand experiences. Word-of-mouth as a result of brand advocacy is the outcome, which in turn increases sales.

Live brand experiences allow you to convey complex messages as well as reposition brands, gain credibility with hard-to-reach audiences, and save money by avoiding the wastage of traditional mass media. Live brand experiences allow brands to handpick the consumers that interact with the marketing communication through 'on brand' activity.

A perfect example of an organization that is properly utilizing customer experience management and experiential marketing is Apple, which creates a truly added-value experience for its customers. The experience starts from the very beginning of their relationship with the brand, to every touch point along the way, from in-store, to online, to its customer service. It ensures a positive added-value experience in the form of brand immersive stores, free in-store workshops that bring to life all the available software and staff who are themselves brand advocates. All of its efforts are designed to create lifelong advocacy inspired by its interaction with customers.

In this case, the consumers are not just shoppers who purchase the products: they are the people who sing the brand's praises, converting endless computer users by preaching the benefits of an alternative. When you go into a branch of Apple stores worldwide, you feel as though you are going back to school, only 10 times better. The cinema-style screens and beautiful set is like a technology and music-gadget candy store. It is a playground for the modern adult and teenager alike. By educating and informing consumers through brand-relevant, engaging experiences, they create brand evangelists. The word-of-mouth, inspired through personal recommendations and lifestyle aspirations, is priceless.

Apple has managed to hit the nail on the head, not only because it uses an experiential philosophy at its core, but also because it uses it as part of its retail environment. With cutting-edge design, education, added service and sensory elements, its stores are the platforms for inspiring customer experiences and the store staff are like the Brand ambassadors. But this is not the only brand to take experiential marketing to the next level and keep the experiential strategy at the core of its overall strategy. Countless global brands such as Nike, Singapore Airlines, Sony, Bombay Sapphire and Smirnoff position brand-relevant experience at the core of their entire communications.

It is not uncommon for marketers to approach experiential agencies with briefs that describe in detail the above-the-line campaign that they are about to run. This is because there is a tendency to ask the agency to implement experiential marketing activities that reinforce the above-the-line message and bring it to life. Often, they want to do this through a live brand experience that either replicates a TV advert creative or amplifies a similar theme that is a common thread throughout a planned campaign. This campaign is likely to be based on concepts and ideas that work best with broadcast media, so in this instance the creative team at the ad agency has been working within a very specific framework (broadcast media) that can limit the opportunities of creativity.

The live brand experience campaign's ultimate purpose in these scenarios is to create an experience that is similar to the type of creative message in the above-the-line campaign. But live brand experiences can provide deeper levels of engagement and a higher quality of interaction than any other marketing channel. Later in this book, when we discuss experiential strategies, the different approaches to the relationship between the live brand experience channel and other channels will be explained in detail.

Many campaigns can bring good results, even if they were executed following a brief to bring above-the-line messages to life (this will be discussed in more detail in Chapter 9). Likewise, there are larger and very significant benefits to be gained when the initial concepts and ideas for an integrated campaign are geared around a big idea inspired by the live brand experience. This is especially true where the live environment is utilized as a platform and the other channels, such as broadcast media, work hand-in-hand with the experience to expand its reach to a wider audience. The overall exposure is higher than if the live brand experience were implemented independently, and the effect on consumers is more engaging and adds more value than if the media campaign were implemented alone. The real gain from such an approach is that it also tackles one of the major barriers and misconceptions that many experiential marketers face when implementing live brand experiences: the criticism regarding numbers and the volumes of reach that can be achieved.

The amplification process has traditionally involved the live brand experience bolstering the other channels, and more specifically, the above-the-line creative. Though this can be effective, it is important to remember that significant benefits can be gained when the above-the-line creative takes the live brand experience channel to heart, and uses the live brand experience channel as inspiration for the creative in the other channels. The other media channels can also add live brand experience elements by working interactively with consumers through two-way interaction with the media and through the broadcasting of experiences.

Recently, a strategic media agency ran a campaign promoting an experiential TV show hosted by a celebrity UK chef. The Michelin-starred chef was participating in a highly publicized TV series involving three of Britain's best, exposing the perils of the chicken farming industry, amongst other creative and/or controversial topics. The TV show being promoted was the finale in this series, and was broadcast on primetime British TV in 2008. It was the first of its kind. The concept behind the show was that the chef cooked a three-course meal live on TV in an hour-long broadcast, inviting the public to join in, to actually cook alongside him in real time. It was a big challenge to pull off a show with such an innovative format, so to increase the interest and make it even more exciting, a famous London radio DJ cooked alongside him.

The media agency asked an experiential agency to bring the show to life, reinforcing the experiential message by encouraging consumers to purchase the ingredients needed for the three-course meal in their local supermarkets. The experiential agency recruited 200 lookalike chefs from their database of promotional staff – Brand ambassadors who were kitted out in chef's whites, black trousers and latex masks, as well as a wicker basket for their ingredients. They hired space at three of the bigger supermarkets in the UK, across 50 stores nationwide, positioning four lookalikes at each, purchasing the ingredients for the following night's programme and showing them to consumers in the stores. The Brand ambassadors also brought to life the chef's personality through a bit of friendly banter. The Brand ambassadors spoke in first person, as if they themselves were celebrities, inviting shoppers to cook along live with them, and greeting consumers as they entered the shopping centre with messages such as 'Are you going to cook along with me tomorrow night?' They were also giving out shopping lists of the exact ingredients and had an invitation printed on the reverse. The teams of four chefs per supermarket generated hundreds of smiles from surprised shoppers. One lookalike was the team leader and was responsible for the ingredients basket, while others were giving out the ingredients lists/invitations to cook live.

Over 200,000 invitations/lists were given out on the day before the show, supported by above-the-line print and TV adverts as well as radio mentions broadcasting constantly in the week before. The live show was a major success, with a record-smashing 4.4 million viewers on the night. As well as turning the campaign around with excellent viewing results for the show, the experiential agency also had the 50 team leaders participate at home the following night. By recording the whole experience both in writing (filling in the qualitative and quantitative data report forms) and through visual evidence (photos), they succeeded in adding a research element to the campaign. By providing the client with data that served as a valuable insight into how much the audiences that participated in this TV experience enjoyed the new innovative format, they added value to the campaign. Customer research is something that can be gained from running experiential campaigns without incurring any significant extra costs (for details of this case study, see Chapter 16).

This TV show and campaign is a great example of how, when the live brand experience (in this case remotely) formulates the big idea, and that big idea is placed at the core of an overall strategy, fantastic results can be achieved. The public feels they receive a beneficial, engaging and exciting experience that brings them closer to a brand they already appreciate and aspire to. In fact, not only was the show a success, with the chef's brand increasing in popularity, but millions of consumers nationwide learnt to cook a fabulous three-course meal of scallops, steak and chocolate mousse, all in one hour, cooking with a celebrity they would never have 'met' otherwise. All of this is more than the average Friday night of TV can achieve, and more than a printed sheet of paper ever could on its own.

Summary

This chapter has examined how and why people have been daunted by the differences between the obvious tools and live brand experiences. It has also demonstrated how the experiential marketing campaign should feature a live brand experience at the core of the overall strategy and then use the other selected channels to amplify the big idea. When planning experiential marketing, it is of vital importance to remember that the live brand experience should be considered at the beginning of the strategic planning process.

We have looked at how to use live brand experiences in processes such as AIDA, and we have seen how experiential ideas can increase their effectiveness. We've also had a look at traditional tools and why some are losing effectiveness, because of several factors such as Generation X and Y becoming more media savvy, and having higher demands from brand communication. Technology is rapidly snowballing in growth and innovation, constantly providing customers and the general public with even more choice about which messages they consume and when.

We have seen how fragmentation of media channels has led to too many options for marketers to choose from when it comes to their advertising schedules, increasing the cost of reaching a wide audience. We have examined how commoditization has led to a lack of differentiation between organizations that previously succeeded in using service to add value. This led us to note the change in the business era we have entered, from one where added service meant added value, to an era where the traditional product and service concept has gone through its own commoditization, and that this has resulted in the dawn of the new business era.

Experience-driven organizations are rising to the top. They not only offer their consumers great products and services (or vice versa) but are also providing a superior customer experience at every touch point. They have seen how brand-relevant experience acts as a unique differentiator, and how this enables a competitive market to maintain standout players that can get away with premium prices, and maintain a loyal customer base and stable market share. Additionally, we have addressed a few common misconceptions about live brand experiences, and some of the myths about its limitations, specifically the supposed lack of ability to reach volumes, and a false problem with measurement.

It has been clarified that field marketing is a sales-driven activity that has a commonality with live brand experiences only in that it can involve people (promotional staff or Brand ambassadors) working on behalf of a brand or agency in the field. Experiential marketing is the process of identifying and satisfying customer needs and aspirations, profitably, engaging them through two-way communications that bring brand personalities to life and add value to the target audience.

With that said, we have found that field marketing can be appropriate in certain situations, and has benefits of its own. It is a different discipline and should be viewed as such: field marketing activities should come from a sales budget, while live brand experience budgets should be allocated as significant portions of the marketing communications budgets. We've summarized the benefits of experiential marketing, such as bringing to life a brand personality, conveying complex messages, creating interactive memorable brand moments, driving word-of-mouth, creating brand advocacy and brand evangelists, increasing sales, driving traffic to websites, shifting people's perceptions of a brand, positioning or repositioning a brand, creating customer loyalty and more. To sum up the difference between live brand experiences and field marketing: as long as the campaign has two-way interaction between the brand and the consumers through brand-relevant experience that adds value, it is a live brand experience.

This chapter has shown how two-way interactions with consumers are fantastic and genuine ways of building consumer relationships. They are central to the concept of designing experiential marketing plans that integrate experience at their core, creating long-lasting brand advocacy that drives positive word-of-mouth amongst the target audience.

We have examined data that prove marketers are spending more on experiential marketing than ever before, and that the effectiveness of the live brand experience channel, when measured against any of the other media, is rating sky-high. We have seen how experiential marketing can be used creatively across all sectors, from financial to retail, from cosmetics to entertainment. With a creative ideas process that involves bringing to life a brand personality, experiential marketing is not just for FMCG brands, as some have previously supposed.

We tackled some of the negative perceptions that some people have about experiential marketing, such as criticizing it for a perceived high cost, lack of volume reach, or ability to effectively measure ROI or the achievement of specific objectives. While we can agree that the marketing industry doesn't have common metrics upon which it benchmarks the live brand experience part of its experiential campaigns, the effects of each interaction, and the practice of tailoring systems and mechanisms for measurement, is an approach that lends itself very nicely to detailed and in-depth evaluation of this relatively new discipline.

Experiential marketing can be implemented successfully, with great benefits, no matter what the size of the organization. They key point is that live brand experiences need to be integrated as the core of the overall marketing communications and organizational strategies across brands and global high-performing organizations. The size of the budgets allocated to live brand experiences has risen in reflection of this awareness. There has been change in recent years regarding the integration of live brand experiences earlier in the planning stages, usually when a brand is planning for the year. This is clearly the key time to allocate a reasonable portion of the marketing budget to live brand experiences, allowing the other channels enough time to design their creative in a way that amplifies the big idea. Most beneficially, many marketers are keeping experiential marketing at the centre of their thinking.

Though previously wrongly positioned as a tactical field sales support activity, which was very much a more junior decision made by middle management, experiential marketing is moving to front-of-mind with senior members of an organization. This is even true of marketing directors and other high-level executives. Therefore, the budgets allocated to live brand experiences, compared to other communications channels, are growing rapidly.

Finally, we saw how integrated experiential marketing involves the amplification of live brand experiences through effective and innovative use of other channels, and how this can be extremely effective. Even though amplifying the other channels with live brand experiences can bring good results, we must not lose sight of the difference between the two amplification processes.

The following chapters will describe a very useful model for brainstorming creative ideas that will help to tie all these broader concepts together when coming up with ideas for experiential marketing that tick the important boxes. BETTER is the acronym: it stands for Brand personality, Emotional connection, Target audience, Two-way interaction, Exponential element, and Reach.

Notes

1. Jack Morton Worldwide studies show that each person who interacts in an experiential campaign tells an average of 17 people (source: Kevin Jackson, at Jack Morton). An executive summary of this survey is available online at www.JackMorton.com

2. Jack Morton Worldwide. An executive summary of this survey is available online at www.JackMorton.com

3. Schmitt, B H (2003) *Customer Experience Management: A revolutionary approach to connecting with your customers*, p 17, Wiley, Chichester
4. MICE survey, as cited on http://www.prnewswire.co.uk/cgi/news/release?id=178594 (accessed 18/05/08)
5. MICE survey, as cited on http://www.prnewswire.co.uk/cgi/news/release?id=178594 (accessed 18/05/08)
6. Jack Morton Worldwide. An executive summary of this survey is available online at www.JackMorton.com

2 Outsourcing vs in-house

When thinking about planning an experiential campaign, you might be considering whether you want to try and organize it in-house or hire either your normal agency or a specialist agency. Additionally, you may consider sourcing an experiential agency specialist to do the planning and implementation. Usually, it is important to use experts in this field who have set up infrastructures and systems geared towards handling the complex environments that many live brand experiences tend to have. Live brand experiences require not only great attention to detail in the planning stages, but also great knowledge of footfall and demographics in a plethora of locations, as well as the need for your agency to have good relationships with specialist suppliers and experienced promotional staff. All this requires a very specifically trained and experienced team to manage effectively the smooth running of campaigns, which have so many external factors that can potentially cause things to go wrong.

If you compare live brand experiences to adverts, the process of logistical planning is very different. An advert has to be designed and improved sufficiently before it is scheduled for broadcast. But once it is scheduled, there are very few things that can stop it from happening. On the other hand, a live brand experience can involve hundreds of thousands of people interacting in real time, and there are many things that can go wrong. In addition, many external factors come into play – political, economic, social, technological, environmental and legal (PESTEL), and, of course, the weather. Every aspect of the PESTEL mix can, at any point during the live brand experience, place things in jeopardy (this will be addressed in detail later in the book).

Even though it is advisable to appoint an experiential agency that is expert at successfully handling these variable environments, there are nonetheless several options to consider. While at brief stage, you may want to evaluate what you want to do in-house and what is more effectively done externally. It is usually best to employ people in-house for the customer experience management (CEM) programme and to employ an experiential marketing agency for the live brand experiences. The other agencies can then work in partnership to amplify the live brand experience, forming the integrated experiential marketing campaign.

Companies go to many different types of agencies with live brand experience briefs. Frequent choices include PR agencies, advertising agencies, media agencies, direct marketing agencies, field marketing agencies, sales promotion agencies and, obviously, experiential marketing agencies. They sometimes even go to creative shops or event-planning agencies. In other words, companies have been known to invite pretty much any of their agencies to pitch for the live brand experiences they want to implement. Therefore, it should be of no surprise that the experiential marketing medium as a whole has been subject to criticism when at least half of the time, live brand experience campaigns are implemented by non-specialist agencies rather than experiential marketing experts. With that said, a lot of the time the live brand experience part of the experiential marketing campaign will eventually be outsourced to an experiential specialist anyway for activation.

There are pros and cons to every approach, and when considering each different agency type for experiential marketing, we need to be aware of what those are. It is of ultimate importance to make the right choice in terms of which agency to appoint to run your live brand experience campaigns. If live brand experience becomes the core of your experiential marketing strategy as a brand, you will need to consider whether you will invest in the resources required to bring experiential marketing in-house. But this discipline is complex for internal management, and an internal team of sufficient experiential marketing capability in terms of creative strategy, activation of live brand experiences and evaluation, may prove too expensive in resources compared to using outside expertise.

This chapter looks at the external factors that inevitably put at risk the success of every live brand experience campaign. When it comes to the creative process, there may be similarities with the activities involved in other marketing communications channels. You can look at a brand personality and come up with an emotional message, and likewise, you can look at a product's features and benefits and come up with a more rational message. The creative approach that reflects the brand, the target audience and the product, taking into consideration the situation, can be applied across all channels. But while we can probably apply a similar creative process in a way that is relevant and relates to many forms of marketing and advertising, we cannot apply the same execution or evaluation processes. Therefore, the creative process is where the similarities between planning live brand experiences and planning other communication channels ends.

Live brand experiences are very different to any other forms of marketing, in terms of the number of different factors that come into play and affect the outcome of a campaign. To understand the difference, think of a magazine advert that is due to be printed, or a TV or radio advert that is due to be broadcast, and think of how many things can go wrong (technically) once that creative has been produced, the advert shot or designed and slotted into the media schedule. It is very likely that it will be printed or broadcast as planned, as there are not a huge number of things that can happen to interrupt that process. In contrast, while a live brand experience campaign can be planned creatively, then logistically, once the campaign goes live there are so many things that can then still occur to affect the success or failure of the entire venture.

Successful live brand experience planning and execution requires a complex mix of individual skill sets and existing relationships. It needs to be in the hands of the right people to bring results, rather than potentially becoming a logistical nightmare. In the hands of the wrong people, campaigns can become impossible to execute effectively, with so many complexities factoring into the equation. Activation requires careful operational logistics planning, detailed execution schedules, and a fanatical attention to detail to be a success. This is of course additional to the fact that the experiential idea should be powerful in the first place. It should also carry strategic insights from previous campaigns, regarding selection of the locations and people. This type of specific planning is something that we will examine in detail later on in the book. The planning system, SET MESSAGE, which forms the structure of this book, is geared around integrating the right systems into your experiential marketing plan; systems that have been tried and tested by leading experiential marketing agencies.

Once you decide that you want to change your approach and use live brand experiences at the core of your communications, using the other communications channels to amplify the live brand experiences, you might consider the possibility of bringing the live brand experience team in-house. Alternatively, when you outsource the live brand experience programme, do you outsource it to a full-service, specialist or experiential agency?

If you are on the client side, working for a brand, or in a full-service agency, it is very likely that you are already working with a wide array of agencies. Maybe you have a PR agency that handles your below-the-line marketing and an advertising agency that you work with to raise awareness. Or maybe you work with integrated marketing agencies who manage the other agencies for you. No matter what your situation, if you have decided that you would like to use live brand experiences, and place them at the core of your marketing communications, you will need to decide who will be responsible for them. This is crucial, because for your experiential marketing to be most successful, the selected channels should be in place to amplify the live brand experience channel, with appropriate people accountable for it. Let's look first at some of the pros for a large organization bringing an experiential marketing team in-house.

In-house

Pros

You understand your own industry and products better than an external entity. You understand the decision making and buying process in your organization very well. If you recruit a skilled specialist experiential marketing team to work in-house, they will work only for you, because you are their only 'client'. The people who you bring in to be responsible for experiential marketing will get to know key players within your organization and have a greater understanding of the internal politics.

On the other hand, bringing an experiential marketing team in-house is not usually advisable because you would need an experienced team with backgrounds in live brand experience creative, strategy and activation. This is something that should only happen if, after spending several years heavily committing to customer experience management and experiential marketing, you are ready to make a big investment of time, money and people. With that said, there are obvious advantages in doing so. If you are looking to make this serious move and bring experiential marketing teams into your organization, this commitment is representative of the overall orientation and philosophy of the organization. We have seen in Chapter 1 how businesses and brands have differentiated themselves from their competitors by shifting from a product orientation, to a service orientation, to a customer relationship orientation. It is clear that now we are at the dawn of an era where organizations are differentiating by shifting once again, this time to a customer experience orientation. By bringing experiential marketing teams in-house, not only will your external marketing communications benefit, but your internal marketing will too.

If your experiential marketing teams are in-house, then it should become their responsibility to ensure that all the departments within your organization have an understanding of the importance of the customer experience, and that management understand how the employee experience will filter through and affect broader stakeholders and the public. This focus on the customer experience is not only one for the marketing and sales department. It should apply to everyone, from the call centre personnel who answer your phones, handling customer service enquiries, to the staff in the retail environment, right through to the finance department. No matter which sector or industry your organization focuses on, or which department your employees work in, collectively they form the orientation of your organization, and they need to be trained by working with the experiential marketing (or customer experience) part of your organization. This will enable them to complete the shift to a customer experience and experiential marketing focused outlook.

Many of the agencies that you work with are aware of the experiential marketing revolution, and they are noting a high demand for live brand experiences from their clients. That is why many of them have adapted their agencies, to enable the provision of live brand experience services to their existing clients. Though these agencies may apply an experiential marketing philosophy to the channels they were already offering, the live brand experience channel is one that they are still likely to outsource to an experiential specialist (after marking up the fees). Another phenomenon, in a smaller number of cases, is that agencies are recruiting teams of specialist personnel who are experienced in experiential marketing, or buying existing independent experiential agencies, allowing the integrated agencies to provide their clients with experiential marketing solutions.

The main advantage of bringing an experiential marketing team in-house is that they will know the key players within your organization much better than any agency ever could. This results in them being far more familiar with the buying and decision-making process. Intimate with key players, stakeholders and politics within the organization, they will be able to adapt the customer experience to be in line with the overall organizational goals, as well as designing the experiential marketing programme to achieve marketing communication objectives. In-house staff will be more familiar with the organization's ethos, plans and goals, as well as with who makes which decisions when, why and how. Obviously these considerations are of key importance because this information can help the team to integrate an experiential philosophy into many facets of the organization.

Another positive factor is that the in-house experiential marketing team will spend every working day and all their energy focused on the organization and its goals without other commitments or priorities. Their 'clients' are all internal, and therefore the experiential team's energies are divided only between the key decision makers and satisfying them and the agreed projects at hand. The alternative is an agency scenario where the agency teams will have to focus on many different clients, of which your organization is only one.

Another factor to look at is the proprietary rights or the intellectual property of the experiential strategies. Imagine a situation where your experiential agency team comes up with creative strategies for a campaign, and you want to approve these plans because the ideas are good, but you cannot go ahead with them until the following financial year (for copyright or contractual reasons). You would want to put the strategy on hold for reconsideration 12 months down the line, or maybe you would like to test the water with market research and pilot the idea before committing to it on a large scale. If the ideas and intellectual rights belong to your organization, you would have full confidence that you could implement them now or at a later stage without much risk of the ideas going to your competitors. It doesn't matter whether you are ready now or later, because the team that developed the strategies is yours. If the ideas belong to the agency and the concepts were proposed to the client, then the client would have the opportunity to go ahead or not. There are many people at the agency who would have already been exposed to these strategies and would have the opportunity to talk about them to other clients; therefore, the chances of the ideas escaping into the public arena prior to execution are far greater.

Cons

As previously stated, this approach is not recommended unless you are willing to invest a huge amount of time, money and people in the process. It is extremely costly to set up experienced internal teams and systems, and this part of this chapter will focus on why.

First, for live brand experiences you will need a creative team and an operational or project management team, as well as the large numbers of specialized Brand ambassadors and suppliers that require an enormous amount of management. Therefore, you would also require a promotional staff booking team, and in many cases warehousing, storage and logistics facilities, so the investment should not be underestimated. And the cons are not only financial but resource-based.

Another con is that if you are not running live brand experiences all the time, the logistical and activation part of the team will be doing nothing in the interim period. If you have experiential campaigns on all summer long, and then there is a break for three or four months, the activation part of your experiential team, with maybe five or more employees, will have nothing to do apart from attempt to assist those people in the experiential marketing team who are responsible for CEM. In this case, you will have invested a great deal of time, money and effort, but when there are no live brand experience campaigns running, many members of the activation and staff-booking teams will become idle.

Understandably, if you do decide that you want to bring your experiential marketing in-house, then you will want the best people to be part of the team. However, can you find those best people straight away? Not only will this major specialist recruitment become a challenge, but you will face other issues. Competent executives with superior creativity in experiential marketing will be less likely to want to join an organization as an employee, because they are likely to already own or manage an experiential agency, or be in a senior role where profits will be higher for them. In addition, creative people within experiential marketing are more likely to want to work on the agency side than be an employee in an organization. They will want to be more senior in an organization, and it is unlikely that you will be able to offer senior roles when experiential marketing is such a new division within your company. Therefore, the types of people that you are likely to attract for an in-house experiential marketing team are going to be comfortable working in middle-level positions and as a result not the highly creative executives you seek.

It is important to note that it is not only the profits and seniority that will attract these individuals to work in the agency side but also the variety of work. By working with a range of clients across many different sectors, creative experiential marketing executives will have the excitement and fluidity that they desire. On the other hand, working for one brand or company requires a very different type of person who is attracted to that type of role and has typically come from a client-side background.

In summary, it is important to remember that unless you would like experiential marketing and customer experience management to be at the centre of your organizational marketing strategies, then bringing it in-house is a massive investment that is not likely to be right for you. It is usually preferable to find a specialist experiential marketing agency to work with you or to use your integrated agency on your experiential marketing (especially the live brand experiences). If you do think that experiential should be at the core of your organizational strategy, then it could be worth the time, effort and investment in the long run to bring specialists in-house for the CEM programme. Even in this case, it would still be preferable to hire specialist experiential agencies to work in partnership with the in-house team.

There are companies for whom customer experience is a key part of their organization and identity. Disney, PlayStation, Red Bull, Sony, Nike, as well as brands that originated as start-ups, such as Ben and Jerry's and Innocent Smoothies, are organizations that pride themselves on positioning positive, brand-relevant customer experience at the core of their company ethos. Their CEM focuses on the customer's touch points with the brand, where an experiential strategy leads the way. As a result, these organizations invest heavily in their in-house teams responsible for CEM. Many of these companies still regularly supplement their in-house activities by working with specialist experiential marketing agencies that have benefited greatly from the in-house involvement and importance placed on experiential marketing.

Some companies already have an excellent relationship with the specialist agencies they work with; their media agency or their PR agency, for example, know them very well and understand their brand. The next section of this chapter looks at the pros and cons of outsourcing the live brand experience aspect of experiential marketing to some of the agencies with which you may have an existing relationship.

Outsourcing to your media or full-service agency

Pros

The obvious pro is that the agency will be more familiar with your brand and will have run previous campaigns for you, and therefore have a deep understanding of what you like, the approach of the organization and your brand as a whole. It will also be able to put things into context very well, as it will have been responsible for, or involved in lots of previous strategies for marketing your brand.

Another pro for implementing experiential marketing through your media agency is that it will be easier for it to have control of the integration of the live brand experience strategy into the above-the-line media (advertising). A further pro is that it may be responsible for implementing an integrated campaign with global reach. It will be easier for it to ensure that your live brand experiences also have a consistent global reach by managing consistency across campaigns executed by many experiential agencies. Due to its international resources, it would potentially be easier for it to ensure quality control on such a large scale compared to a smaller specialist experiential agency, which may struggle.

Cons

Media or full-service agencies that you have an existing relationship with are very likely to do their own outsourcing. They will want to move at least the majority of the live brand experiences to experiential agencies or other agencies (such as outdoor specialists) that they work with. There is a certain lack of control in this type of situation, because the agency that you are paying to handle your experiential marketing is not the agency that is actually carrying out the work or managing the campaigns' strategies as a whole. The people that are your client contacts in the media agency will not be as well-placed to give you a realistic picture of what is happening, because they are clients to the experiential agency that is really handling the live brand experience campaign. The experiential agency may paint a certain picture to its client, the media agency, and the media agency may paint yet another picture for you as a client. The more agencies involved in the outsourcing chain, the more honesty and control are in jeopardy.

Another factor is cost. Obviously, the media or full-service agency will mark up unit costs significantly, not to mention the agency commissions on top, so you will be paying more for your live brand experiences than you need to, especially when several agencies are involved.

Large media agencies are used to doing things on a large scale. Therefore, they will usually recommend that your live brand experience should be on such a scale and similar to your media. You may not have done any live brand experiences in the past, and if you want to start then it may be better to test your ideas on a relatively small scale.

Most important, experiential marketing is not the media agency's area of expertise. In fact, people who are trained, educated and predominantly have experience in media are not likely to be people who have significant experience in live brand experiences. It is therefore not ideal to assign them as the agency responsible for managing your experiential strategy as a whole because they may be less likely to position the live brand experience at the core of the campaign.

Another factor is that media people are less likely to appreciate live brand experience as a serious discipline and internalize an understanding of its true benefits and fantastic future in marketing. Media agencies win prizes for advertising, and historically they tend to see live brand experiences as a part of the field-marketing arena, a discipline perceived as tactical and unsophisticated. For the average media professional, there are too many uncertainties in live brand experiences, and it can sometimes be too small scale to interest them

Media agencies are used to media metrics and try to measure live brand experience campaigns similarly, without taking other factors into consideration. It is unlikely that media agencies will note things such as the effect-per-interaction and the word-of-mouth reach. It is more likely that they will use opportunity to see (OTS) and cost per thousand (CPT). If only 50,000 people can directly interact with a live brand experience compared to 5 million people watching an advert, it is likely that, from a media perspective, the live brand experience campaign will appear to have a less effective reach. In comparison, an experiential marketing agency or an experiential marketer will understand that not only do those 50,000 people interact with the experience, but that each of them is likely to tell an average of 17 other people about it, and therefore the overall reach of the campaign becomes significantly larger.

An experiential marketer will also understand that the effect per interaction is very significant, that many of the people that interact with the experience are converted into brand evangelists, and they will understand that this dynamic results in increased customer loyalty and positive word-of-mouth. The experiential agency would be able to demonstrate these results, showing how the campaign is achieving objectives that advertising simply cannot currently achieve.

The final con for placing experiential strategy and live brand experiences in the hands of your media agency is that they will be more used to budgets that are based on simple unit costs, which are multiplied based on the number of exposures or display opportunities. For example, they know what it costs to broadcast adverts in 30 seconds on a specific scale, with a specific media owner. They can then multiply that unit cost by the number of times it will be displayed or broadcast on that channel, add in agency commissions, and they have the cost. This is something they will do regularly, with the same costs applying to many of their clients. They will do this across all the media channels that the advert will broadcast. It is a simple mathematical multiplication. On the other hand, costing the live brand experience part of experiential marketing campaigns requires a far more detailed, complex and variable approach. An experiential agency knows this complex and bespoke costing process is a necessity, and will not be fazed by it, while the media agency will be daunted as it will not be part of the normal parameters it is used to when budgeting.

Working with a PR agency

Pros

The next option is the PR agency. For many companies, this is the first point of call when they think of experiential marketing. To begin with the pros: obviously the company can integrate the live brand experience with the PR strategy and therefore maximize the reach of a campaign, which is fantastic.

For example, a UK-based PR agency managed the strategy of an experiential marketing campaign for a popular brand of chocolate bars, and outsourced the activation of the live brand experience to an experiential agency. The experiential agency's staffing division deployed 30 'hunks' dressed in branded outfits with the chocolate bars attached to their chests, to amplify the above-the-line campaign whose intention was to target a new audience for the chocolate. The target audience was females aged 20–35. This was at a time when it became illegal to advertise certain foods to children, and the company had to completely shift its marketing to a different audience and reposition the brand.

The hunks were kitted out and hit the streets of London, distributing 60,000 chocolate bars and engaging the female consumers with the key communication message: 'A little bit of what you fancy' while inviting them to rip the chocolate bars from their chests. They reinforced the above-the-line message and visited media houses with a campaign finale at the famous Eros statue in Piccadilly Circus. The finale, which was a publicity stunt drawing in many members of the press, saw photographers snapping away at the hunks, who were catwalking up and down Piccadilly, chocolate bars strapped to their chests, female members of the public trying to grab the chocolate. The coverage that resulted was enormous because the PR agency secured millions of pounds worth of press coverage, including an appearance on the news that night (one of the key terrestrial TV channels in the UK). Not only did the campaign gain national television coverage on the news, it also gained a front-page spot on a London paper, as well as other relevant press mentions in media that catered directly to the target audience (such as a leading online woman's e-zine).

This campaign is just one example of hundreds showing how when a PR agency is appointed to manage the experiential marketing channel, it can deliver a successful campaign, even if it is outsourced. The benefit of doing this through the PR agency is that it can utilize press and media contacts to expand the reach, so that the campaign is exposed to millions of people, in addition to the people that actually interacted with the experience (and spread word-of-mouth). As you can see from this example, the activity was still outsourced from the PR agency to a specialist experiential marketing agency, marking up costs along the way, but there was added value to be gained.

As well as the fact that the experiential campaign can be integrated with the PR campaign, you will also maximize the value for money. In the example of the chocolate bar campaign, the PR agency spent a relatively low amount with the experiential agency to execute this short-term campaign. The reach of the campaign was nonetheless huge, providing a great return on investment for what they spent. Ferrero achieved optimum results by appointing a PR agency for the Bueno campaign.

It is assumed that if you are thinking of outsourcing experiential marketing to a PR agency, this is likely to be because you already have an existing relationship with them, and therefore similar and comparable benefits can be gained as in previous strategies and campaigns. Because you and the agency will be familiar with each other, it will understand your brand and already work with you on other campaigns, creating a good understanding of the context of the live brand experience that should be at the core of the experiential marketing campaign.

Another positive element in favour of outsourcing to PR agencies is that they tend to understand word-of-mouth dynamics very well, because they are used to targeting key influencers and opinion leaders. By reaching key people in specific communities or the public eye, they succeed in disseminating information and positioning brand messages through specific peer-to-peer, celebrity or expert channels. This understanding of social networks is in line with some of the specific skills required when planning successful experiential marketing strategies. They have already come a long way in understanding how experiential marketing, when correctly targeted, triggers the exponential dissemination of information from specific seed groups of people to broader target audience groups and the public.

PR agencies are usually in tune with and understand how celebrities can play a key role in influencing the perceptions that specific publics have of a brand. The PR agency will have the relevant contacts with agents, and know which stars are already positioned similarly to a positioning that the brand desires to achieve in the eyes of the same target audience. The PR agency understands that credibility can be given to a brand by affiliating it with something or someone that is perceived in this desired way. Therefore, they can integrate celebrities, star appearances or sponsorship into experiential marketing campaigns, greatly helping to achieve objectives such as changing public perceptions or positioning the brand for desired effect.

PR agencies understand how a live brand experience activity (or stunt) implemented on a small scale can influence and reach a massive number of people. It is likely that the PR agency will be flexible in its planning approach because it is usually experienced in running face-to-face campaigns, whether in the form of live events and parties or a press meeting, such as a launch or photocall. Therefore, it will be familiar with the process of catering for and aiming to predict uncertainties and external factors that must be taken into consideration, ensuring contingencies are in place for impeccable execution.

Many brands turn to their PR agencies when outsourcing live brand experience activity because PR agencies are often assigned responsibility for all the events, sponsorships and live consumer interactions that the brand is involved with. PR agencies will have good relationships with many of the relevant suppliers needed. If they can't run the live brand experience campaign in-house, they will already know and have relationships with experiential agencies to outsource to. Sometimes they may choose to outsource different sections of the campaign activation to different suppliers, after doing the strategy part in-house. For example, they might outsource the promotional staff to a staffing agency, the production to a set building company, and so on. They are likely to know what they need to achieve best prices from individual suppliers, and will have internal project managers or event coordinators who could coordinate the process effectively.

Another positive point in favour of outsourcing experiential marketing to PR agencies is that they are familiar with crazy deadlines, working around the clock and doing things for clients at the last minute. They will have the ability in many cases to handle out-of-hours live brand experiences with high levels of uncertainty and will be more likely to have the problem-solving skills required than an above-the-line agency. Planning contingencies and looking at all the potential problems that need to be addressed in advance contribute greatly to the effective activation of live brand experience campaigns.

Cons

Having carefully examined the positive side of outsourcing experiential marketing to a PR agency, it is time to flip the coin and take a careful look at the cons involved in this mode of delegation. The first negative is that most successful PR agencies in the UK are based in London, where the main media owners, publications and journalists are. It is the obvious place for all the media to be located, and certainly all the national media are based in the capital. As a result of this geographic limitation, PR agencies will not have the same level of expertise and understanding of the complexities of executing a national live brand experience campaign.

The same can be said for all big cities around the world. A New York City PR agency will be much less likely to successfully handle a live brand experience campaign across 20 states, from a logistical perspective, than an experiential agency. This is because the PR agency will be familiar with working within New York City and not have as much relevant expertise when it comes to working nationally across the whole of the United States.

This leads us to the second con. PR agencies are focused on small 'important' groups of people such as key members of the press or highly influential individuals. They are much less comfortable with focusing on reaching consumers directly and achieving volumes of direct consumer interaction on a large scale. Live brand experiences have the effect of driving word-of-mouth. Therefore, the consumer is king and the media is prince, and should only be used to amplify and maximize the reach of a campaign. The press should not be prioritized above personal recommendations, which are the most valuable form of marketing. This is an approach to experiential marketing that some PR agencies will find hard to grasp, and will have less understanding of when compared to an experiential marketing agency.

PR agencies also have a tendency to pigeon-hole the live brand experience campaign as 'content' for a broader PR campaign. They place higher focus on the media coverage than on the initial campaign and the brand relevant two-way interactions with the consumers who experienced the campaign first hand.

Working with a sales promotion agency

Many marketers misunderstand experiential marketing and think of it as purely live brand experience or field marketing (which is part of sales promotion). This misunderstanding arises because they are used to field marketing activities, designed to support sales in retail, and tend to place experiential marketing and field marketing in the same category. This confusion stems from the fact that direct contact with consumers is normally the responsibility of the sales or customer services departments, and live brand experiences are sometimes funded by the sales promotion budget, especially when they feature special offers or discounts.

Pros

A sales promotion agency will have an existing relationship with the sales department in your organization. The fact that the sales department and therefore the sales promotion agency would, in this case, be responsible for the experiential campaign should not necessarily mean that the marketing department will not play a role. The sales department is likely to communicate with the marketing department to a greater or lesser extent, and can potentially have more flexibility with its budgets, providing an opportunity to spend more on experiential marketing by using budgets specifically allocated to achieving sales objectives where there may be more room for movement.

Moreover, your existing sales promotion agency will have solid relationships with the outlets where the product is sold (assuming your product is sold in a retail environment). The live brand experience part of the campaign could then be positioned in the same or in neighbouring locations to where the product is positioned, and therefore have a greater chance of directly influencing the sales of the product. Because consumers will participate in the live brand experience in close proximity to the point of sale (POS), they are provided with the opportunity to purchase the product while the experience they had is still memorable, with a significant and lasting impact on their thoughts and feelings.

Cons

A sales promotion agency will have a strong sales orientation and therefore will be less interested in achieving marketing objectives that are complex and more elusive. These benefits include word-of-mouth, bringing brand personalities to life, as well as more long-term objectives such as customer loyalty. Moreover, by having a sales focus, the sales promotion agency may not design the experiential campaign in a way that is integrated properly with selected channels and geared towards reaching the optimum potential of the campaign.

Summary

In summary, there is no clear recipe for appointing a non-experiential agency to handle your experiential campaign, because every situation, relationship, company and agency is different, with each type of partnership having its unique pros and cons.

The safest option is the experiential marketing agency. With that said, experiential marketing agencies differ greatly from each other, some specializing in strategy with others having originated and evolved from being staffing or logistic specialists. These days many small creative shops and suppliers are repositioning themselves as experiential marketing agencies, and it is hard to know which agency can really offer a full service, from strategy and creative to activation and evaluation. There are experiential agencies that have spent many years preparing and improving every area of their organization around ways to best design, implement and evaluate successful experiential campaigns. These specialist experiential marketing agencies work in close partnership with the other channel agencies and therefore they can ensure seamless integration, with the live brand experience at the core of the overall strategy. Experiential marketing agencies with a long history of successful live brand experiences have systems and mechanisms for measurement in place, and they have long-term relationships with locations, suppliers, Brand ambassadors, etc.

When choosing an agency, ensure it has case studies of other campaigns and strategies it has implemented across brands. These could be your competitors or be in a relevant sector, have a comparable brand personality, or target a similar audience to yours. A good experiential marketing agency can inspire your overall marketing strategy to become experiential, as well as ensure smooth, flawless delivery, because it will be familiar with all the external factors that can arise within the complex arena of live brand experience (especially those that are delivered face to face).

As organizations continue to move from a service orientation to a customer relationship orientation, and on to a customer experience orientation, we will continue to see a growth of investment in experiential marketing. Gradually, the practice of bringing customer experience management programmes in-house, and working directly with specialist experiential marketing agencies, will accelerate.

3 BETTER

To make the process of brainstorming top-line experiential marketing ideas easier and more systematic, a brainstorming model called BETTER has been developed; see Table 3.1.

Table 3.1 The BETTER model

Brand personality	Three brand values that sum up the brand's human-like characteristics
Emotional connection	Multi-sensory and/or authentic, positively connected and personally meaningful
Target audience	What they like, their lifestyle, their aspirations, the time they have available
Two-way interaction	A live brand experience [face-to-face/remote] that combines the above B, E and T
Exponential element	A trigger mechanism that encourages participants to pass on their experience
Reach	Two-way interaction, word-of-mouth and amplification channels

BETTER enables you to bring the Brand personality to life, and create ideas that are experiential in nature and dazzle your target audience. This is best achieved when the big idea is centred in the live brand experience, which is usually sensory and always interactive. BETTER ideas focus on engagement that drives word-of-mouth, gaining maximum

Reach for the campaign. By following this brainstorming process, you are completing the first steps towards creating your own experiential marketing concept. The BETTER brainstorming model is inspired by the fact that when creating a genuinely engaging, memorable experiential marketing campaign, the ideas need to be multi-facetted and better than many used in traditional marketing approaches.

How do you use BETTER?

When using the BETTER brainstorming model to come up with top-line concepts for experiential marketing (see Figure 3.1), you first complete the B, E and T stages, and then combine the results as components for the second T: the Two-way interaction. Then you build in E, an Exponential element, and then the R, trying to achieve the best possible Reach (a combination of the initial Reach of the live brand experiences, the word-of-mouth Reach, and the Reach of the amplification channels).

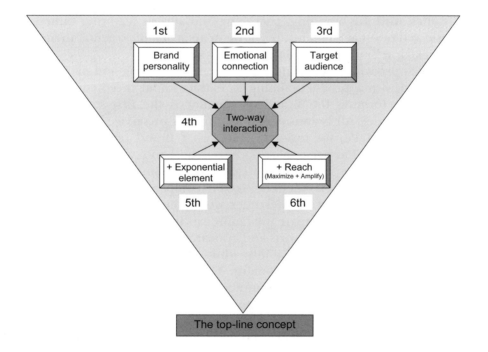

Figure 3.1 Top-line concept using the BETTER model

B for Brand personality

The B stands for the Brand personality. Some people might find the concept of a brand having a personality slightly confusing and may not differentiate between the brand and the product. For example, if you look at a brand such as Coca-Cola, the product itself is Cola, so from a consumer perspective there is confusion regarding the difference between the product and the brand. To understand more about what is meant by a Brand personality, we should first think about personality in the context of people.

Different people have different personalities. For example, there is Frank: he is my neighbour who is always chatty, bouncy and happy while on the go (he has a happy, chatty, bouncy personality). Similarly, you might know somebody else who comes across as sophisticated, smart and talks directly 'to the point'. He lives in the city and has a fast-moving lifestyle. Now try to look at brands in the same way. What personality does your favourite brand have? Is your washing powder's Brand personality fragrant, natural and caring? Or does it have an exciting, bright and energetic personality? Recently, a well-known company launched a new brand of washing detergent featuring essential oils and the smell of jasmine. The liquid is packaged in small, attractive see-through capsules, with the branding, packaging and adverts featuring calming music and oriental elements, resulting in an aromatic, oriental themed and relaxing Brand personality.

This approach to dissecting the imagery, advertising and packaging associated with a product, aiming to extract about three core brand values and forming the Brand personality, is the first stage of the BETTER model. All brands across all product or service sectors have personalities. Take, for example, cars: what Brand personality does your car have? What personality does your husband, wife, girlfriend or boyfriend's car have? Do both your cars have the same personalities, just because they are cars? If you were asked to compare the personality of a Volvo to the personality of a Mercedes, would they be the same? Even in a situation where you compare two family cars that are similar in product specifications, one car's adverts and appearance communicate a Brand personality of trust and reliability, while the other has a pragmatic, logical and simple Brand personality. The core values embedded and encoded in existing brand communications should be decoded and extracted, forming the Brand personality. This will be the first point of inspiration for the experiential marketing idea.

As a marketer you are likely to be very familiar with the concept of brand values and you probably have a good understanding of branding.

If you are unclear about this concept, you may find the task of extracting the Brand personality daunting, or you may be unsure where to start. Try practising this process the next time you watch TV commercials. Watch an advert and sum up, in 20 seconds, what you think the Brand personality is that the people behind it were trying to encode. What was the agency responsible for the ad attempting to communicate? Next time you see an ad, regardless of whether it's for a financial services product or a candy bar, brainstorm which different human-like values come to mind, as if the brand itself were a person with its own unique personality. Try to think, what type of brand is this? Is the person in this ad the type of person I want to be friends with? Is this brand representative of values or a lifestyle that I aspire to? Or is this brand like somebody else I know; somebody I like, or somebody I don't like? Is this brand nice? Is it honest? Is it sexy? Is it smart? Is it trustworthy? Is it adventurous? Is it fun? Is it sophisticated? Is it cheap? Is it active? Is it relaxed?

There are many different personality facets to take into consideration, many different values that a brand can have, because Brand personalities can be as complex as human personalities. Brands can have their own intricate personalities and core values. The first stage of BETTER is about figuring out what the brand stands for. Try to analyse and dissect the adverts and other marketing communications and packaging, to bring it down to the core brand values. This process will help you to get into the habit of extracting the most important brand values, which you will then use as inspiration throughout the rest of the BETTER brainstorm and during the more detailed planning process (according to the SET MESSAGE model, to be outlined later in the book).

After completing the first step of the BETTER model, you should have narrowed down two or three core brand values that you will then use to bring to life the Brand personality. For example, Brand Z, a fruity breakfast cereal, has a healthy, fit and natural Brand personality.

E is for Emotional connection

In the BETTER brainstorming model, the first E stands for Emotional connection. It is important that we form an Emotional connection with the target audience since we need to engage them in a way that will touch them beyond their conscious thoughts. The reason why this stage of the brainstorming process is so vitally important is that, by appealing to people's emotions and creating genuine Emotional connections, the experience is likely to embed itself in their memories. Studies have shown that vivid autobiographical memories are usually of emotional events. These emotional events are likely to be recalled in more detail, and more often, than emotionally neutral events. Emotional stimuli can heighten memory retention by triggering neuro-chemical activity affecting certain areas of the brain that are responsible for encoding and recalling.[1, 2, 3]

The Emotional connection stage of the BETTER brainstorming model is designed to gather inspiration for emotionally stimulating elements that integrate the results of the Brand personality and will combine with the Target audience stage to form the Two-way interaction part of the brainstorm (the top-line concept for the live brand experience). The two approaches that can best form inspiration for Emotional connections are the 'three key attributes' and multi-sensory elements.

Three key attributes

Experiential marketing should always make a deep Emotional connection with the target audience through their feelings. To achieve this connection we should apply elements that have the three key attributes to the live brand experience, which have to orchestrate in real time, 'in the here and now'. These attributes when integrated into the concepts for all live brand experiences, whether they are delivered remotely (through technology or communication platforms) or face to face, result in experiences that are more memorable. The three key attributes that should be thought about during this stage are authentic, positively connected, and personally meaningful. In essence, these attributes summarize what the concept should be to ensure that it connects with the emotions of the participant. If the live brand experience is not delivered face to face, a multi-sensory approach is less appropriate, but by applying the three key attributes you will still be able to create a genuine Emotional connection and embed the memory of the experience into the participant's mind. To create an Emotional connection, we therefore need to apply the three key attributes to the concept, and if the live brand experience is going to be executed face to face, then we do this in combination with the process of establishing a multi-sensory connection.

Multi-sensory elements

By adding into the concept multi-sensory elements (allowing consumers to touch, taste, smell, hear, and see) that are product-relevant, consumers can experience and most importantly feel an Emotional connection with the brand. In achieving a multi-sensory and immersive live brand experience, we are triggering emotions that traditional marketing and advertising approaches will struggle to reach. The multi-sensory approach is appropriate for live brand experiences that are set in face-to-face environments, and should be applied in combination with the three key attributes. By adding product-related multi-sensory elements we will utilize elevated platforms that engage emotions through the senses. Experiences that engage the senses affect the right brain hemisphere and create lasting impressions.[4]

People often ask, 'How do I decide which senses are appropriate for which live brand experience?' The answer is to refer to the product and the Brand personality for inspiration. Think of the sensory elements that are appropriate in each case, and think of how to apply the three key attributes, making the experience authentic, positively connected and personally meaningful. This will form the basis of a multi-sensory Emotional connection.

Example of the Emotional connection part of a BETTER brainstorm

A good example is a brainstorm that was conducted for a fruity breakfast cereal product (it was already established earlier in the brainstorm that it has a fit, healthy and natural Brand personality). The next step, after deciding that the live brand experience was going to be implemented face to face, was to brainstorm which senses would be appropriate. Taste was obvious here; it was important to allow the target audience to experience the superior taste of the fruity cereal. Touch, sight, smell and sound were also deemed relevant to the product and Brand personality, so it was concluded that all five senses would be stimulated. Some of the multi-sensory and three key attributes elements that came up during the Emotional connection stage were formatted into a table for easy reference later in the brainstorm; see Table 3.2.

The table demonstrates how to complete the Emotional connection stage while incorporating the Brand personality and the product into the multi-sensory elements and the three key attributes. In the example of the fit, healthy and natural Brand personality, it was clearly demonstrated how the brand values were integrated to create an Emotional connection through the multi-sensory and three key attributes elements. Because the creative team free-associated words that represented being healthy, natural and fit, they thought about taking care of the body, being healthy, things that represent being natural and in touch with nature and, as a direct result, many elements were suggested. Exercising, eating fruit and drinking plenty of water are some of the signs of a healthy lifestyle, therefore these actions were some of the sources of their inspiration. It was concluded that the brand values of being fit and healthy could be conveyed by a yoga exercise that the consumers could participate in.

Table 3.2 Emotional connection brainstorm

Multi-sensory element	Ideas
Touch	Consumers can participate in a yoga class inside the live brand experience set, to reflect the healthy brand value. They can also receive a goody bag to take home.
Taste	Consumers can be invited to eat the cereal prior to completing the main part of the experience, and we can give them fruit-flavoured water and a cereal sample in their goody bags.
Sight	People walking past the set can see the people who are participating in the experience on external plasma screens that can be built into the set. Also the appearance of the set can reflect the brand personality and product packaging.
Smell	In front of the entrance to the live brand experience set, we can place a big sculpture (like a water feature, but with milk instead of water) and emit the aroma of fruit using essential oils.
Sound	Once people enter the experience, we can play music that is recorded sounds from nature, to reflect the natural brand personality.

Three key attributes	Ideas
Authentic	The cereal product range is genuinely healthy (we have conducted tests that show it is healthier than rival brands), and we only use natural ingredients to make the product. Therefore, the healthy and natural themed experience *is* authentic.
Positively connected	We can take a photograph of participants while they are engaging, and then print their photo, putting it into a branded frame.
Personally meaningful	We can run a competition (this can link up with the PR amplification channel), asking participants to tell us about their 'get fit' stories, and ask them to explain how getting healthy and active has made their lives happier. We can also link this up with a competition prize.

Table 3.3   Emotional connection brainstorm

Multi-sensory element	Ideas
Touch	Consumers can go online to fill in a form that allows them to order a 'baking experience kit', which could include a branded apron, cake mix, and branded cookie tin.
Taste	Consumers can be invited to bake the cookies from home, obviously eat them, and then maybe even give some to their favourite neighbours.
Sight	People can upload photos of themselves baking, and of their finished cookies onto the live brand experience webinar site
Smell	Obviously the cookies have a lovely smell, but maybe we could send people that complete the experience a branded letter and envelope set, where the stationery carries the scent of brownies.
Sound	The webinar site, which is the location for the live brand experience, can feature a retro song in the background.

Three key attributes	Ideas
Authentic	The instant brownies and cookies company has been around since the 1950s, so the retro and neighbourly baking experience is definitely authentic. To convey this further, on the webinar site we can allow participants to download wallpapers featuring some of the original ads from the 1950s, which showed a happy woman giving cookies to her neighbour.
Positively connected	We can encourage all the participants to bake their cookies on the same day and at exactly the same time. We can incentivise them to comply by having a cut-off time after which they cannot submit their photos. Also we could have the same celebrity chef (that is in their current adverts) participate in the webinar baking experience at the same time.
Personally meaningful	We can run a competition (this can link up with the PR and TV amplification channels), inviting participants to create the next cake mix produced by this brand, by running a press and TV ad competition for the best homemade cake recipe. The amplification channels could also show imagery from participants of this live brand experience.

The combined elements were then used to think more explicitly of how the two-way connection could be carried out.

In another situation, a manufacturer of brownie mixes had a home-made, friendly neighbourhood and retro Brand personality and it was decided that the live brand experience should be carried out remotely from people's homes; see Table 3.3.

The emotional connection stage of the BETTER brainstorm for the brownie mixes live brand experience was still able to produce ideas for multi-sensory elements and the three key attributes even though the live brand experience was designed to be executed remotely (from home and online). Both the Brand personality and the product itself contributed to the suggested elements, which would eventually be combined and refined to further develop the Two-way interaction that the consumers would participate in. The activity can connect emotionally with the consumers, and the live brand experience (even though it is not face to face) would vividly remain a part of their memories. The multi-sensory elements of taste, touch, smell, sound and sight and the three key attributes – authentic, positively connected and personally meaningful – can, in combination, create memorable emotional connections with the target audience.

T is for Target audience

Besides brainstorming the core brand values that create the Brand personality, and thinking of elements that create an emotional connection, understanding the Target audience is essential in formulating the Two-way interaction, which should be at the heart of every experiential marketing campaign. It is of the utmost importance to know the target audience and make sure that the live brand experiences are relevant to them. What they like and what they dislike are crucial considerations. The market research does not have to be expensive, nor does it always have to be carried out by a market research agency. As long as you have insight into the Target audience (for example, how they behave and what their needs are), you are halfway there.

The experiential marketing must add value to their lives while exciting them and engaging them with the brand itself. If the product is, for example, a saving bond with a fun Brand personality, and the Target audience is affluent, conservative bankers, it would not be relevant to bring to life the featured product through a punk-rock themed live brand experience. Research shows that a conservative Target audience is unlikely to appreciate this type of activity and, therefore, even if this activity is relevant to the fun Brand personality, it is nonetheless irrelevant to the Target audience. Thus, before you finalize and confirm the emotional connections that you will create with your consumers, by bringing to life the product and the Brand personality with the three key attributes and multi-sensory elements, make sure that your Target audience will find these elements relevant to their lifestyle, their aspirations, their goals and their daily lives.

The ultimate aim is to create a golden bond with the participants of the live brand experience. The Emotional connection with the participants should be designed to create genuine, strong, deep relationships. How do we create relationships with people in real life? We build foundations for relationships by engaging likeminded people in Two-way interaction or dialogue that is relevant and interesting to both parties. It is a 'safe bet' to conclude that talking to people without listening to them would not facilitate a genuine relationship. In fact, this could annoy people and make them want to avoid the brand, or even spread negative word-of-mouth. Experiential marketing aims to convert consumers into brand advocates who love and champion their favourite brands. By using both qualitative and quantitative research you can learn more about what will appeal to your Target audience in a live brand experience.

At this stage of the brainstorm, check that any elements you have thought of are relevant to the Target audience, and think carefully about what will drive consumers to be enthusiastic about the live brand experience and inspire them to talk about the brand. The dialogue that you will create in the Two-way interaction (the talking and listening/ giving and taking process) is very similar to how relationships between people are formed, and admiration grows for a loved one or friend. Therefore, any insights into the target audience should be summarized here, and used to contribute to the Two-way interaction.

T is for Two-way interaction

Experiential marketing is the future of marketing because of the focus on Two-way interactions. The aim of the Two-way interaction (the live brand experience) is to create a foundation for all your integrated marketing communication channels that lets your target audiences know that your brand cares about them. Consumers are likely to reciprocate, as they would if it were a relationship with another human being. In a human relationship, one person must not take and take from the other person without giving back. Similarly, when creating an experiential marketing campaign, the live brand experience activity must engage, excite and dazzle the target audience: giving something back. You need to make the live brand experience a Two-way interaction in real time in order to engage and excite consumers. No matter how exciting and amazing a one-way communication, it will not create as deep and genuine a relationship with the receivers, regardless of whether they enjoy it. They will not feel like they participated in it and therefore they will not care. Just imagine an Average Joe who is invariably on his own until suddenly he begins dating a model. At first, she seems captivating and beautiful. However, time reveals that she never listens to anything he says. She does not seem to care about him and all she does is talk about herself. Sooner or later, she will start annoying Joe and his impression of her being beautiful will dissolve. He may stay around and suffer further because she is beautiful, but when another pretty woman moves into his neighbourhood, carefully listening to him and laughing at his jokes, he will leave the model and appreciate the Two-way interaction developing with the new woman.

This metaphor illustrates why it is important to have a Two-way interaction with consumers. It is vital to listen to them and have input from them, otherwise the communication is one-way and no matter how theatrical or entertaining the campaign may be, it will simply be entertainment, and the consumer will not truly connect with the brand and its personality. So how does one go about creating a Two-way interaction within an experiential marketing context? The answer is in the live brand experience. For example, there could be a game, service or an interaction where brand ambassadors and consumers engage, talk and listen. Experiential marketing has the potential to form the foundations of a life-long friendship where the consumer develops high loyalty for the brand. He or she then becomes a brand advocate who will recommend the brand and spread word-of-mouth. He or she is your brand evangelist.

The following is an example of how the dialogue develops. Harriet is the marketing manager for a new product that comes in three basic flavours: strawberry, orange and banana. The product is a delicious candy that is available in fresh new packaging. Harriet wanted to create a Two-way interaction with consumers and engage them, while discovering which flavours are the most popular (achieving market research objectives). Harriet decided that brand ambassadors positioned at the live brand experience could ask consumers what their favourite flavour was. By renaming each flavour so that it formed its own identity, she hoped to strengthen the impact of the interaction between the brand and the consumers. The brand ambassadors invited the target audience to identify with each flavour by asking if they are a 'sexy strawberry' person, a 'brave banana' person or an 'organized orange' person. Depending on their answers, the participants were led into a different part of the live brand experience set, and participated in an experience that was geared around their selection. It may seem that asking the target audience their favourite flavour was a simple and boring way to interact. But in actuality, the brand ambassadors asked them something about their identity. This made the consumers feel good because it showed that the brand cared about them as individuals.

The moral of this story is that the Two-way interaction should be as personalized to the Brand personality, the Emotional connection and the target audience as possible. Interactive questions, where answers then create a variation in the live brand experience and formulate research data, are a good approach to getting to know your consumers, developing a real relationship, and making them feel listened to. As long as the interaction is not a one-way venture, and it takes on board the previous three stages of the BETTER model, then you are on the right track to creating a fantastic and successful experiential marketing campaign. The Two-way interaction forms the basis of the top-line concept for the live brand experience, and will be further developed into a strategy during the experiential strategy part of the SET MESSAGE planning system.

E is for Exponential element

Thus far in the BETTER model, you have integrated the Brand personality, Emotional connection, Target audience, and a brand-relevant, Two-way interaction, which brings the Brand personality to life and adds value to the consumers' lives. Via these means, you are on your way to building valuable consumer relationships, creating brand loyalty and dazzling the hearts and minds of your consumers. Even though these benefits are superb and yield results that traditional approaches are less capable of achieving, an experiential marketing idea can be even better.

The experiential marketing idea (focused on the live brand experience) should integrate an Exponential element in which participants are encouraged to tell others about the brand experience. As previously mentioned, word-of-mouth is one of the most powerful tools, and one of the most solid benefits of experiential marketing. The Exponential element in an experiential campaign often happens by default, as the live brand experience part is extraordinarily powerful and exciting as is. The consumer who participates in the activity will tell other people about the live brand experience because the engagement excited and benefited him or her. However, anything that can be done to encourage them to spread the word is an added bonus, and should also be used in the amplification channels.

A live brand experience was designed to bring to life the bubbly, jovial Brand personality of a new orange-flavoured soda. The live brand experience part of the experiential marketing campaign encouraged consumers to play a juggling game with real oranges while bouncing on a giant orange trampoline. While they were engaging in the experience, brand ambassadors took their photo and told them that they could go online later to download it. When they got home and downloaded the photos of themselves trying to juggle and jump at the same time, they were able to send their picture to a friend. Participants were also prompted to play a flash game. This game represented the same experience that they enjoyed earlier, this time they could practise juggling and bouncing to try and get the highest score. The flash game brought the Brand personality to life again and further deepened the two-way relationship that was established in the live brand experience. The online site became an integral part of the Exponential element. When you give game-players a competitive incentive to invite their friends to compete at playing the game and to view their photos, the digital channel amplifies the live brand experience. In this case, the digital channel was home to the Exponential elements. These Exponential elements (forward the photo to a friend, and invite a friend to compete on the flash game) drove word-of-mouth, or in this case, WOW (word-

of-web). You may wonder why one would do this. Why is it necessary to have an Exponential element in the campaign? The answer is to obtain high 'Reach'.

R is for Reach

As discussed in Chapter 1, experiential marketing is sometimes subject to faulty assumptions such as: 'Experiential marketing is incapable of reaching a large number of people.' You may have a live brand experience in a shopping centre that creates quality interactions with 5,000 people per day, while a TV ad may deliver a one-way communication to 5 million people per day. If you are an ATL (above-the-line) marketer, you may be sceptical of the experiential marketing landscape because the live brand experience often reaches fewer people than the former approach. However, we must take into account the fact that each of the 5,000 people who interacted with the live brand experience is, on average, likely to tell 17 others. This experience will thus Reach a greater and greater number of people, as each will tell another, and each of those will continue to tell another. One can quickly see how the word-of-mouth generated from the live brand experience increases the Reach of the experiential campaign.

The Reach quality of one-way communications is far less likely to create a genuine relationship than that of live brand experiences. It is rare that we will see an ad in the paper or watch an ad on TV or prior to a movie and, later on, tell anyone about the 'experience'. In contrast, participating in a live brand experience through an experiential marketing campaign is exciting and we are very likely to tell many people about it. When coming up with an experiential marketing concept, always take into consideration both the initial Reach (the people who interact with the live brand experience) and the combined Reach of the experiential marketing campaign as a whole (including the amplification channels). Your live brand experience channel does not have to compete with the other channels, some of which can have a very high Reach. We know that other channels can be less effective when implemented traditionally, so for best results it is recommended that the live brand experience idea is integrated into the other selected channels. As a result, the experiential marketing campaign can Reach the highest possible volumes.

When you are in the Reach part of the BETTER brainstorming process, first take into consideration factors that affect the initial Reach of the live brand experience: where would be the ideal location to hold your experience? If we decided that the best place to hold the experience was the middle of a park, but there was no footfall in the park, then the

Reach factor is not addressed, making the initial Reach of the campaign unsuccessful. On the other hand, if we researched brand-relevant events where thousands of people attended and the target audience is consistently present, then this could be a more appropriate set of venues. Secondly, you should think of integrating additional channels that will ensure that the Reach of the complete experiential marketing campaign is high (ie, you could broadcast the live brand experience on the radio). Always remember to consider the word-of-mouth Reach (try using the Jack Morton statistic that is based on the number of interactions) generated from the live brand experience.

Summary

In summary, one must brainstorm and consider six stages when developing a top-line concept for an experiential marketing campaign. The BETTER brainstorm involves covering the following bases:

- Brand personality. Two or three main brand values, human-like characteristics that are extracted to form the Brand personality
- Emotional connection. The brand must strive to connect on an emotional level with its Target audience. This is best achieved through a combination of multi-sensory elements and the three key attributes: authentic, positively connected, and personally meaningful.
- Target audience. The Target audience is key when brainstorming the idea. Lots of research about the lifestyle of the target audience should be brought to the table, to ensure the right experience for the right people.
- Two-way interaction. The live brand experience involves interaction between consumers and brands in real-time (either remotely or face to face). The first three stages, Brand personality, Emotional connection and Target audience, should inspire this.
- Exponential element. The Exponential element should be designed to encourage participants to pass on their experience, spreading word-of-mouth.
- Reach. Clearly, gaining maximum Reach for the experiential marketing campaign is crucial. The initial Reach of the live brand experience, the word-of-mouth Reach and the combined Reach of the selected amplification channels should be taken into consideration. The right amplification channels should be there mainly to expand the Reach of the live brand experience, thus allowing the campaign's concept to engage more people.

The total BETTER brainstorm process should be completed in the following way. Begin by collecting any existing research and having it handy. Start with the B stage (thinking of the Brand personality, which you identify from the three main brand value and human characteristic components), then think of how to create an Emotional connection (multi-sensory and/or the three key attributes; authentic, positively connected, and personally meaningful), then take into consideration the Target audience (their likes, dislikes and lifestyle). Combine the first three steps to create the Two-way interaction. Then build in an Exponential element (taking into consideration the amplification channels), and think of how to maximize the Reach (the initial inter-actions with the live brand experience, the word-of mouth Reach, and the Reach of the most appropriate amplification channels).

Notes

1. Bradley, M M, Greenwald, M K, Petry, M C and Lang, P J (1992) Remembering pictures: Pleasure and arousal in memory, *Journal of Experimental Psychology: Learning, memory and cognition*, **18,** pp 379–90
2. Schacter, D L (1996) *Searching for Memory*, Basic Books, New York
3. Hamann, S B (2001) Cognitive and neural mechanisms of emotional memory, *Trends in Cognitive Sciences*, **5,** pp 394–400
4. LeDoux, J (1999) *The Emotional Brain: The mysterious underpinnings of emotional life*, Phoenix, London

4 IDEA

Having utilized the BETTER model, this chapter is about presenting the top-line ideas so that favourites can be identified for development. Whether working at an agency, business or brand, it is always best to present at least two or more ideas – you never know how people will take to your initiatives. There are several factors to be taken into consideration when choosing an idea. For example, cost for an adventurous concept can be complicated. It can be tricky to implement the live brand experience idea, especially considering integration with the other marketing channels you are using. The IDEA format is an effective way to present several top-line ideas, and it will allow you to create presentations that display top-line ideas without having to go into a detailed planning process for each one. Once an idea has been chosen, it should be developed further using the SET MESSAGE format, which will be explained in depth throughout the rest of the book.

The purpose of the IDEA format is to create presentations that allow shortlisting of top-line ideas for experiential marketing campaigns; see Table 4.1.

Table 4.1 IDEA

I	Inspiration and illustration	Summary of BET stages in BETTER and a visual of the idea
D	Details	Description of the activity
E	Evaluation	How you would evaluate the campaign
A	Approximate budget	A top-line, ballpark budget

Using IDEA

I is for Inspiration and illustration

The first phase in the IDEA model corresponds with the first three steps of the BETTER model, referring to Brand personality, Emotional connection and Target audience. These are the categories that inspired the idea. Start by creating a slide (in the presentation) in which you summarize in one short sentence where your inspiration came from. For example, if there is a concept for a new brand of plant fertilizer that has a magical brand personality and targets housewives, this would be outlined at the bottom of the slide. The rest of the slide should be a visual illustration. Here, it is advisable to use a professional graphic designer, agency, or your in-house creative team to prepare the illustration. This is a visual representation of what the idea will look like in real life, and it needs to be good.

It is usually preferable to present your idea's visual in 3D because it can demonstrate the concept more clearly than a 2D one. You do not have to spend much money preparing your illustration; if you do not have the resources in-house, graphic design graduates are normally more than happy to work with you on a freelance basis and prepare cost-effective illustrations, as it adds to their portfolio and provides extra cash. If you are part of a big organization, you will already have graphic design facilities, either in-house or through a creative agency and you may prefer to use them. In summary, the I in IDEA stands for Inspiration and illustration. This will be the first slide of your presentation. You should begin with a visual representation and the inspiration behind the idea, including the Brand personality, Emotional connection and the Target audience.

D is for Details

The details slide is the core of the presentation, where the real concept of the top-line idea is explained. First, the Details slide should have one or two paragraphs that provide an overview of the experiential concept and describe what elements are in place. For example, if we were to create a live brand experience for a Chinese food chain, we could set up a Chinese-style set in busy areas around a town centre. The Details slide would explain what this comprises. In other words, we could say the live brand experience for the Chinese food chain will be located in busy town centres and will be comprised of a Chinese-style set. We would also

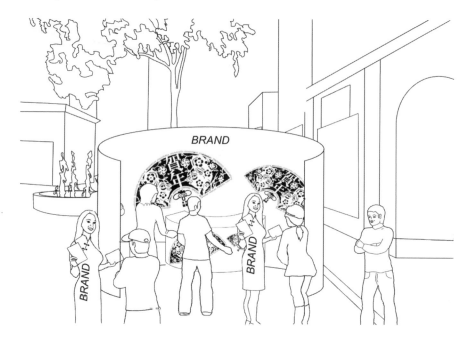

have a team of Brand ambassadors participating in the campaign. These are the people who communicate directly with the consumers, in this case wearing traditional Chinese clothing.

After introducing the set and team of Brand ambassadors, you will describe the action segment of the activity. For example, the Brand ambassadors could give away fortune cookies with sales promotion vouchers inside, as well as showing consumers how to paint with Chinese watercolours inside the Chinese set. After the first paragraph of the Details slide introducing what elements are present (in other words, the Chinese set and the team of Brand ambassadors), we would then have a numbered list that explains the timeline for the consumer interaction with the brand. Once consumers enter the experience, the Chinese Brand ambassador team approaches the target audience and invites them to participate in the live brand experience. The target audience enter the set and are invited to sit down and participate in a Chinese watercolours lesson. While having their watercolours lesson, they can view the food-chain's menu shown on plasma screens on a loop. After listening to gentle Chinese music, watching the adverts and having a watercolour lesson, they will receive a fortune cookie containing a sales promotion voucher for the restaurant chain. By creating a numbered list for this activity in the Details slide, you will explain how the consumer will participate in the experience and the idea itself.

The final paragraph in this slide summarizes what benefits and objectives will be met by this idea. For example, 'After the consumer has engaged with the Chinese live brand experience campaign, they will associate the food chain with traditional Chinese culture. It will position the chain as a brand of authentic Chinese food, which brings a touch of China into the city life. The activity will also drive sales to the restaurant as a result of the incentives provided by the sales promotion fortune cookies.' In summary, the Details slide of IDEA begins by introducing the elements of the campaign, continues with a numbered list explaining exactly how the idea will work in practice, and culminates in a summary of what benefits and objectives the experience facilitates.

E is for Evaluation

The Evaluation slide of the IDEA presentation is essential because it gives the audience an understanding of how you will measure the success of your campaign. Everybody wants to know how an idea will be evaluated because when spending money on a campaign, people need to know they will get results and that these results are measurable and explicit. It is important to build on ways of measuring the success of your campaign in the planning stage. Even at the concept stage, where you are presenting your top-line idea, it is important to let people know that it is possible to measure the effectiveness of the campaign.

The Evaluation slide should be formatted as an overview when providing multiple ideas in top-line format. However, once an idea is chosen, you will plan in more detail using the SET MESSAGE methodology (to be described later in the book) to cover a much more in-depth analysis of how to evaluate this experiential campaign. When preparing the Evaluation slide, there are standard metrics that should be included. It is recommended to present this in a formatted table, the first column showing the title 'metrics' and containing the following rows:

- OTS (opportunity to see);
- number of interactions (in the live brand experience);
- word-of-mouth reach (which should be calculated as 17 times the number of interactions);
- number of samples/or promotional merchandise distributed (if relevant to the live brand experience);
- any other elements that are relevant, depending on your objectives and amplification channels. For example: number of hits to microsite, number of text message responses to the billboard (amplification channel), number of data captures, number of

market research responses, number of sales, increase of footfall in-store – all depending on your objectives.

The second column of the table should read 'Total estimates'. Each row should correspond to its appropriate metric. It is important to state whether these numbers are per day or per week, while also including the total estimates throughout the entirety of the campaign.

A is for Approximate budget

This leads us to the final question, 'What is the cost of the campaign?', which is presented in the final slide, Approximate budget. The reason the budget is estimated is that, at this stage, you do not want to spend a huge amount of time planning the costs in great detail. That said, it is important that your costs are still realistic and based on genuine units, as your final confirmed budget should fall within plus or minus 10 per cent of the approximate budget.

The Approximate budget should be split into relevant cost categories, usually between five and six for the live brand experience plus estimates for amplification channels. Category 1 should include the live brand experience set production costs, such as the Chinese-style set for the Chinese restaurant in the earlier example. Category 2 includes all merchandise needed for the campaign, such as the fortune cookies, the uniforms for the Brand ambassadors, and other giveaways. Category 3 is staff costs. This should include the cost of the Brand ambassadors, as well as anyone needed to implement the campaign, such as drivers and riggers. Logistics is Category 4, which includes the costs of transporting the set and all of the other items, as well as rigging and de-rigging the set. This will also include any storage and packaging and postage costs. Category 5 is for expenses, which accounts for things such as hotel rooms, food budgets and travel costs, as well as the phone bill for the staff, which you will be paying. Your sixth category could be space hire, which will include the cost of permits for positioning the live brand experience campaign in places such as town centres. Your seventh category could cover costs associated with the amplification channels (for example radio competitions and print ads).

In each of these categories you should have realistic approximations of the costs, and these costs should be based on real quotes from suppliers. In each category, give an indication of how many days the cost is for. The final cost will be your management fee, which should be calculated at about 20 per cent of the cost of the campaign. If you are using an external agency, then obviously you will need to incorporate the management cost according to the pricing structure that they use.

To summarize the IDEA presentation: there is the Inspiration and illustration slide (with the graphic image), the Details slide (with the meat of the idea), then the Evaluation slide (estimates and metrics), and finally the Approximate budget (showing ballpark costs for the live brand experience and amplification channels). These four slides in the IDEA format are representative of the top-line idea for an experiential campaign and are necessary to narrow down the top-line ideas and develop them further.

Choosing the idea

There are different factors that should be taken into consideration when choosing the top-line idea, such as the components of the BETTER model: Brand personality, Emotional connection, Target audience, Two-way interaction, the Exponential element, and the Reach of the campaign, as well as making sure that the concept is right for the objectives. It is also very important to take into consideration the budget, how realistic the idea is and the timescale you are able to roll out on. It is therefore important to prepare three ideas that vary, from a simple to a more complex one, always keeping your focus on both the Brand personality and the Target audience.

5 Situation and background

Up to this point we have gone through the BETTER brainstorm process, created the IDEA presentation(s), and shown them to the decision-making unit, boss or client. As a result, a decision has been made about which top-line idea is to be developed in further detail, since a more detailed idea, strategy and plan are required prior to implementation. This is where the SET MESSAGE model comes into play. SET MESSAGE is a more detailed planning system, which ensures that both your Experiential objectives and Experiential strategy are supported by built-in systems for systematic planning and Evaluation, enabling you to keep your campaign on track. These systems will allow the people responsible to assess the plans in depth prior to implementation and to gauge effectiveness during the campaign, as well as effectively evaluate it afterwards.

SET MESSAGE

The SET MESSAGE model stands for:

Situation and background;
Experiential objectives;
Target audience;
Message – key communication;

Experiential strategy;
Selected locations and Brand ambassadors;
Systems and mechanisms for measurement;
Action;
Gauging effectiveness;
Evaluation.

It is important to carry out a systematic planning process, so that once you've completed it you have a very straightforward framework to follow. The campaign plan becomes a blueprint for implementation success, in which delegating tasks and managing different segments of your campaign becomes simple. It has been said that 'If you fail to plan, you plan to fail.' This is definitely true for experiential marketing. The live brand experience should be at the core of the experiential marketing idea, and as with any live event, there are many more factors, both external and internal, to make things go wrong. Detailed planning is the only way to avoid the detrimental effects of unexpected eventualities occurring during a live brand experience. Also, by having a detailed plan that addresses every element of the campaign, you will have answers to many of the questions that will arise from those who may be sceptical about experiential marketing. Whether these inquisitive people are internal to your organization or part of a client team, it is important to show that you have covered all bases from the campaign's inception.

Consequences can be grave if planning is not carried out properly. As a busy individual, you will not have time to plan as you go along. If you fail to plan systematically, there are areas of your campaign that are doomed to be neglected, and sacrifices will have to be made. For example, if you do not decide what the measurement metrics for your campaign are in advance, then although your campaign may be successful, it will be impossible to prove that the benefits were a direct result of the campaign.

Imagine that you are working in an agency. One of your clients has a website and it has given you the task of creating an experiential marketing campaign designed to promote its website. If you failed to plan, how would you track visitors to the site? There would be no way of proving the direct correlation between the increase in site visitors and the consumers that engaged in the experiential marketing campaign. There is no guarantee that your client would not claim the increase was due to the £5 million it spent on traditional TV advertising. Even if you were sure that at least 60 per cent of this increase in traffic was due to the exciting and engaging experiential campaign you implemented, it is not a fact until you can prove it to your client or stakeholders. The Systems and mechanisms for measurement part of the SET MESSAGE plan would have enabled you to plan how to communicate to stakeholders what portion of the increase in web traffic was due to the experiential marketing campaign. Something as simple as a promotional code or unique URL would suffice. Moreover, the client would have agreed to this form of measurement in advance and would, therefore, appreciate the significance of the results once the campaign has been implemented.

Not planning a live brand experience in detail can mean staffing inappropriate Brand ambassadors. No matter how amazing the idea for the live brand experience is, if the wrong team of Brand ambassadors interacts with the consumers, the concept behind the live brand experience could be nullified. Along with providing the right Brand ambassadors (to match the brand personality and target audience), detailed project management systems, budgets and schedules are essential in attaining success. If one were to miss important deadlines and have bad project management as a result, the campaign would inevitably lead to a below-par execution. Similarly, if the amplification channels are not properly integrated in the planning stages to maximize the impact of the live brand experience, a lot of money can be wasted on traditional media that does not contribute significantly to the overall success of the experiential marketing campaign.

The rest of this book is formatted according to the SET MESSAGE methodology, with each chapter focusing on a different letter of the planning system. By the time you finish reading, you will be able to see the importance of, and have a clear framework for planning an experiential marketing campaign in detail. The first step is discussed below.

Situation and background

The S in SET MESSAGE stands for Situation and background. This is the first category of your detailed experiential marketing campaign plan. The purpose of the Situation and background category is to give an overview of what the company and brand have been doing up until now and the relevance of this background to the current experiential marketing plan. This category should also detail information about competitors' previous experiential marketing programmes.

It is best to begin by including data on the history of the brand. For instance, there is a brand of energy drinks that targets people who play sport or live an active lifestyle. The energy drink was invented around 50 years ago and was originally targeted at sick children. However, after the realization that the drink is more effectively targeted towards people with active lifestyles, the energy drink changed its positioning. This type of information is worth mentioning in the Situation and background part of the SET MESSAGE plan.

In addition to the historical background, you should also mention things such as the size of the market and the market share currently held by the brand. Any other key information about the philosophy and ethos of the brand, such as 'The brand is owned by a family business that operates with fair trade policies', would be excellent to mention in this category. It is also recommended that you look at the types of marketing carried out over the last five years and provide a brief summary, preferably in one or two paragraphs, indicating which marketing channels have been used (especially those that have been used with the most success or where there was a lack of impact on the brand performance).

Research the factors that have led this brand (your organization or client) to use experiential marketing. Where relevant, you should mention whether you or others have done any experiential marketing for this brand in the past, and if so, how successful the campaigns were.

For example, Jessica has been the brand manager of a denim company for the last five years. The majority of her marketing budget had gone into TV advertising, with some print advertising, and a bit of digital over the last year. The reason that she is now thinking of placing live brand experiences at the core of the marketing communications strategy is that the live experience channel is superb at driving word-of-mouth, can change the perception of the brand and reposition it as being trendier. After exploring tools like sponsorship, she has decided that an integrated experiential marketing approach will give the most credibility and the live brand experience channel, when amplified by the other selected channels, will be most effective in attaining her objectives. In Jessica's case, this is the first time she will be implementing an experiential marketing strategy. If, however, she had already done some experiential marketing for the brand, then it would be important to mention what the Strengths, weaknesses and insights report (this will be explained in detail later in the book) from the previous effort had shown.

Robert is a brand manager of a beer company. The beer is imported from Asia and has a very different taste to other beers. Robert has consequently run field marketing programmes to encourage product trial, which conveyed the strength of the product in the last three years. The previous field marketing initiatives have successfully driven product trials, but they have not really succeeded in conveying the Asian heritage of the brand. Therefore, if you were Robert, at this stage in the SET MESSAGE method, you would explain that while the field marketing campaigns have been successful, they have not achieved all of the objectives. This is why Robert now wants to try an experiential marketing approach, replacing the field marketing with live brand experience programmes, and integrating the live brand experience into the other marketing communications channels to form the complete experiential marketing programme.

In the Situation and background, you should also mention any important changes that are relevant. Sometimes an experiential marketing methodology marks the introduction of a new strategy for the complete communications mix. The reasons for this could vary; for example, it could be a reaction to a customer experience management orientation developing throughout the organization.

In another example, Frank was the marketing director of a condensed milk drink brand. In response to a recent decision to adopt a market development strategy in which a new hard-to-reach audience of Caribbean males would be targeted, Frank decided that a traditional approach would not be appropriate. By using media, there would be a lot of wastage and Frank's market research agency felt that Caribbean males would not be as responsive to above-the-line methods. Therefore, he signed a significant portion of the marketing budget to a live brand experience programme and chose PR along with radio to amplify it and form the complete experiential marketing campaign. Frank explained this when he was preparing the Situation and background part of his SET MESSAGE plan.

Another element that should be included in the Situation and background category is research on your competitors and what experiential marketing they have done. When you were brainstorming using the BETTER model and presented the concepts using the IDEA format, you looked at competitors with the same type of Brand personality, product or Target audience, and what experiential marketing they have employed. This includes the Emotional connection they used and which senses they stimulated. Keep in mind: this is research that should have already been completed prior to coming up with the topline concept, so at this stage of your plan you are simply referencing it.

Summary

In summary, the Situation and background part of your SET MESSAGE plan should provide an overview of the brand's history, its current situation or brief, what has happened before, why it was or wasn't successful, as well as any interesting and successful experiential marketing campaigns that other brands with similar Brand personalities or Target audiences have executed.

6 Experiential objectives

The second step in the SET MESSAGE planning methodology focuses on which Experiential objectives to choose at this stage of the plan. You will already have an idea of the type of objectives you would like to achieve, because you will have decided that as part of the broader marketing communications strategy. When you are coming up with your Experiential objectives, you can often be more creative than with traditional approaches because experiential marketing facilitates meeting many objectives that can be harder to attain otherwise. As previously discussed, there are many benefits to be gained from running successful experiential marketing campaigns and, as a result, there are many exciting objectives to choose from, but you should stick with no more than three.

It is important to include all the relevant information when presenting your experiential objectives. Try presenting in this format: To achieve objective x, for brand x, with target audience x, in location x, by date x. For example: To increase sales for Barley Bars with 20–30-year old women in France by January 2011.

Prior to embarking on the SET MESSAGE planning system, you will have already completed several BETTER brainstorms, presented the top-line concepts using the IDEA format, and selected one for detailed development. At this stage you may need to adapt the top-line concept to ensure that it is appropriate and fits in with the Experiential objectives. The following are examples of some experiential marketing campaigns that were geared around specific objectives.

Examples of experiential marketing campaigns

Bringing the Brand personality to life

John is a marketing manager who is responsible for a breakfast bar with a sporty and active brand personality that targets healthy males and females aged 18–35. John wanted to bring the bar's Brand personality to life in the United States. His experiential marketing agency designed a sporty live brand experience that ran for one month in each of the eight largest parks across the North-east. The live brand experience set featured circuit-training elements, where consumers were invited to participate in a circuit challenge across several exercise stations, such as a jogging machine, a rowing machine, a push-up bench and monkey bars. They were then invited to have their pulse taken and heart rate tested. A branded wall that showed the breakfast bar, its logo and colour scheme surrounded the circuit equipment. Consumers who completed the circuit challenge in less than two minutes won a goody bag containing: a sample bar, a sales promotion voucher (to entice them to purchase in the future), a branded T-shirt, and a branded stopwatch.

After the experience, research showed that the Target audience associated this breakfast bar brand with a sporty and active lifestyle and therefore the campaign achieved this objective. It also achieved its second and third objectives of driving product trial (with the sample in the goody bag) and driving sales (with the voucher in the goody bag). The experiential marketing agency worked on the campaign in partnership with John's media agency, which is responsible for the brand's media (creative, planning and buying). The live brand experience was filmed by the media agency and clips were edited, contributing to a 30-second advert promoting both the product itself and the upcoming live brand experiences. The ads were broadcast during carefully allocated slots prior to sporting events on TV. The successful integration of the live brand experiences, sales promotion vouchers and TV adverts was a result of good communication between John's experiential marketing agency, sales promotion agency and media agency, which worked together to deliver the integrated experiential marketing campaign.

Drive word-of-mouth

Mark is the brand manager for a new basketball computer game with revolutionary features. He wanted to drive word-of-mouth about the game among 16–21-year old city-based males. His PR agency created a gaming experience held outside basketball courts in his target cities. They hired an experiential marketing agency to design branded 'chill-out zones' with comfy couches, large surround-sound plasma screens, gaming consoles, and fridges containing free soft drinks (branded with the video game imagery). The participants were asked to provide their contact data upon entering the chill out zone, prior to playing the video game. High scorers (around 40 per cent of participants) were offered the opportunity to receive free (branded) business cards with their own contact details printed on them. Each high-scorer had a special status as a 'team member' of the video game manufacturers' 'preview team'. The Exponential element was very strong, because the Target audience used the business cards when socializing and giving their phone number out to their peers. Every time that they gave a business card to someone, they were likely to mention the video game and their involvement with it (especially because their membership in the preview team was a cool talking point).

The PR agency invited a famous basketball player to launch the first day of the live brand experience every time it visited a new city; as a result, they succeeded in gaining a large amount of publicity and drawing large crowds. When the same video game manufacturer wanted to achieve its market research objectives, they invited the 'preview team members' to exclusive video gaming preview sessions and gave out demo versions of the games. Again, this activity created a talking point that drove word-of-mouth among the Target audience. As well as achieving the primary word-of-mouth objective, this experience achieved secondary objectives: gaining PR coverage, capturing data and positioning the brand as the basketball videogame with the best street credentials amongst a media-savvy young target audience, who would have been less likely to respond to traditional channels.

Create a memorable brand experience

Sandy owns a travel website that sells holidays to exotic locations in the Caribbean and warm places around the world. She had spent a significant amount of money with her advertising agency and had benefited from a healthy increase in web traffic when they ran print ads, but as soon as she stopped paying for ads, her site traffic would plummet. She wanted to utilize a marketing approach that would have a longer-lasting effect. Her main objective was to create a memorable brand experience. She also hoped to convey the exotic Brand personality of the travel company through the campaign, with the aim that after participating in the live brand experience, her Target audience would continue to think of her business when booking their next holiday. She wanted them to remember her company and the experience they had.

She designed a live brand experience that featured a touring Caribbean beach set with Brand ambassadors dressed in traditional Caribbean clothing. The live brand experience toured around the country during the summer and targeted families. Carefully positioned Brand ambassadors invited consumers to have their photos taken while visiting the 'beaches' (which were also artificially warmed using special lamps). The participants were handed glossy brochures that both promoted the travel website and invited consumers to visit a micro-site, where they could download their photos. Once the consumers visited the micro-site, they were prompted to enter their contact data prior to downloading their photos, after which they had the option to forward their photos to friends and family, as well as order free hard copies in branded frames. This live brand experience campaign proved to be highly memorable, and it also achieved secondary press coverage and data capture objectives.

Drive product trial and sign up members

A market-leading natural skincare brand from Asia launched in the UK. They approached an experiential agency to work on their launch, as well as ongoing live brand experience activities. The agency built an experiential set that featured a counter for signing people up to the brand's monthly beauty magazine, and sampling counters at the rear for product testing and demonstrations. The set also had display stands that featured the magazines along with highly visible branding and signage, which reflected the brand identity and Message – key communication.

The experiential set toured around brand-relevant beauty shows and events. A carefully trained team of Brand ambassadors visually reflected the brand (and had relevant experience in the beauty sector) and were the interface between the brand and the guests of the shows. The Brand ambassadors wore tailor-made uniforms that fused Japanese and English style. By engaging consumers with the offer of product consultations and free four-step skincare samples, the team were able to sign up large numbers of the Target audience to the brand's monthly magazine. The experience also featured multimedia messages that were transmitted to guests' phones via Bluetooth technology. The Bluetooth messages featured a product showcase and allowed consumers to respond and sign up to the magazine.

The live brand experience achieved objectives of driving product trial amongst the Target audience, as well as signing membership for the magazine. The activity also resulted in an increase in website traffic and sales, thus achieving other objectives.

Increase sales

When Mary, a brand manager for a popular yoghurt brand, was assigned the task of increasing sales and engaging mums with young children, she asked her sales promotion agency to come up with a creative live brand experience concept. Her sales promotion agency worked closely with an experiential marketing agency because they knew that live brand experiences are more likely to drive purchase consideration than any other channel.[1] The experiential marketing agency created life-size versions of the fruit characters that were usually found on the yoghurt pot packaging. Brand ambassadors who stood outside supermarkets (where the yoghurts were sold) wore the costumes. The fruity characters engaged young children, asking them what their favourite fruit was, and provided them with a free sample of yoghurt (in the flavour of their chosen fruit). The Brand ambassadors also told the mothers about the

nutritional value of the yoghurts, while giving them a nutritional booklet that featured scratch and sniff stickers (for the kids), and a discount coupon (that they could redeem inside the supermarkets).

This campaign increased sales by an average of 80 per cent in participating stores. It also achieved the secondary objectives of driving product trial and delivering complex brand messages about the nutritional value of the yoghurts.

Communicate complex brand messages

Vladimir is responsible for marketing a premium brand of vodka, and he approached an experiential marketing agency with the task of communicating complex brand messages about the product. The vodka has a unique five-step purification process. The agency helped him to design a campaign in which that complex brand message was brought to life symbolically. The live brand experience was implemented at upmarket nightclubs, where consumers were invited to sit on a larger-than-life luxurious 'purification chair', put on a silk blindfold and proceed to be 'purified' with an aromatic, facial cleansing wipe and a head and shoulder massage from a 'purification angel'. Then, each

participant received a shot of vodka to complete the 'purification process.' During this experience, the consumers were informed that they were going through a 'five-step purification process', just like the vodka did. This live brand experience successfully communicated the complex brand message, which other marketing channels would have been less likely to convey with such ease and tangibility.

Position the brand

Savio is the marketing and sales director of a sportswear company that sells comfortable, sporty clothing in Australia. He wanted to position the sportswear brand as a trendy and preferred option for comfortable streetwear with influential opinion leaders aged 16–25. He knew through market research that his Target audience enjoyed street dance, and he decided to gain credibility with his audience by holding a live brand experience tour. The campaign featured dance competitions at music festivals across Australia, where all the visitors had the opportunity to enter and compete. The competitive spirit attracted big crowds to cheer their respective dancer friends, while giveaways were thrown into the crowd. The dancers who competed wore the sportswear clothing, and danced for five minutes each while trendy music was played by popular DJs.

These dance competitions were some of the biggest talking points of the music festivals. Gaining credibility is hard with a media-savvy audience; this was a success, as were the word-of-mouth and free publicity that the campaign generated. All of this would have been much more difficult to achieve through traditional media channels or sponsorship alone.

Target a new audience

When a new mobile phone offering was launched by one of the biggest mobile phone providers in the world, it wanted to attract a consumer audience to purchase a phone that had previously been targeted at the business market. Grace, who was responsible for the marketing of the phone, wanted to create personalized interactions that tailored which of the product's many features and benefits were to be demonstrated to the Target audience. She wanted to communicate that the phone was ideal for organizing consumers' busy social lives. She hired an agency to provide Brand ambassadors (who went through intensive training so as to understand the product features and benefits and learn how to demonstrate the phones). During the live brand experience activity, the Brand ambassadors wore Adscreens (17-inch plasma screens/sound system backpacks). The Adscreens were connected to the phones to demonstrate the features, as well as to show a tutorial on loop. The Brand ambassadors were positioned outside participating stores on weekends and were tasked with attracting the new consumer to participate in a tailor-made demonstration. The Brand ambassadors asked the consumers questions such as 'Do you go on Facebook?' and 'How often do you check your e-mail?' The answers gave the Brand ambassadors an indication of which features to demonstrate. Consumers who were interested in finding out about the different packages available were directed to sales advisers in-store.

By tailoring the demonstrations, the product's features and benefits that were showcased were specific to the needs of the consumer. The live brand experiences successfully achieved the main objective of the campaign: attracting a new consumer Target audience to purchase the phone.

Increase customer loyalty

Marco is the owner of a family pizza chain and wanted to increase customer loyalty. He had previously been offering a one-off 30 per cent discount to customers who had visited the restaurant 10 times, but his margins were tight and he soon found the promotion was not worth the investment. Mario's consumers were not overly excited by the prospect of the 30 per cent discount, and the loyalty scheme was largely unsuccessful. After hearing from a friend about the benefits of experiential marketing approaches, he concluded that he should start by implementing a live brand experience. He decided to try out the innovative approach to increase customer loyalty.

He designed an experiential incentive of a free 'pizza-making workshop' with his well-known pizza expert Chef Tony. The incentive was awarded to all customers who visited the restaurant 10 times (this was monitored with stamps on a card). The new experiential loyalty scheme worked out well. Not only did the prize encourage customers to complete 10 visits, but also once they had experienced a workshop, they told all their friends about it with excitement. Marco thus achieved his primary objective of increasing customer loyalty while achieving his other objectives of driving word-of-mouth and differentiating the pizza chain brand from its competitors.

Increase footfall in-store

Amanda is the brand manager for a popular high-street retailer. The retail outlet sells inexpensive fashion garments and targets teenage girls. After a retail slump in 2008, she was tasked with increasing footfall in-store. After fitting new footfall detection devices into all the outlets, Amanda's bosses were keen to see an increase, fast. She had read in recent trade press that experiential marketing was delivering both instant and long-term results when it came to driving traffic into retail outlets and decided to give it a go. She did not have a huge budget and resolved to cut funds from some of their print advertising. She decided to use her remaining print budget to run ads in a magazine that was frequently read by teenage girls. The ads featured a competition, inviting readers that wanted to become a 'window model' for the day (and win a mini shopping spree) the chance to be part of the campaign. The readers of the magazine were more than enthusiastic at the chance to become a model for the day, with thousands applying after seeing the ads. She hired an experiential marketing agency to look after the experiential marketing campaign, and had them train 100 lucky competition winners to become 'window models' (like live mannequins posing in the store windows). All the competition entrants that 'failed to win' the opportunity to be a 'window model' were invited to preview the new season's collections on the day before the campaign went live. They were excited at this privilege and the thought of previewing the collection before the public drove them to tell all their friends about their honour. As well as having the winners modelling in the windows, the agency also hired professional models to parade on mini-catwalks that they raised outside the stores, with Brand ambassadors distributing invitations for fashion consultations inside. Each store manager was invited to a weekend training session prior to the campaign in which they were taught how to spend time training their best internal store staff on giving fashion consultations. The store staff (who received good sales commissions) were attempting to consult customers on fashion advice anyway, so the training programme was well accepted. Amanda also got her PR agency involved, which sent members of the local press to flash away and add buzz to the catwalk outside.

The integrated experiential marketing campaign resulted in a consumer frenzy, with queues of teenage girls (members of the target audience) waiting to have fashion consultations, a flood of excited shoppers entering the stores, and an increase in sales because of the consultations. Everybody was happy. There was an 80 per cent increase on the newly installed footfall devices. The 'window girls' spread word-of-mouth about their experiences as models and their shopping sprees. The preview girls spread word-of-mouth. The consumers were happy to be treated like celebrities with personal stylists. And finally, the store staff were pleased with the extra commission that they earned.

Summary

It is really important to adapt the content of your idea to match the experiential objectives. Ultimately, the experiential objectives are the reason that you are implementing experiential marketing and live brand experiences and therefore achieving them should always be the focus of your campaigns. For example, there is no point in aiming to increase sales in the short term if the campaign is located far away from the retail outlets (detailed information on selecting locations is provided later in the book).

Experiential marketing can achieve many objectives, but do not overload your plan; stick to three main aims at most, and make sure that all your objectives are measurable. As we saw, experiential marketing is especially good at achieving the following objectives:

1. Bringing the Brand personality to life.
2. Positioning or repositioning the brand.
3. Creating a memorable experience.
4. Communicating complex brand messages.
5. Gaining high long-term ROI (an LROI formula is given later in the book).
6. Increasing customer loyalty.
7. Gaining credibility with specific Target audiences.
8. Driving word-of-mouth.
9. Creating brand advocacy.
10. Increasing sales.
11. Raising brand awareness.
12 Driving website traffic or driving traffic in-store.

In fact, the measurable objectives are infinite. Later in the book you will learn how to build into the plan Systems and mechanisms for measurement that directly relate to each experiential objective.

Note

1. Jack Morton Worldwide. An executive summary of this survey is available online at www.JackMorton.com

7 Target audiences

As with all marketing, it is crucial to know your Target audience. If we don't know who we are selling to, then it is impossible to tailor our campaign accordingly. It is important to clarify Target audiences so that we can create the right experience for the right people.

As we discussed earlier, experiential marketing is adept at reaching large volumes of people through word-of-mouth. It is not simply that the live brand experience can reach a huge number of people directly, but that the impact of the communication is exponential. As we have seen, while reaching a relatively small number of people, the impact on those people is such that an average of 17 more are also reached through word-of-mouth recommendation from each person directly affected by the live brand experience.

To capitalize on this word-of-mouth process, it is important to know that the initial group reached is really the best group; best because they are the group who will influence the rest. Sometimes known as 'opinion leaders', the initial group should be people who are used to disseminating information to their peers, and who are already seen as credible sources of information. If this targeting is done effectively, the initial reach and word-of-mouth reach will be far greater and brand advocacy will be the engine fuelling the campaign towards success and achieving objectives.

Before continuing with the SET MESSAGE planning model, it is important to really think about and research the lifestyle, or the day-in-the-life of your ideal consumers, as well as looking at their aspirational lifestyle. By this, I mean that it is advisable to look at their aspirations, who they look up to, and the lifestyles of the people that they aspire to be like. We thought about the Target audience while using the BETTER model, but during this stage it was only a top-line concern. Now we must conduct a much more in-depth analysis to provide us with important answers for the rest of the SET MESSAGE model. For example, when selecting locations and Brand ambassadors, we will be directly inspired by the data we will gather at this stage of the plan. As well as always being best suited to communicating with consumers in their real daily lives and appealing to their lifestyle aspirations, experiential marketing is especially effective at reaching specific Target audiences. It has been proven effective for all groups, especially niche audiences and, as discussed previously, Generations X and Y.

Analysing Target audiences

The following are examples of how we would go about analysing particular Target audiences in the context of specific ideas and varying sectors. To begin, let's look at young British mums with kids aged between 1 and 6. This Target audience has been colloquially named 'yummy mummies'.

To carry out an experiential campaign for this group, we would have to analyse the group through market research. It can be expensive to conduct primary research, so secondary data can be a good option. We would only conduct primary research if we had significant budgets for this stage of the plan or if the secondary research was insufficient in providing the data we needed. There are several resources online that can help in providing existing in-depth research of different niche groups. Even though these reports cost money, the information is very valuable and will be key in the success of the campaign. Therefore, it is worth investing in acquiring this data.

A day-in-the-life analysis of a yummy mummy

She wakes up and prepares a packed school lunch for her son. She may also ensure that he has the relevant stuff he needs, including his books and gym kit. Once the child is ready to go to school, she is likely to drive him there, possibly bringing a younger child or baby in the car with her. As a more affluent mother, she possibly has a childminder or somebody to look after her younger child during the day. Once she has dropped both children off, she will probably go for a morning coffee with other young mothers in a café or restaurant. She may do some shopping during the afternoon or go to the gym. After going to the gym and doing some shopping, and possibly having lunch with another friend, she is likely to head home prior to picking up her son from school. Then, once she has collected him, she may drop him off at some kind of extracurricular activity, such as a sport group, or at a friend's house. Once at home, she is likely to prepare dinner, and possibly watch television before her husband returns from work. Once the husband is home, and their son is back from his extracurricular activity, the family may sit down together for a meal. Alternatively, she and her husband may go out to dinner while the children are looked after by a babysitter or a live-in housekeeper. When they go out for dinner, they are likely to go into town and eat somewhere a bit more intimate or fashionable, not the same restaurant where they eat when they bring the children along on the weekend.

This is a typical weekday. On the weekend, things will be very different. It is likely that the family will all go out together on a Saturday. They may stay at home, but she will be with her husband throughout the weekend. They may even all go away for the weekend, possibly to visit relatives or go to the countryside as a rest from the city. They may all go shopping and visit a local mall, an exhibition or show, as well as possibly going to the cinema.

The school holidays will greatly influence this target audience, because if there is a break, the family is likely to either go on holiday or visit child-oriented attractions such as a zoo, an amusement park or the local leisure centre.

Aspirations of a yummy mummy

There is also the question of who the yummy mummy will look up to. Research showed that it is likely that she will look up to celebrities who also have children but are able to maintain a busy lifestyle and an attractive appearance. The research also showed that the mums aspire to have highly intelligent and creative children.

As you can see, it is not possible to predict exactly what will happen in everybody's life, because no two people are the same. But by painting a picture of a typical day-in-the-life of your target audience, you will begin to understand when, where and how to engage them.

How does the analysis influence an idea for a yoghurt brand?

With this background information in mind, we can focus our minds on the yoghurt brand mentioned in Chapter 6. They targeted young mums with kids aged 1 to 6, and used live brand experiences to increase sales at supermarkets. The brand manager, Mary, worked with her agency that used the BETTER model to come up with more ideas for live brand experiences (this time with the main objective of creating a memorable experience). After presenting the ideas using the IDEA format to the marketing director, it had been narrowed down to one idea for further development using the SET MESSAGE model.

The idea chosen involved having the same Brand ambassadors dressed up as fruit characters, this time engaging children and inviting them to have their pictures taken together with the fruit characters. But then, rather than being able to take their photos home on the spot, the Brand ambassadors would give nutritional information booklets to the mothers, as well as discussing the nutritional advantages of the yoghurt. The booklets were reprinted with additional information and directed the yummy mummies to a micro-site that had been specially created for the yoghurt experience. Once on the micro-site, the mothers would be prompted to enter their contact information, at which point they would be able to log in and download the photos of their kids with the fruit characters.

After having looked carefully at the day-in-the-life of a yummy mummy, Mary decided that it would be best to implement the campaign during school holidays. This would be the best time to reach large numbers of influential mothers and children. After carefully researching the footfall

of the locations likely to be visited on school holidays, it was concluded that zoos and amusement parks would be the best locations for the live brand experience. It was also discovered that the Target audience looked up to other mothers who had maintained a good physical appearance, and therefore the Brand ambassadors should reflect that image and personality. Mary decided that she would use this information when she reached the Selected locations and Brand ambassadors part of the SET MESSAGE planning process (this is covered in Chapter 10).

An alternative to Mary's approach would have been to spend extra money on traditional adverts that promoted the yoghurt. This could have been less effective, because as well as being less engaging and therefore limiting impact, it would not have inspired the yummy mummy or the young child to tell anybody about the yoghurt. Can you imagine somebody telling 17 people that they saw a traditional advert on a billboard, on TV, or in a magazine? It is doubtful, unless it was a particularly miraculous, revolutionary or disturbing product or advert. On the other hand, it is easy to imagine how this live brand experience could reach another 17 people for every person who interacted with the experience.

As we already saw from the mother's lifestyle, she spends a lot of time meeting people, whether it is a friend over coffee or lunch, the people she sees every day at the gym, or the mothers at the school. Inspired by his child's picture with a fruit character, her husband may also tell his colleagues and show them on the web. They may forward this picture to family and friends, especially if they also have the opportunity to download a sales promotion voucher. The next time the mother visited the supermarket, she would probably use the voucher, found in the nutritional booklet. Finally, the child would tell his or her friends at school or extracurricular activities about the fruity characters. He or she may even forward the picture to friends, or upload it to a social networking site such as Bebo or Facebook. We can now see that Jack Morton's estimate of 17 for word-of-mouth Reach may even be conservative.

How does the analysis influence an idea for a brand of educational toys?

When Harry was planning a campaign, promoting educational toys to yummy mummies and their children, he came up with an idea using the BETTER model. After presenting it in three variations to the rest of the decision-making team, they chose one idea for the launch of a new child's toy. The toy looked similar to an easel, but had multifunctional elements with a calculator, touch screen and special slots for different art materials. The idea for the live brand experience involved a design competition, where kids would have the opportunity to use the product and create pictures, which would be hung up on a gallery wall as part of the experiential sets. The pictures could also be scanned and shown in a slideshow on a large plasma screen. Kids would also have the opportunity to use the touch screen to format their pictures into greeting cards for their mums and dads. These greeting cards would be available to download online and forward on to other family members or friends of the family.

Harry concluded that based on the 'day-in-the-life' analysis, it would be best to target the whole family together on the weekends. The weekends would allow continuity. He also concluded that shopping centres would be the best locations for this campaign, partly because the research showed that the yummy mummies and their kids would visit the shopping centres, but also because the product would be available to buy there. He also noted from further research into yummy mummies' aspirations that many were focused on the intelligence of their children, and that they admired other mothers whose children showed signs of early intelligence and creativity. This led him to decide that his Brand ambassadors would not only have experience working with children or have their own, but would also be representatives of

intelligence and creativity. Some Brand ambassadors would form 'The Tech Team', which would represent intelligence, and some of the Brand ambassadors would form 'The Art Team', which would showcase creativity.

Harry wondered what he would have spent the live brand experience budget on if he had not discovered this innovative new technique, and he remembered the other option: traditionally advertise in publications that targeted yummy mummies. He was confident, however, that this would not have been as effective, because the yummy mummies did not all read the same magazines. And anyway, they would not have remembered the ad for long, and when it was time to purchase the toy for a birthday present or Christmas, they would not necessarily be inspired by the magazine. On the other hand, he was very excited about the current live brand experience plans and was already in talks with his full-service agency to discuss the amplification channels that would be integrated to form the complete experiential marketing campaign for the launch.

He knew that the children would enjoy playing with the creative toy, as market research and focus groups had already proved that children responded remarkably well to the product. He knew it was likely that after the children played with the toy, they would ask their mums and dads to buy it, possibly nagging them until their next birthday or holiday. He was also confident that after seeing their children engaging in an educational experience, stimulating their creativity and intelligence, the yummy mummies would feel this toy bringing them closer to their aspirational lifestyle.

How does the analysis influence an idea for a brand of girls' dancewear?

When Maggie, a marketing director, was planning a campaign to launch a new line of kids' dancewear across 20 of their stores, she knew that it might be hard to achieve the results that she was looking for with a limited budget. She considered advertising but knew that she would not be able to afford more than two months' worth. She was not too confident that placing adverts in the magazines and local newspapers read by her Target audience of yummy mummies (and their daughters) in Southeast England would actually have any impact on sales. Though they might raise a certain amount of awareness about the range, it would not create a demand with the girls, and therefore the girls would not be likely to pester for the clothing.

Maggie wanted to reach the children, but she did not know where to start. Besides, she felt under-financed. A colleague had told her of the successes her husband had when using live brand experiences to launch his trendy and exclusive new restaurant. His PR agency had even secured lots of press coverage off the back of the experiences. They had worked with an experiential marketing agency that created tasting experiences that invited consumers to interact with the restaurant's brand and taste canapés at fashion shows.

The colleague convinced Maggie that she should try an experiential strategy, and after learning about the BETTER model, she came up with an idea to create an interactive ballerina experience. The experience was to be positioned at local shopping centres, where the retail stores were located, with specially created pink ballet-theme experiential sets. The sets were to comprise a branded pink floor that featured the logo of the clothing line, along with a ballet bar and mirrors. She would have the clothing collection present, including leggings, leotards, legwarmers, dance cardigans and tutus. She planned to invite mothers to book their kids into a ballet session, while the mums could go and shop for half an hour.

The idea was simple: the young girls could learn some ballet and try on the funky new dance clothing mid-launch. She also would offer them the opportunity to receive a free goody bag, which was a drawstring backpack branded with the dancewear logo. Inside the bag would be a sales promotion voucher. After using the BETTER model to generate her idea, Maggie began to plan in further detail using SET MESSAGE. After looking at the day-in-the-life of the mums, along with the primary Target audience, their young female daughters, and analysing their aspirations, she found they looked up to older, pretty girls who were good at ballet. This is how she established the identity of the Brand ambassadors. She decided to hire an experiential agency to manage the campaign. She briefed the agency to recruit girls in their late teens with a passion for ballet. The Brand ambassadors would wear the dance clothing and teach ballet techniques. Her research also revealed that there were local dance competitions, and she briefed the agency to roll out the live brand experience at these events as well.

Maggie decided to reinforce the experiential concept further. She would hire dancers in their late teens to work in the stores. These dancers would preferably be the same staff who would become her Brand ambassadors during the live brand experience campaign. This way, after the young girls learnt ballet from the older girls (the Brand ambassadors) they could be invited to come back to the stores for more advice on ballet and dancewear. This would further strengthen the relationship between the brand and the Target audience, while bringing a customer experience management outlook to the brand.

Maggie then completed the rest of the SET MESSAGE planning system (with the help of her agency) and found that she still had a small

budget left over. She used this with her PR agency. It had an excellent relationship with a TV production company that made shows for young kids. The TV production company liked the concept of the live brand experience campaign so much that they agreed to create a reality TV show to broadcast the campaign as a series of branded content. Maggie was confident that this experiential marketing campaign for the dancewear range would not only bring the brand personality to life, but would raise awareness, increase sales, and gain credibility with the Target audience. When she compared her campaign idea with her initial thoughts of running a relatively small-scale magazine ad campaign, which would be expensive and raise a relatively small level of awareness, she was very happy about the potential of the experiential marketing campaign.

A day-in-the-life analysis of an affluent professional

This demographic goes to work in the morning, probably in rush-hour travel by public transport or car. They possibly skip breakfast or grab a quick pastry snack on the way, and perhaps a cereal bar or breakfast bar when they get to work. They tend to be busy checking e-mails, answering and making phone calls, rushing to meetings and are often too busy to have lunch. They may simply grab a sandwich and bring it back to the office. Alternatively, they may go out to lunch and eat in a restaurant, possibly as a business meeting. They will then go back to work and, depending on how busy they are, they may leave at 6 pm. If they stay late, they might head straight home as soon as they can. Alternatively, they may attend a social engagement with work colleagues at a local bar. They could have a business dinner or event, such as an awards ceremony, to go to. Sometimes they might be networking in the evening. If they do have a social engagement, they may be meeting their partner for dinner or drinks.

At the weekend, affluent professionals are likely to unwind and relax from their busy week and could participate in leisure activities which, depending on their interests, will vary greatly. These might include golf, shopping, or entertainment such as theatre or concerts. In fact, interests vary across the board.

The affluent professionals also travel sometimes, some more than others. This could mean travelling business class or economy, depending on their status. Their socioeconomic stature could depend on how senior they are in a particular organization. When at the airport, they could have a long time to kill before the flight, as most airlines require people to arrive two hours before the flight leaves. During this time they could shop or perhaps sit in the business lounges available to those in business class. They may have nothing to do during this time and grow bored. They could possibly use their laptop or make some last-minute calls, again depending on their schedule and interests.

Aspirations of an affluent professional

Looking at who affluent professionals look up to is key. Normally, they would look up to successful entrepreneurs and business people prominent in the media. They may look up to people who have been successful in the business world, especially in the sector they work in. For example, if an affluent professional works in IT, he or she could look up to Bill Gates. If he or she were a marketing professional, he or she might look up to somebody well-known and successful in the marketing industry. The aspiration may also involve very successful entrepreneurs whose lifestyle is one of luxury, comfort and convenience. These entrepreneurs tend to travel in chauffeur-driven cars and dine in elegant restaurants, live in beautiful homes with several cars parked in the driveway, and have staff at their disposal. The analysis also showed that many male business executives look up to colleagues and acquaintances that demonstrate good business acumen, and they themselves aspire to hold conversations that demonstrate a comprehensive knowledge of successful businesses and their practices. The research into the life of our target audiences, in this case the affluent professional, gives us the opportunity to influence and develop existing ideas while planning using SET MESSAGE.

How does the analysis influence an idea for an airline brand?

Rob was a marketing manager responsible for promoting a new improved business class offering for an airline brand. The whole organization was beginning to shape its actions around the customer experience, and the philosophy lent itself particularly well to experiential marketing. Rob's boss wanted him to push the message that the new business travel experience was far more comfortable than previous offerings. Rob used the BETTER model to deliver some top-line experiential concepts, and he came up with four options. He narrowed them down to a favourite concept after careful deliberation with the rest of the marketing team at the airline. The concept was simple, but Rob was confident it would be effective. It involved setting up 'business zones', which were enclosed experiential sets. Rob decided to replicate the business section of the planes in the experiential sets. The zones would feature replicas of the special new 'experience chairs' installed in the airline's business class sections. Rob thought it would be a great idea to integrate food into the live brand experience; that way, he could convey the improvement in the quality of the airline menus. The affluent professionals could sample delicious canapés and food while relaxing in the experience chairs, which featured a special shiatsu massage. The trained Brand ambassadors would reflect the calibre of the newly trained airhostesses. Overall, the brand experience would take five minutes to complete. The consumer would be invited to sit down in the experience chair, eat a starter, have a glass of champagne and have a quick chat with one of the Brand ambassadors about the new business class offering. The consumers would also feel invigorated by the aromatherapy emissions.

Even though Rob had the top-line idea approved by his team, he was still unsure of the implementation until he began his Target audience analysis. When using the SET MESSAGE method, he looked at the day-in-the-life of his Target audience and their aspirations. This led him to understand that these affluent professionals did not have a lot of time to lunch. As they were especially busy people, they would not venture far from the office to eat in the day. He also realized that people working in business office parks lacked many options at meal times. Therefore, he decided to position the live brand experiences in business parks, allowing people to have a five-minute business class lunch. This would not only add value by satisfying their hunger, but would communicate all the benefits and the Brand personality of the new experience-oriented

business class service. When he looked at the aspirational lifestyle of the target audience, he noted that they looked up to successful business people and high-profile individuals in their sectors. He then decided to add another aspect to the live brand experiences. He would take the 'business zone' set on tour to visit conferences and seminars where opinion leaders, such as speakers and organizers, could also participate. He knew that association with these credible individuals would impress his Target audience. He also knew that if the speakers participated in spreading word-of-mouth, their stamp of approval could go a long way.

After completing the plan in SET MESSAGE and hiring an agency to implement the campaign, Rob saw excellent results. Following the great success of the launch of the improved business class offering, Jake (the new CEO) was over the moon. Rob also continued to work closely with his advertising agency, hired to prepare more innovative adverts that would go in business-related magazines and on business-related TV channels, promoting the opportunity to 'trial the new business travel experience'. After the initial live brand experience campaign, he began integrating all the marketing communications channels to amplify the live brand experiences, whilst allocating a large portion of the total budget to future live brand experiences. Since the airline adopted a customer experience management programme and Rob pioneered the use of experiential marketing to promote the new and improved services, the brand has benefited from increased market share, and hasn't looked back.

How does the analysis influence an idea for a retail clothing brand?

Francesca, an account manager at an integrated full-service agency, received a brief from one of its biggest clients. The client is a chain of successful clothing shops, providing smart, fashionable clothing. Ideal for the office and evening entertainment, the clothing is of a reasonable quality at an affordable midrange price. The brand targets young female professionals who want to stay in fashion and change their wardrobe for each season. The clothing collections mainly cater to females, but also have a small range for men. The concept behind the clothing range is that the consumer can wear an outfit to the office, jazz it up in the evening, and even wear it at weekends. The client wanted to communicate to its customers that the clothing is adaptable for many environments.

Francesca was far more familiar with coordinating advertising campaigns than live brand experiences, so when the client gave her the brief, assuming that the advertising agency could also be responsible for integrating advertising and live brand experiences to form a complete experiential marketing approach, she turned to an experiential marketing agency for specialized help. The creative team inside the experiential agency suggested a top-line idea, which they had brainstormed using the BETTER model. The idea was for an integrated experiential campaign involving live brand experiences, billboards and bus shelter ads. The live brand experience channel, in the form of a roadshow vehicle, would travel around city areas, giving professional women a mini after-work makeover (perfect for going out for drinks). The billboards would promote the makeover roadshow while showing images of a woman quickly transforming her outfit, from office to eveningwear. The bus shelters would feature interactive technology that allowed consumers to press a button to transform a woman from being appropriately dressed for the office to being fashionably dressed for evening drinks.

After Francesca decided the idea was good, she wanted to develop the concept further in SET MESSAGE before presenting to the client. She completed the day-in-the-life analysis and researched the aspirational lifestyle of the Target audience. She found that the experiential marketing idea was actually perfectly suitable for her Target audience. With the office women she was targeting, she found that they tended to go out in the evening, straight after work. They wanted to go out looking great without having to go home first. Thus, the adaptability of the clothing range was a major selling point: you could quickly transform an outfit from smart office chic to sophisticated city glam for the evening. She developed the live brand experience idea further by adding an element: Brand ambassadors would visit offices at lunchtime, bringing with them branded coffee and invitations to the makeover roadshow. Straight after work, the roadshow bus would park outside large office blocks at a specified time. Many women would be made over and instructed on how to go from office to evening glam with this clothing brand.

She was confident that the client would love the idea and she was right. It really brought to life the Brand personality and demonstrated to the Target audience what the brand was all about. This real-life context is hard to achieve with traditional media alone. Because Francesca worked in an advertising agency, she knew she had access to something very powerful: the wide reach of advertising. She felt that the concept of the live brand experience campaign could be amplified by traditional advertising, as suggested by the experiential marketing agency. She spoke to some of the creative and media planning teams and convinced them to run the billboard and bus shelter ads to amplify the big idea. The billboards then drove people to participate in the live brand experience. Even those who had not necessarily participated in the live brand experience were very excited by the thought of this brand reaching out to people just like them.

After the campaign had been implemented, Francesca's client was very pleased. Not only had the client received the experiential marketing campaign that they were after, but Francesca had managed to maximize the impact that each channel had by integrating them to form a unified experiential concept. The market research that the brand of clothing conducted after the campaign showed that the Target audience's perceptions of the brand changed significantly after the campaign, because consumers could understand its proposition from a completely different perspective. The campaign was tailored around the busy lifestyles of female professionals, and by feeling that the brand had catered to them, they developed a real bond with it. The experiential campaign implied that the clothing brand understands and appreciates their daily lives and connected them with the identity of the glamorous businesswomen, whose lifestyles they aspired to live.

How does the analysis influence an idea for a gambling website?

Owing to changes in advertising regulations, an online gambling company wanted to reach out to its target audience of affluent British males, without advertising. Short of ideas, it contacted its PR firm with a brief to generate press coverage. The client suggested a PR survey as a method of achieving its objectives. Unfortunately, the PR company was less than enthusiastic. They said it would be difficult to get any press at all because of the negative perceptions of gambling amongst the media. Also, they were worried that promoting gambling could attract negative attention from the press and they did not want to risk generating unwanted coverage. They said that no matter how much money the client spent implementing an elaborate stunt, it would be hard to control the coverage and it could potentially become a wasted effort. The PR agency bosses passed on the brief to Larissa, an Account Executive who had come from an events background. She recommended that the gambling company drive people to its website and collect member registrations using live brand experiences. Larissa then approached an experiential marketing agency with whom she had an existing relationship. Together, Larissa and the experiential marketing agency brainstormed to come up with a creative idea.

The Brand personality of the online gambling website was all about bringing good fortune to others (the target audience was affluent male professionals). The word 'fortune', which was central to the brand identity, and was usually represented by Oriental imagery in advertising, became the focal point of the live brand experience campaign. Using the BETTER brainstorm, they came up with an idea to target businessmen with an Oriental-style experience. It was designed to target affluent males and involved a guessing game about Fortune 500 businesses. After completing the BETTER brainstorm, and presenting the idea using the IDEA format, the concept was still not fully developed, but everyone was keen to present a proposal as soon as possible. There was mild panic spreading through the PR firm, which knew its client would struggle to maintain its market share without a good campaign. It worried that the client may go elsewhere if Larissa did not propose something good.

Larissa and the experiential marketing agency then continued to plan the idea in further detail using SET MESSAGE. When they got to the Target audience part of the planning stage, they identified a few key points. After doing a day-in-the-life analysis and identifying key aspirations of the Target audience, they discovered that affluent professionals spent a lot of time travelling and waiting for flights. It was identified that waiting and boredom were negative factors that businessmen associated with catching flights, and that they would be potentially open to engaging during that time. In addition, because the client was targeting the more senior end of the demographic, the professionals would be travelling business class. This insight was essential in inspiring the ideal location for the idea: business lounges in major airports. It was also suggested that a common aspiration of the businessmen was to receive attention from glamorous females.

Building on the insights and pushing the 'fortune' theme a little further, Larissa decided that they would hire small sections of the business lounges for the duration of the campaign and they would theme these areas with plush Oriental décor, subtle branding, and install wireless computers (with internet browsers that would be preset to the gambling website's homepage). Attentive female Brand ambassadors, dressed in classic Oriental dresses, would greet the business travellers who were waiting for their flights. The Brand ambassadors would give the businessmen fortune cookies containing promotional codes that enabled participants to play with varying amounts of 'free money' when gambling on the site. Brand ambassadors would then invite the target audience to participate in a Fortune 500 quiz game, which would be most entertaining for those waiting for their flights in the business lounges. The game would also provide the target audience with the opportunity to showcase their business knowledge (a process identified earlier as being enjoyable to them). JC Deceaux, leader in experiential space at airports confirmed that it would be feasible.

The live brand experience would simultaneously drive memberships to the site, and relevantly engage the target audience (while they had a

lot of disposal time on their hands) with the website's brand personality. After the PR agency completed the SET MESSAGE plan and presented it to the client, it received a delighted response to the proposal. The client did, however, state that it still wanted the PR agency to amplify the live brand experience and gain press coverage for the gambling site, because that was the original objective.

The PR agency was by now in a completely inspired mode, and was looking at the campaign very differently to when it had first received the brief. Colette, a senior member of Larissa's team, was now involved and had a good contact: the editor of a leading airline's in-flight magazine. Colette resolved to wine-and-dine the editor, convincing him to write an article reviewing the most up-to-date, revolutionary business lounges around. Once the client signed off the activity, and the brand experience went live, Colette and the editor visited one of the business lounges that featured the live brand experience. The editor was so enthused with the activity and the immersive stylish environment that the gambling brand had created, that a photo of the experience made it onto the front cover of the in-flight magazine. This achievement amplified the reach of the live brand experience and generated huge interest amongst the Target audience.

The number of new members that signed up to the gambling website as a direct result of the experiential marketing campaign was record-breaking. It far exceeded the numbers the client had previously received from running traditional print advertising campaigns. The CEO of the gambling website decided it had been a 'blessing in disguise' that the advertising regulations had changed, because otherwise he would never have considered such an innovative channel, which has been placed at the core of their marketing communications strategy ever since.

We started by conducting a day-in-the-life analysis of a yummy mummy and saw how by completing this process during SET MESSAGE different brands from different sectors could develop their top-line concepts, improving them with insights about the yummy mummy's lifestyle and aspirations. We have also looked at how conducting a day-in-the-life analysis of an affluent professional can influence the plans of three very different companies. Those mentioned above are obviously not the only potential Target audiences. In fact, it has been known that live brand experiences generate a good response from Target audiences across the board.[1] The Target audience part of SET MESSAGE can be very useful, no matter who the campaign is targeting. With that said, live brand experiences can be particularly effective at targeting a trendy youth demographic. A Jack Morton survey shows that 60 per cent of Generation Y consumers (aged 18–23) say live brand experiences are very influential in their brand perception.[2] Trendy youths tend to prefer organic, grass-roots tactics, and they often shun any marketing that does not benefit them in some way or have relevance to their lifestyle.

A day-in-the-life of a trendy youth

This hard-to-reach 18–23-year old demographic is most likely to be comprised of university students or recent graduates. They start off by waking up late and possibly going to a lecture. Then, they meet up with friends and hang out through the night, most likely attending a party or going to a bar, as this is a very social target population in terms of fashion. They shop at underground boutiques and other places where trendy clothing and individual street-wear labels are sold. Global brands, such as Levis, Diesel and Nike have always managed to maintain a good presence and credibility with the trendy youth.

It is hard to generalize about this group because members vary across different socioeconomic backgrounds and world cultures. Music and fashion play a big role in influencing them, however; gigs, music festivals and nightclubs will be their favourite social outings, as well as extreme sporting events such as skateboarding and snowboarding. Music and fashion, being the key influences here, lead us to their aspirations. Usually the trendy youth will have musical icons and interest-based role models. For example, a rock fan is likely to aspire to live the lifestyle of a rock star; a nightclub fan will look up to a DJ's lifestyle; and a 'fashionista' will admire the life of a fashion designer. Also within their university or social community there will be peers who are higher in their social circles and are very influential in terms of what their friends and others think, say and do.

Several brands target specific trendy youths in order to reach wider demographics, because the carefully identified groups of trendy youths can be key influencers. Brands such as Apple, Nike, Facebook, MySpace, Levis, American Apparel and Sony are some of the brands that are popular and well perceived by this audience. All of them have used experiential marketing and customer experience management philosophies to maintain their credible positioning and customer loyalty amongst trendy youth.

How does the analysis influence an idea for a vodka brand?

When Dan, the marketing manager at a vodka brand, was tasked with launching a new ready-mixed-cocktail version of the product targeting trendy youth, he immediately conducted a brainstorm with the creative team at his full-service agency to generate ideas. It wanted to position a live brand experience at the core of an integrated experiential marketing campaign. This direction for the launch was decided collectively amongst the team members, because of research showing that this Target audience would respond exceptionally well to experiential marketing.

The brainstorm generated a favourite idea that was well liked, but needed further development in the SET MESSAGE methodology. The idea involved driving product trial of the cocktail version of the drink, which was already popular with the Target audience. Inspired by the fact that the drink comes in three different cocktail flavours, the creatives wanted to communicate the key message 'What's your flava?' throughout the live brand experience and all the amplification channels. They wanted to play on the word 'flava' and its double meaning, insinuating both a statement about style and culture, as well as a preference for specific tastes. The concept involved encouraging people to have a mood test that would determine their particular flavour. The mood test would involve a colour-sensitive drinks bar, which consumers could touch, and it would change colour according to their mood (actually to the heat of their body). They would then be served a sample of the drink in the 'flava' that corresponded to their mood (the colour that the bar changed into when it was touched). This experiential concept was both interactive and fun, and Dan was confident that the trendy youths would buy into it. He thought they would enjoy the free samples and the added interactivity would strengthen the relationship further. It would show them that the brand was taking their preferences and state of mind into consideration. In other words, it would subliminally say 'We care' and 'We understand.' The core concept was originally developed during the Emotional connection stage of the BETTER brainstorm.

After deciding to use SET MESSAGE to develop the idea further, Dan and his market research agency conducted a day-in-the-life analysis of the Target audience. The integrated agency also consulted several of its own real-life sources to discover more about the lifestyle of trendy youths. They kept stumbling upon the same facts: music festivals were very popular and brought large numbers together in one place. In addition, the aspirational analysis revealed that many of the two main groups of people the consumers aspired to, DJs and fashionable peers, would be present at festivals. The festivals would allow the brand a scenario where it could reach both. At the same time, Dan was confident that the word-of-mouth effects would be high, because the live brand experience would target the right people at the right places.

Dan and the agency team developed the idea further using the key insights; just having a bar would no longer be enough. They decided to build branded 'Flava Tents', themed around music and fashion, and position them at music festivals. By having its own areas, the brand would have more control over the Target audience's experience. For example, the bars would be completely interactive and the only drink served would be the new vodka cocktail in its several different 'flavas'. Additionally, the live brand experience would feature nightly fashion shows (from up and coming avant-garde designers), as well as popular DJs, and live music performances (from underground talent). The other marketing communication channels that would be used to amplify the live brand experience were advertising (in the festival guides and online), and PR (targeted at fashion and music magazines and websites). The online ads would link to live broadcasts from the 'Flava Tents', the ads in the festival guides would promote the opportunity to visit the 'Flava Tents', and the PR activity would be geared around the DJs, fashion designers and musicians that would be performing at the 'Flava Tents'.

The launch plan was completed and Dan's boss loved it, signing it off immediately. The integrated experiential marketing strategy was a big hit and though the integrated agency outsourced some of the campaign to an experiential marketing specialist agency, it did a fantastic job of ensuring consistency across all the selected channels and leveraging the live brand experience for maximum exposure. The Target audience part of the SET MESSAGE planning process facilitated a better understanding of how to develop the initial concept into a complete, relevant plan, and proved to be a crucial step in the development of this exciting campaign. Dan was very pleased with the outcome of his initiative when comparing this engaging campaign to some of the possible alternatives, including the launch campaigns of some of the vodka-cocktail brand's competitors, such as field marketing and traditional advertising.

How does the analysis influence an idea for a microwave meal brand?

Craig is the marketing manager at a microwave meal manufacturer. He was briefed to plan and implement a face-to-face campaign that would target students. He knew that it was of great importance to come up with an idea that related to the lifestyle of this niche audience. As a former student himself, he was already aware of some of the habits of this demographic. After he came up with a few ideas using the BETTER format, he showed them to his boss in an IDEA-formatted presentation for input and feedback. One of the ideas stood out and he suggested developing it further using the SET MESSAGE methodology. He had completed the S and E stages, and was pleased with the plan thus far, but knew that it was still missing a certain relevance to the Target audience. The concept involved giving out free microwave meals to students in return for them filling in a questionnaire. This questionnaire would obtain valuable insights into their eating habits, which could be beneficial for the product development team, who had contributed some of the budget for the experiential activity.

When Craig began planning using SET MESSAGE and got to the Target audience section, he carefully looked through several sources of secondary data about students and their eating habits. He also conducted primary research by arranging focus groups and acquired enough data, allowing him to prepare a day-in-the-life analysis, as well as identifying the aspirations of the Target audience. He realized that student lifestyles did not tend to involve cooking, and that students, who were often supported by their parents, preferred to spend their spare money on entertainment and socializing rather than proper meals. They often bought cheap takeaways because they did not usually know how to cook the meals that they were familiar with from home. The analysis also showed that the students had a desire to cook themselves and looked up to peers who were good at cooking, but their lack of expertise was the main barrier to the attainment of these culinary aspirations. He found that they sometimes missed the nourishing home environments that they knew before they went away to university

This information inspired Craig to develop the idea further. Instead of simply giving away the microwave meals, he would hire a specialist agency to create a home-themed live brand experience at the universities. There would be small house-shaped sets with 1950s-style decor, representative of a traditional family kitchen. The students would be invited to visit the 'homes' and enjoy home-style meals, which were then revealed to be easy to make, microwave meals. This would show the students that they could still experience home-style cooking, simply by pressing a button on the microwave. While the trendy youths would wait for their meals to be prepared, they could fill in the questionnaire. Therefore, in the setting of the comforting environment and with the promise of a delicious meal arriving, the form would not seem like such a chore, and the experience would be relevant to their lifestyles. After completing the remaining planning stages, Craig was confident that the microwave meal brand would benefit greatly from the live brand experience strategy.

Summary

We have now seen how to conduct a day-in-the-life analysis, and explain the insights generated in the Target audience part of the SET MESSAGE planning process. The process is simple. During the Target audience stage of the SET MESSAGE planning methodology, you carefully research the Target audience's lifestyle and aspirational lifestyle, then analyse the data to extract core insights. Later in the planning process, these insights will allow you to double-check that the experiential strategy has all three key attributes (authentic, positively connected and personally meaningful) and adapt it if needed. Overall, experiential marketing is most successful when it features a live brand experience at its core, creating the right experience for the right people. In other words, this stage of the planning process will help you to ensure that the experience matches the Target audience's lifestyle and aspirations.

Careful targeting is very important, especially when 10 per cent of a Target audience (opinion leaders) usually shape the opinions and purchases of the other 90 per cent (opinion followers).[3] This is why it can be highly beneficial to target an influential group of the Target audience, identified as opinion-leaders, who will proceed to influence the remainder of that population, spreading word-of-mouth and expanding the reach of the campaign. By applying the techniques covered in this chapter, your plan will remain relevant to the consumers with whom it wishes to engage, bringing you a step closer to building strong relationships between your Target audience and brand with the aim of generating and maintaining brand advocacy and customer loyalty.

Notes

1. Jack Morton Worldwide. An executive summary of this survey is available online at www.JackMorton.com
2. Jack Morton Worldwide. An executive summary of this survey is available online at www.JackMorton.com
3. Weimann, G (2203) *The Influentials: People who influence people*, University of New York Press, New York; and Keller, E and Berry, J (2003) *The Influentials: One American in ten tells the other nine how to vote, where to eat, and what to buy*, Simon and Schuster, New York

8 Message – key communication

This chapter strives to improve the ways in which you communicate with your Target audiences, providing a planning framework that facilitates a superior level of consumer engagement through experiential marketing campaigns.

In this part of SET MESSAGE we will look at the importance of your campaign Message – key communication, covering the process of integrating components of your brand message into your experiential marketing campaign, starting with the live brand experience. It is then recommended that you utilize the other marketing communication channels to amplify the live brand experience, which in itself becomes content for the broader campaign message.

The purpose of the Message – key communication section is to provide you with a systematic approach for ensuring that participants interpret your live brand experiences as intended. Then, when the other marketing communication channels are integrated to form the complete experiential marketing campaign, the Message and key communication of those channels will be led by the live brand experience. When members of your Target audience see or hear of your live brand experience, even if they themselves are not participants, they will still identify that your brand is reaching out to them, trying to benefit their lives. The feeling that the brand cares for them enough to go out of its way to create a positive experience that is catered to them will be enough to plant the brand and this positive message deep in their memories. This communication process is demonstrated in Figure 8.1.

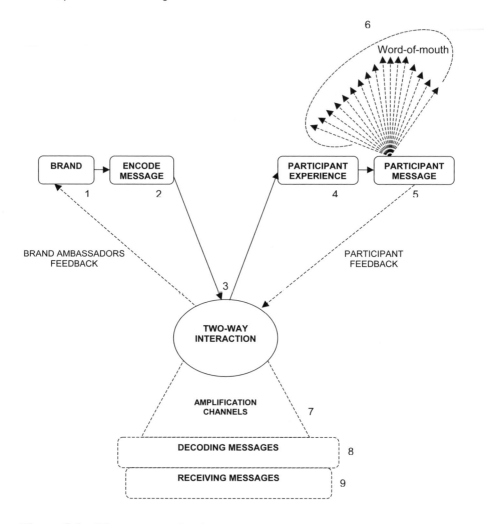

Figure 8.1   The communication process

It may be that you have already planned your brand's Message and key communication, as these messages are usually already integrated across all your marketing and advertising. If you already have a brand Message and key communication, then this is the time to bring it into the planning process.

Verbal Messages (strap lines) and key communications are important in every type of campaign. Marketing materials and adverts translate the Messages and key communications of the brands they are promoting into emotional messages, rational messages or a combination of both. Rational messages tend to focus on conveying the features and benefits of a product or service, and are therefore product-focused. Emotional messages tend to relate to the aspirational lifestyle of the Target audience as well as aiming to generate moods and feelings, and are therefore customer-focused. This choice between a rational or emotional message often relates to whether the product or service is a low-involvement or high-involvement purchase. Often successful communications combine both emotional and rational messages.

Whether you decide to use a rational message, an emotional message, or a combination of both, you will need to encode the message that you wish to convey into the two-way interaction (the live brand experience). The message should be consistent and clear enough that the participants properly decode it during their experience. While the consumer is participating in the two-way interaction, the message will need to be successfully conveyed to them both mentally (how they feel and think) and physically (through their senses and the environment).

Live brand experiences provide excellent opportunities for bringing to life the different components that form your brand's Message and key communication. At this stage, you need to dissect your generic messages to extract their very essence. By breaking generic messages into various essential components, then encoding those components into your live brand experience's interaction and environment, you will increase the likelihood that the participants' experience will embody the message that you aim to communicate. If the live brand experience succeeds in this respect, then you heighten the chances that its participants will proceed to disseminate the desired key communication to their peers.

Ask yourself the following question: what is it that we want our Target audience to understand, believe or identify with about our brand? Once you have your answer, you can identify and focus on these elements and integrate them into the live brand experience. You need to refine your live brand experience to ensure that the brand message is communicated effectively and concisely, in a way that will be correctly interpreted by its participants. The message must also be relevant to the activity they are engaging in, though this should not be an issue because the activity itself should reflect the brand personality. The message should represent the identifying nature of what you want the consumer to know, act on and believe in. You can adapt your brand Message and key communication to suit the capacity of the live brand experience environment. The communication can be different to that of a traditional advertising message, because the message forms part of a dialogue, and allows immediate feedback and input from consumers. It is always important to adopt a coordinated approach; hence, the message used in the live brand experience channel should be consistent with the messages used in the rest of your communication channels. To keep messages consistent across all channels, I recommend that you first adapt the message to suit the live brand experience, and then amplify it across the other selected communication channels.

The authentic, genuine part of your brand's Message and key communication should become the sources of inspiration for many elements throughout the live brand experience. If you understand what your brand truly stands for and believes in, you are on track to reflecting that philosophy through the messages communicated in your campaign.

Bringing the message to life

A brand of vitamin water

A vitamin water brand's message is 'Quench your soul'. Breaking this message down into its essence, these good-for-the-soul components were discovered: rehydration, vitamins, natural extracts, a good body, natural relaxation and invigorating effects. The brand wanted to communicate its message effectively while also promoting three different flavour options. When this brand created a series of live brand experiences at holistic fairs and music festivals, it brought to life the brand message components of each of its products through the atmospheres and interactions of each experience.

One experience featured a 'Relaxation zone' where guests could enjoy a relaxing massage, smell a lavender aroma, and be exposed to relaxing mood lighting and music. At the same time, they would enjoy a sample of the 'Relax' variety of the water. There was also an 'Invigoration zone', where consumers had the opportunity to bounce on a branded trampoline to energizing music, while smelling the invigorating aroma of citrus and rosemary essential oils, prior to receiving a sample of the 'Invigorate' variety of water.

As well as the 'Relaxation' and 'Invigoration' zones, the brand also had a 'Refreshing Zone' where consumers were invited to have a mini aromatic-cleanse facial, before being given a cool-gel eye-mask to wear. While they engaged in the facial, refreshing smells of freshly chopped grass would fill the moist room (the moisture was emitted from a humidifier). After having their refreshing mini aromatic-cleanse facial, they received a sample of the 'Refresh' variety of water.

While festival goers waited their turn, plasma screens showing the brand's TV advertisement (featuring the key communication 'Quench

your soul') lit up the reception areas of the live brand experience tents. In addition, Brand ambassadors wearing yoga-style clothing were inviting festival guests to come and 'Quench their souls' while giving out branded gifts such as cleansing wipes (Refresh), stress balls (Relax)

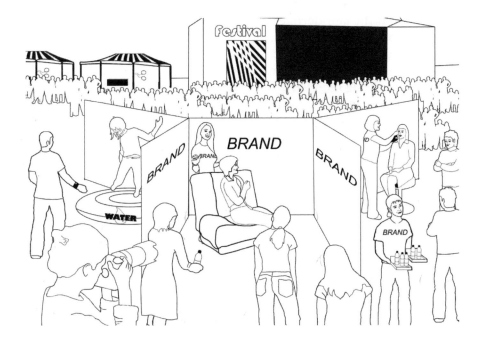

and skipping ropes (Invigorate), all featuring the 'Quench your soul' message.

The overall effect was completely immersive, bringing to life all of the components and elements that formed the Message and key communication of the innovative water brand. This all ensured that when the live brand experience's participants spread word-of-mouth, they would pass on a message that reflects the brand's essence.

A brand of washing powder

An example of a brand that also integrates a rational message into its communication is a washing powder with environmental credentials. Its message 'Get clean, be green' is designed to communicate that the washing powder combines superior cleaning performance with environmentally friendly ingredients and packaging. The key communication aims to relate to two of the key aspects that are important to its Target audience, the first aspect being that it can succeed in cleaning their clothes effectively, the second that it can make them feel that they are doing something positive for the environment.

The washing powder brand's campaign involved converting hundreds of previously coin-operated launderettes into live brand experience sets, where consumers were invited to have their washing done for them. The message's components were brought to life through the environment and service at the launderettes. First, the brand gave the launderettes a design makeover by wrapping every surface with printed vinyl, ensuring that the visual decor matched the brand identity. Then, they emblazoned the key communication 'Get clean, be green,' on every washing machine and dryer. By using recycled wood to construct the waiting benches, and minimizing wastage (by encouraging consumers to bring their own bags to carry their laundry), they succeeded in conveying their environmental awareness. They even installed new, environmentally efficient washing machines, courtesy of a leading white-goods manufacturer with whom the brand had formed a partnership. Aside from the green component of the message, the clean component of the message was also vital to communicate. Therefore, the brand invested in ensuring that the launderettes were immaculately clean with a fabulous fragrance.

The Brand ambassadors, who were responsible for washing and drying the participants' laundry and engaging them in relevant dialogue, had previous experience working with environmental charities. They were carefully selected, and trained to produce perfectly clean clothing and maintain their uniforms in pristine appearance. After completing the laundry, the Brand ambassadors would give the neatly folded 'Clean

and green laundry' back to the consumers, with a frec sample of the washing powder and a sales promotion voucher. The voucher offered a discount against future purchase of the product and a promise that a percentage of sales would be donated to an environmental charity.

In addition to the makeover it provided to the local launderettes, the brand also gave the launderette owners training on environmentally friendly systems, such as recycling and energy-saving practices, and helped to set up donation boxes, allowing their customers to continue contributing to local environmental causes. The relationships that the brand formed with the launderettes and their customers continued, and by helping the small businesses to adopt the brand's 'clean and green' philosophy, they strengthened the impact of their key communication. The participants of the experience had previously been used to manually operating the machines themselves and waiting while they completed their cycles. The immersive environmentally themed locations, combined with clean ready-to-collect laundry were more than enthusiastically welcomed. After the initial setup costs, the ongoing live brand experience proved to be very cost-effective, with word-of-mouth and media mentions (the PR amplification channel generated huge coverage) helping to increase sales for the brand by over 50 per cent.

A skincare brand

There is a skincare brand whose key communication message is 'beauty secrets from Japan'. The message was created with the aim of conveying important concepts that form the brand identity: elegance, beauty and Japanese tradition. The message also implies that beauty secrets are passed on in the form of personal recommendations. The inspiration for this process is the brand's holistic philosophy. Product sampling is in fact one of the main marketing communications objectives. Distributing samples is important to this brand because they found that when people try the product, they discover 'beauty secrets' and then tell those 'secrets' to their friends.

This brand places great emphasis on the live brand experience channel, because it facilitates the tangible communication of beauty secrets (through product sampling) and provides a great platform for bringing the Message and key communication to life. The core elements of the message are integrated, both physically and mentally, into every aspect of the live brand experience's communication, from its Brand ambassadors, their uniforms, and the packaging of its samples, to its literature, verbal dialogue and physical environment.

Summary

When you are at the Message – key communication stage in SET MESSAGE, it is time to refer to your organizational philosophy, existing strap lines, and to key messages that you want to communicate throughout your marketing. You should break down these messages into their most important components and then recode those components into the live brand experience. The live brand experience itself can then become the message for amplification across selected channels.

What you want the participants of your live brand experience to know, believe and do about your brand should be at the heart of the two-way interaction, in order for them to communicate your message effectively through word-of-mouth.

Part of what is so special about having your message recoded into the experience is that your Target audience will have the opportunity to interact with your key messages. The messages will be internalized by your Target audiences through real-life experiences, which they are far more likely to appreciate and pass on than the one-way messages they receive from many traditional media channels.

To achieve this desired response, we need to build multiple sensory or emotional elements (inspired by the brand message) into the concept to create a genuine link between the sensory motor, feelings, and thoughts. These three areas, in harmonious interaction, generate lasting impressions in the mind of the participant that lead to action; this is because they align four of the key areas of the whole person (feeling, thinking, being and doing).[1] The first principle that stems from the psychodynamic theory is that all action that has been triggered by communication is a result of the emotional translation (of the brand's message) because it is perceived, not consciously, but subconsciously through the filtering of the participants' 'inner world'.[2]

Notes

1. Errica Moustaki, Psychoanalytic Psychotherapist MA
2. Isaacs, S (1952) The nature and function of phantasy, in Developments in Psycho-analysis, ed M Klein, Haygarth, London

9 Experiential strategy

Strategy is important to any plan. It is the core of achieving your objectives. This is the part of the plan where you outline your Experiential strategy, the campaign's main concept. It is the answer to the questions 'How will we achieve our objectives, and what is the big idea?' This book recommends that the big idea for the experiential marketing campaign is based on a two-way interaction between the consumer and the brand, in real time; in other words, a live brand experience.

Almost all experiential marketing campaigns include two or more of the 10 experiential elements. These elements can be mixed in any combination to create the experiential strategy. At this point in the planning process, you will at least have a rough idea of the kind of thing you want to do in your experiential marketing campaign, because you will have already brainstormed using BETTER, and presented ideas using the IDEA format. In SET MESSAGE you have already covered the Situation and background, the Experiential objectives, the Target audience, and the Message – key communication stages. In the process, you will have planned your aims, decided on the components of your message that you will integrate into the live brand experience, and carefully analysed your Target audience's lifestyle and aspirations.

STRATEGIES

STRATEGIES is an acronym that allows you to pick your experiential elements and combine them to formulate your Experiential strategy:

Service
Theatre
Research
Adverts
Televised or broadcast
Entertainment
Game (or competition)
Interactive technology
Education
Set

S is for service

Service is something that you can provide as an added-value element for the Target audience. Service can mean many things: a laundry service, car washing, transport, delivery, pampering or a makeover. In this context, anything that human beings (or in some cases, technologies) do as a process that adds value can count as a service. By using the Service element in your strategy, you can bring to life the Brand personality and benefit consumers. Service can facilitate a two-way interaction.

T is for theatre

This is clearly an important element, and there have been many debates about whether experiential marketing is in fact simply 'brand theatre'. It is actually not as simple as a branded performance, but Theatre is a key element of many Experiential strategies, and can be integrated with other elements to create an exciting strategy. This element can be especially successful when integrated with the Adverts element, which we will discuss below.

R is for research

Experiential marketing lends itself perfectly to providing both qualitative and quantitative research as part of the campaign. Research strategies can be integrated easily into the interaction in a way that is unobtrusive to consumers, yet still manages to uncover significantly valuable information. In fact, the Research element is very popular because it is often a shame not to make the most of an interaction with the Target audience. Brands and marketing agencies alike are finding that the experiential marketing campaigns that they run give them insights into the thoughts, feelings, lifestyles and purchasing behaviour of their consumers. It is simple to gather valuable data in the form of consumer conversation and surveys because there is always direct contact with consumers, and many live brand experiences involve face-to-face interaction.

A is for adverts

In this context, the Adverts element is representative of one of several elements that combine to form the Experiential strategy. Just as an advert can amplify a live brand experience, a live brand experience can bring to life an advertising campaign. First, the live brand experience can reinforce advertising that the Target audience may have already been exposed to, and secondly it gives consumers the feeling that they are closer to the brand, and that the brand is a real part of their everyday lives.

Live brand experiences can be used to communicate the content of an advert in situations where it is unlikely that the Target audience will otherwise see the adverts. For example, if there are no billboard sites in a target area or event, then a live brand experience, which reflects the theme and content of the ad, is the perfect alternative. If a sporting event is held and sponsorship is out of budget, sometimes it is more cost-effective (and more interesting) to bring to life the advertising campaign with an experiential element. Also, using an Experiential strategy to convey your advertising message can be a good way to make the campaign more memorable and allow the consumer to interact with the brand, resulting in a deeper relationship that stimulates word-of-mouth.

T is for televised or broadcast

Imagine how much you can expand the reach of your live brand experience by forming a media partnership, and broadcasting it on television, radio, or online channels. A media partnership that informs consumers about a live brand experience prior to it happening and then broadcasts the experience, can be very successful in positioning the brand as one that cares about its consumers. This perception can be achieved with those who do not participate in the live brand experience as well as those who do.

E is for entertainment

This entertainment element is not relevant for all brands, but when it is in line with the Brand personality, then this element of your Experiential strategy can be valuable in terms of adding value, gathering large numbers of people to a live brand experience, and positioning the brand in a certain way. In fact, many companies use brand-relevant music festivals or fairs as core elements in their experiential strategies. Some famous examples of live brand experiences that include the entertainment element are the Ben & Jerry's Sundae Festival and Innocent Smoothies' village fête and Fruitstock. In this context, the entertainment element can represent music, fashion or culture-based activities. It can be a good alternative or partner to sponsorship. Entertainment can provide a fabulous source of word-of-mouth stimulation while building relationships between brands and their Target audiences.

G is for game (or competition)

Games and competitions are great ways to create brand-relevant two-way interactions between consumers and brands. Obviously, if your product is a game, then creating an experience that features a game is a pretty straightforward option. But that doesn't mean that this element should be used for gaming brands alone. In fact, when an experiential marketing agency organized 'business picnics' for a mobile phone brand that was targeting business users, it integrated intelligent games such as chess and Jenga to bring the intelligent brand personality to life.

If you would like to use games as an element in your Experiential strategy, look to existing games for inspiration and make sure that you select and adapt them to be brand-relevant and engaging for your Target audience. Consider researching TV game shows, quiz games, board games, playground games you used to play in school, sports team matches and competitive games. Also consider arcade games, and games that you come across in an amusement park or fairground. Even simple games, or the type you would play using paper, like crosswords, Sudoko and rock-paper-scissors, can be inspirational when relevant.

The great thing about games within the experiential marketing context is that you can personalize them to the brand and the objectives, making them larger than life. Even when a Game element is not wholly relevant or appropriate in the traditional sense, you can build in a competition mechanism where the prize is a means of bringing your brand personality to life. By integrating a simple but effective game into your Experiential strategy, you can create a memorable and fun experience for the participants.

I is for interactive technology

By studying the BETTER model you already understand the importance of two-way interaction in experiential marketing, and the value that can be generated from two-way participation in brand-relevant activity with a Target audience. We live in the age of technology; each day it becomes more and more cost-effective to customize technology to better serve our needs and desires. Think of the interactive technology you can find on a TV set; when a button is pressed a signal is sent, and then the channel or settings are changed in the desired way. Also, think of visiting a museum and participating in an interactive display, lifting flaps, pressing buttons, pulling levers and enjoying the discovery process, presented in a creative way.

The technology can facilitate an amazing range of both face-to-face and remote two-way interactions. When integrated into your Experiential strategy, technology can be a very good way to interact with your Target audiences, whether it is used to gather data, educate, demonstrate, or provoke reaction. Even when your product is in a non-technology based sector, the Interactive technology element can be formulated in an innovative way that is fun and conveys complex brand messages.

E is for education

Experiential marketing is a fabulous way to educate consumers about your product or service. The Education element can be integrated to communicate your product's heritage, its features and benefits, or subjects that reflect its Brand personality and show relevance to your Target audience's aspirational lifestyle. Education-based experiential marketing strategies have been historically popular with government bodies, wishing to educate stakeholders on issues such as voting, health and crime. But likewise, if your campaign is for a car brand that is superior to other cars in its class, one of your main objectives might be to educate your consumers about its technology, in which case Education is likely to be a key element of your Experiential strategy. This element can be especially beneficial when conveying rational messages, and can be an integral part of your strategy, regardless of sector.

S is for set

The Set element of the Experiential strategy represents the purpose-built/designed environment of the live brand experience, and this applies for both face-to-face and virtual settings. The set can form part or all of a retail environment. It could be a converted double-decker bus, or a purpose-built garden in the middle of a shopping centre. The set is any environment that becomes the location for the live brand experience. It should be designed with all the elements of your Message and key communication in mind, and should reflect the visual identity of your brand as well as its personality.

The sets of most live brand experiences attract a lot of interest because they are enticing to the Target audience. A good set, designed as an immersive sensory environment, might be remembered by the participants for years to come. Some experiential marketing agencies outsource the production of sets that are used for face-to-face live brand experiences to companies that traditionally make props and stages for television, film and theatre, or exhibition stands. Similarly, some experiential marketing agencies outsource the production of sets that are used for remote/virtual live brand experiences to digital agencies, web programmers and TV production companies. Meanwhile, some of those digital providers are beginning to offer remote or virtual live brand experiences. This is another reason why, when appointing an experiential marketing agency, it is good to research their company history and understand how they began and evolved, because this will give you an idea of which areas within experiential marketing are their forte.

It is advisable to integrate the Interactive technology element with the Set element into your Experiential strategy, because the more innovative and interactive your set design is, the more engaging your live brand experience will be.

Integrating the selected elements to form the Experiential strategy

It is important to remember that your selected elements need to be integrated to form your Experiential strategy, which will be a combination of two or more of these elements. The Experiential strategy provides a structure for your idea, as well as a clear direction for your plan. When you pick your elements to create the Experiential strategy, keep in mind your original idea and the steps that you have taken thus far to come up with and refine it. The original concept was formulated using the BETTER model; the Brand personality (three brand values that sum up the brand's human-like characteristics), the Emotional connection (multi-sensory and/or authentic, positively connected and personally meaningful) the Target audience (their daily lifestyle and aspirations), the Two-way interaction (the live brand experience), the Exponential element (the word-of-mouth stimulant), and the Reach (the two-way interaction reach, word-of-mouth reach, and amplification channels reach). Since you began mapping out the plan in SET MESSAGE format, you have refined the idea further, carefully considering the Situation and background, Experiential objectives, Target audience and Message – key communication.

As well as ensuring that the Experiential strategy elements you select encompass your idea, it is also very important to remain open to new approaches regardless of any preconceptions that may exist concerning your sector or Target audience. Whether your consumers are affluent executives, or over 50s, or your product is an FMCG (such as a chocolate bar), or a high-involvement luxury purchase (such as a Rolls Royce), Experiential strategy elements can be combined successfully, as long as they are relevant to BETTER. By selecting elements that stay true to your Brand personality, creating an Emotional connection with the participants, and always keeping your consumer front of mind, you can develop an Experiential strategy that creates the right experience for the right people.

You should pick two or more of the most appropriate elements from the STRATEGIES acronym, then integrate them to form your Experiential strategy. Below are sample combinations that mix three or four elements, illustrating how you could go about mixing the selected elements to formulate an Experiential strategy.

Scenarios

Educational + service + research + set

When Sophie, the marketing director of a popular brand of margarine, wanted to show the brand's Target audience how the margarine could be used to lower cholesterol, as well as bring the active, healthy Brand personality to life, she designed an Experiential strategy involving a cholesterol-testing experience in a 40-foot branded trailer. First, doctors and leading experts educated participants about the negative effects and risks of high cholesterol, and secondly they provided guests with free cholesterol and heart-rate tests. Sophie received a contribution from the market research budget towards this campaign and wanted to gather data from the participants (to facilitate tailoring of marketing and distribution to customer needs). She wanted to know which supermarkets the Target audience members shopped in most regularly, how frequently they purchased butter or margarine, and which brands they preferred, and why. The Brand ambassadors, who were assisting the consumers through the cholesterol and heart-rate testing, asked consumers a few quick questions prior to their test. In return for answering the questions, the consumers were given a free heart-rate monitoring wrist strap. The campaign successfully achieved Sophie's objectives: it gathered insightful research, and brought to life the healthy Brand personality. The selected Experiential strategy elements educated consumers about the product's benefits, differentiating it from its competitors, and provided a free relevant service (in order to add value) to its participants in a memorable way.

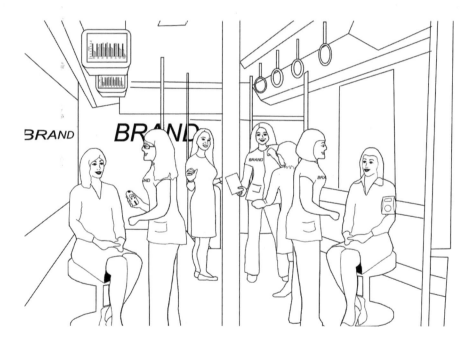

Theatre + advert + game

Mark, the creative director at a leading advertising agency, was informed that a brand of small pocket mints wanted to bring to life its advertising campaign with a live brand experience. The unique selling point of the product (and a key focus in the communication message) was that the mints had a special cooling effect. The live brand experience channel was intended to reinforce the creative from the adverts that Mark's team had designed. Mark wanted to bring the mint's Brand personality to life so he carefully analysed the creative, looking for inspiration on how to do so. The TV advert featured hundreds of life-size mints that visually symbolized 'cooling agents', so he decided that these would be the inspiration for the experience. The strategy incorporated acting, a Game, and the Advert. Professional actors dressed up as the cooling agents in costumes that were identical to the ones worn in the TV advert. The actors, reincarnated as mints, gave out samples of the cooling mints and engaged participants in a game, asking them to guess from three multiple-choice answers what the exact temperature was. Those who answered correctly were entered into a prize draw to win a skiing holiday, which reinforced the cooling USP. The Experiential strategy neatly and relevantly integrated elements of the Advert, Theatre and a Game, which in combination succeeded in bringing to life the advertising campaign.

Service + set

Jaleel, the marketing manager for a brand of paints for the home, ran live brand experiences to position the brand as a colour-matching expert with the Target audience of affluent women aged 25+. His Experiential strategy was designed to convey the colour-matching expertise of the brand, and promote its three main product ranges, Pure, Cirque and Revolution. The first was a range of neutral paints, the second a range of bold paints and the third a range of metallic paints. He combined the most appropriate elements to formulate the Experiential strategy: Service (to benefit and relate to his Target audience's lives), and Set (to demonstrate the appearance of the paint ranges on real walls).

He had already come up with a concept and completed the first four stages of SET MESSAGE during which he carefully researched his Target audience. He discovered that the demographic aspired to having beautiful homes with professional interior design. The women also spent a lot of time discussing their personal appearances and aspiring to look fashionable and stylish. These insights inspired Jaleel's Experiential strategy.

He created a live brand experience involving a set that toured the central atriums of major shopping centres. The set represented three adjoining rooms of a beautiful home, and each room was decorated to reflect one of the brand's paint ranges: Pure, Cirque and Revolution. The rooms featured complementary colours from their respective paint ranges, demonstrating the brand's expertise in colour-matching.

The mini houses had beautician Brand ambassadors positioned in each of the rooms, fully trained on the three paint ranges and on the brand's colour-matching techniques. The Brand ambassadors, who were seated at a branded counter, invited consumers to have their nails painted in shades that matched their outfits. The women were assigned one of three different themes to reflect the neutral, bold, and metallic ranges offered by the brand. Then the consumers were handed a 'Colour-match wheel' and shown how to select the nail polish colour that corresponded best with their outfit. This process closely replicated the process that the brand's website and store advisers used to intelligently match paint ranges and individual colour choices with consumers' style and home furnishings. This Experiential strategy successfully combined two elements: Service (colour matching and painting nails) and Set (a beautiful home environment) to achieve Jaleel's objectives.

Research + entertainment + advert + game (competition)

James, a brand manager at a well-known bank, was tasked with generating leads for a new unsecured loan product that targeted lower-income families. The brand's advertising agency created a TV advert that showed staff from the bank's branches dancing and singing (in the style of a Broadway musical) about an unsecured loan product that the bank had launched. James decided to reinforce the TV campaign with experiential marketing. He hired an experiential marketing agency to produce a series of live brand experiences that would replicate the advert as a live performance, thus bringing to life the advert's creative.

During the Target audience stage of SET MESSAGE James referred to data that indicated that the demographic were most susceptible to applying for loans during school holidays, because these periods were most popular for expensive holidays abroad. Taking this insight into consideration, he decided that the performance should be presented as a 5-minute live advert, shown during the commercials at cinemas during school holidays. A host manned the microphone and introduced the musical performance. Before the performance began, he encouraged the families to complete a quick 'Dream holiday survey', handed out by Brand ambassadors, which asked them about their ideal holiday destinations and activities. In return for completing the survey, the kids received free popcorn (in a branded container), and the families were entered into a competition to win their dream holiday.

This successful and simple live brand experience was performed many times a day during the winter and summer holidays at over 20 cinemas, entertaining families that might not have been able to afford to go away on holiday. The Experiential strategy combined Advert, Entertainment, Game (competition) and Research elements to achieve the brand's experiential objective of lead generation whilst also reinforcing the impact of the advertising campaign through a memorable experience.

Game + televised/broadcast

Andrew is the sales and marketing director at a drinks company. He was planning the launch of a new brand of Caribbean rum. The brand had a pirate-themed brand personality, and Andrew was keen to launch it with an integrated experiential marketing campaign. The objectives were to bring to life the Caribbean and pirate themed Brand personality, drive product trial and generate word-of-mouth. After carefully analysing the concept to determine which strategy elements it combined, he decided on the Televised/broadcast and Game elements for his Experiential strategy.

Following a BETTER brainstorm session with his creative team, he selected a pirate-themed one-hour 'Treasure hunt challenge' with prizes of cases of rum and Caribbean cruises. The campaign ran six 'Treasure Hunt Challenges' simultaneously, one in each of the six main regions in England. Each city had its own branded treasure hunt map, with key points identified as locations to pick up clues. Andrew's PR agency secured local press coverage in advance, ensuring a high level of participation in the live brand experience. The articles instructed readers to form teams of five with their friends before meeting at the start points in each city. Advertising was also used as an amplification channel, with print and billboard ads promoting the 'Treasure hunt challenge' during the week prior to it happening.

On arrival at the meeting points, participants were greeted by Brand ambassadors (wearing pirate hats, fake parrots and eye patches) who registered them for the game and gave them their kits containing treasure maps, rum samples, and branded T-shirts. Off they went racing round the cities to hunt for clues, in the hope of finding the treasure chests that contained prize tickets, within the allotted hour. Andrew secured a media partnership and the nationwide 'Treasure hunt challenge' was broadcast live on television in a one-hour slot, showing the teams running around each town hunting for clues and treasure chests. A 30-minute special the following week showed the winners enjoying their rum cases and Caribbean cruises. In addition to the 10,000 registered consumers that participated in the actual Challenge, another 3 million people tuned in and watched the live brand experience on TV, and almost 1 million watched the special the following week.

The Game element enabled a high level of two-way interaction between the brand and participants, while the Televised/broadcast element enabled the live brand experience to have a massive reach. The experiential marketing campaign brought to life the rum's Caribbean and pirate-themed Brand personality, drove product trial and generated massive word-of-mouth at the same time.

Educational + interactive technology + set

Adriana was responsible for launching an innovative mobile phone that had a built-in, high-quality video camera. It also had a revolutionary function that allowed consumers to edit their videos on their mobile phones using the built-in editing software and effects suite. The product was the first of its kind, and Adriana wanted to create an experiential marketing campaign that would educate consumers on its special features.

Her Target audience, fun loving Generation Y-ers (18–25), inspired Adriana to hire an experiential agency and create an innovative live brand experience on US beaches. They created a giant set, a 'Mobile-video-phone zone' shaped like the mobile video phone itself, and positioned it on beaches that attracted the young, fun demographic. Brand ambassadors were trained and armed with the mobile video phones. They approached groups of friends who were sunbathing on the beach or playing sport such as volleyball, and invited them to be filmed by the Brand ambassador holding the videophone. The groups of friends were excited at the thought of making their own mini beach-movie, and were keen to oblige and participate. Beachgoers were then encouraged to enter the 'Mobile-video-phone zone' to watch a demonstration and tutorial that educated them about the video-editing features of the phone. Brand ambassadors encouraged them to participate in editing the movie clips in which they starred, using life-sized buttons on the sets walls that visually replicated the buttons and features on the device itself. Thousands of excited consumers from beaches around the United States edited their movie clips, which they received on the spot on a branded DVD. The participants had the opportunity to give their contact info and receive the clips by e-mail for use on YouTube or Facebook. As well as being given the DVDs, consumers received branded beach balls and fake tattoos, which raised brand awareness to other beachgoers.

Adriana's Experiential strategy was Educational, and used Interactive technology built into a brand-relevant Set. The live brand experience was also amplified with digital ads, showing some of the live brand experience highlights and social network groups. The experiential marketing campaign achieved its objective of educating consumers about the phone's video-editing features. The memorable and fun two-way interaction also succeeded in generating brand advocacy and driving word-of-mouth amongst the young, fun, Target audience.

Make the experience memorable and ongoing

Keep in mind that even without any additional actions or triggers, a live brand experience is by its nature more memorable than any other form of marketing, and the live brand experience should be at the core of the experiential marketing campaign. Memories themselves do not merely exist across time, linking the past, present and future, nor are they only alive within the individual's consciousness. Memories exist at the very heart of 'lived experience', whether collective or individual.[1] To ensure that the experiential marketing campaign is remembered for the maximum possible length of time, you can create external aids that reinforce the memories of the people that it reached.

A great option when the live brand experience is executed face to face is to provide participants with visual evidence such as photos or videos of their experience. For example, you can take the consumers' photos while they are in or on the set and then let them download their photos online, give them printouts in branded frames or even print their photos onto mugs/magnets/stickers, etc. Visual evidence is a great way of triggering positive emotions in the memories of the participants by reminding them of how much they enjoyed the experience (the souvenir may also become sentimental and lead them to romanticize their experience). When provided in a digital format, the visual evidence can incorporate an Exponential element such as a 'forward to a friend' feature.

Relevant branded gifts are another great way of triggering memories. The gift then acts as an external aid, and an 'important reason for why external aids facilitate memory is that the physical presence of an object usually stimulates memory more than imagining or thinking'.[2] They can either be given in person (when the live brand experience is face to face) or by inviting consumers to order their free gift themselves by text or web form (when the live brand experience is remote). By providing the participants with a call to action prior to receiving their gift, therefore making it necessary that they actively request the gift, you stimulate their intention to remember the experience.

It is recommended that you provide participants of the live brand experience with a trigger mechanism that makes it easy for them to pass on their experience, and then support that system with an incentive for doing so; this forms the Exponential element for the campaign. When the incentive is a gift, the recipients of the participant's message should also have the opportunity to receive a gift, as should those who heard about the live brand experience from an amplification channel. Even though the individuals in these groups did not all participate in the experience themselves, they have the opportunity to receive something tangible, symbolizing the experience that they heard about from a peer or amplification channel. In this way the external aid does not only serve as a tangible reinforcement of the participant's memory, it also provides the recipient of the message with the opportunity to engage further with the brand and form their own personal connection with it.

By creating a further interaction between the brand and both the participants and the recipients, the relationship continues beyond the initial campaign. Ongoing positive interaction is key to establishing long-term customer loyalty, this being the ultimate aim of experiential marketing. By collecting the contact data of the participants of your experience and the recipients of the experience message, and then contacting them with invitations to future experiences (perhaps invitation only), you can convert recipients of a second-hand message about a live brand experience into participants of a live brand experience. By continuing the ongoing experiential marketing communication with a live brand experience at its core, you can build golden bonds with your Target audience and strengthen the feeling that you want to add value to their lives. As a result, the consumers will remember that the relationship that they have with you are long-term and two-way, and that it does not end when the first experience or purchase does. The other phenomenon that can occur as a result of inviting consumers (participants and recipients) to future live brand experiences, is that bonds will form between the individuals in the groups of those invited, and the memory of the group realizes itself in individual memories.[3] This long-term view should be considered when formulating your long-term Experiential strategy, which when coupled with a customer-experience orientation within your organization will build the foundations for brand advocacy and long-standing customer relationships.

Summary

In summary, there are 10 basic elements in the STRATEGIES acronym: Service, Theatre, Research, Adverts, Televised or broadcast, Entertainment, Game (or competition), Interactive technologies, Education, and Set. You should take your existing experiential concept and check which elements from the STRATEGIES acronym best define it, then develop it further by combining two or more of those strategy elements. All Experiential strategies should bring the Brand personality to life, create an Emotional connection with participants, and be relevant to the Target audience's lifestyle and aspirations. You should always have an Exponential element or a talking point that inspires word-of-mouth, and strive to attain maximum Reach (combining the initial reach of the live brand experience, the word-of-mouth reach and the reach of amplification channels) whilst maintaining quality engagement. The Experiential strategy should be fitting to the Experiential objectives, and should integrate the brand's Message – key communication. Use the BETTER model as your checklist to ensure your Experiential strategy is as effective as possible.

Notes

1. Middleton, D and Brown, S D (2005) *The Social Psychology of Experience: Studies in remembering and forgetting*, Sage, London
2. Gruneberg, M and Morris, P (1992) *Aspects of Memory: The practical aspects*, Vol 1, p 154, Routledge, London
3. Halbwachs, M and Coser, LA (1992) *On Collective Memory*, p 40, University of Chicago Press, Chicago, IL

10 Selected locations and Brand ambassadors

You've probably heard the popular sayings 'Location, location, location!' and 'People buy people!' many times. These two statements may be most frequently used in retail, property and sales environments, but they apply to every touch point that a consumer has with an organization or brand during his or her journey with it. This journey includes the marketing communication that the individuals participate in. As previously explained, it is suggested the big idea in your experiential marketing campaign is based on a two-way interaction, in real time. This live brand experience needs to be positively managed by people, and whether they are your employees or part-time representatives, they should be Brand ambassadors. The synergy between participants, locations and Brand ambassadors is very important. Therefore, to be successful in experiential marketing you must strive to create the right experiences for the right people, and those experiences need to happen at the right place, at the right time.

When you completed the Target audience part of the SET MESSAGE plan, you completed the day-in-the-life analysis, also looking at the aspirational lifestyle of your Target audiences, taking time out to truly consider where to find them and how best to appeal to their desires. Therefore, finding the ideal locations (whether face to face or remote) for the experience and setting it up effectively is key. There are many factors to be taken into consideration when selecting locations for live brand experiences. This chapter will give you an in-depth understanding of what needs to be considered at this stage in your experiential plan, and how the choice of locations can make or break an experience.

The Brand ambassadors, also of ultimate importance, are the second facet of this chapter. During the live brand experience they become the identity of the brand, because they are the only human interface between the Brand personality and the consumer. They are the people who have the potential to appeal to the desires of the participants and strengthen their relationship with the brand. You can spend all the time in the world planning your live brand experience and ensuring that everything is logistically perfect, but if a Brand ambassador is not carefully trained or not properly matched to the brand and the Target audience, then the live brand experience will not be a success.

To help you to avoid wasted efforts, this chapter looks at how to plan and carefully select the right locations (whether face to face or remote) for live brand experiences, how to choose the right Brand ambassadors, and how to train them and ensure flawless problem-free delivery.

Choosing locations

There are five factors to consider when evaluating possible locations for your live brand experience:

1. Demographic (of the location's visitors).
2. The state of mind (of the location's visitors)
   – are they seeking to purchase/socialize/be entertained/learn?
   – how much dwell time do they have available; are they in a rush or in leisure mode?
   – and if they are with others, who are they with?
3. Footfall (number of visitors).
4. Practical and logistical considerations.
5. Cost (which should be related to the spaces, footfall, ambience, attributes and positioning).

Since different locations have different demographics, it can be difficult to know exactly where to place your live brand experience. Some places, such as business districts, have an affluent population. This could suit a live brand experience for a credit card, if it wished to reach an affluent Target audience. Areas with large universities will have a strong student demographic, and could therefore be ideal for a brand that wanted to create brand experiences for students or the young, hip and trendy. Likewise, some areas are very 'middle England/middle United States' and could be ideal for targeting the middle-class family demographic, yummy mummies or housewives (and househusbands). No matter who your Target audience are, there are locations (whether face to face or remote) such as venues, events, or institutions that are perfect for reaching them in their natural environment. This applies to every population, no matter how niche or mainstream they are.

When scouting for Selected locations for your live brand experience, it is of vital importance to ensure that the location's visitor demographics match your Target audience's demographics. At this stage in the plan you have already covered analysing or conducting market research into the Target audience's lives, and you should now be referring to those key insights and findings to extrapolate the perfect settings for your live brand experience. The day-in-the-life analysis should be referred to at this stage. If you are working with an agency, this could be its role, but you as the client should still be checking that it has selected the right locations for the interaction.

The second factor to be considered when selecting your live brand experience's locations is the state of mind that the Target audience is in while they are visiting. In this instance, the state of mind refers to what they are seeking (to purchase, socialize, be entertained or learn), the dwell time that they have available (whether they are in a rush or in leisure mode) and whether they are alone or, if not, who they are with.

If it takes five minutes to engage with the experiential interaction, then it is important the participants have five minutes to spare in the selected locations. For example, people at airports have lots of time available. They are often bored and it is most likely that they would welcome an interactive added-value experience with open arms. On the other hand, commuter points, rail stations and transport hubs are high-footfall locations where a live brand experience will not always succeed in capturing a consumer's attention. Twenty seconds' interest may be the maximum here, and it is important not to be a nuisance to participants by attempting to keep their attention for longer than they desire. Trendy music-lovers at an outdoor music festival are likely to have lots of time available and to be open to interactive experiences, especially ones that relate to their state of mind. Imagine you have been camping at a festival for three days with no laundry or cleaning facilities, and a Brand ambassador representing a denim brand approaches you, offering to wash and return your jeans to your tent. This is an added-value experience that relates to the state of mind of the festival-going Target audience, there and then. It is easy to imagine this person putting on the crisp, freshly-washed jeans and telling all his or her peers about the excellent experience he or she just had with the denim brand. This word-of-mouth marketing dynamic would not have been created if the experience had been positioned in the wrong locations. The research that you analysed earlier, in the Target audience part of the planning stage, will be crucial now. By understanding the state of mind of your Target audience while they are in their natural locations (the ones you noted while doing the day-in-the-life analysis), you will be able to ensure that your live brand experiences are relevant, appropriate and welcomed.

The third factor to take into consideration is vital: footfall. The reach of your live brand experience will largely depend on the number of people that visit the locations. Busier locations tend to be better for live brand experiences as they allow a larger number of interactions, and therefore both the initial and the word-of-mouth reaches will be higher. Some live brand experiences that target niche audiences might have to compromise and use locations with a high concentration of the target demographic, but which sacrifice high footfall. Either way, footfall should be taken into consideration, as it ultimately affects the return on investment (ROI) and long-term return on investment (LROI) of the live brand experience.

The fourth important consideration when selecting locations is the logistical or practical factors. There are legal implications when setting up an experience, and depending on who owns the space, permission will need to be granted, hire fees may need to be paid, insurance may need to be in place and all health and safety and risk assessment paperwork (when the experience is face to face) will need to be complete. When the experience is delivered face to face, weather is also a serious consideration, especially when deciding whether to position the live brand experience internally or externally. Sometimes the space may not be practical for the set that you have in mind. If you planned to have a luxury experience located in a park, for example, then under-planning for rain and mud could potentially ruin everything. If you are thinking of hiring space in a shopping centre, that ideal spot located just outside the store in question, which would show your product in its best light, may already be contracted to someone else. If you want your live brand experience to be held on your brand's website homepage but the set is a flash game or gallery zone that takes up more space than is available, then a micro-site may be better. If you want to set up your live brand experiences within a short timescale but you want the experience to be positioned at airports, then it may need to be re-thought because in airports you will face weeks of applications and bureaucracy, not to mention countless security checks prior to and during the live brand experience. If you want to target young children face to face, then the locations must always be safe and appropriate, with a set made of soft, non-harmful materials, without intrusive or flammable surfaces, and the Brand ambassadors will need to be police-checked and experienced in working with children. Keep in mind that the set (its size, look and purpose), whether it is a physical or virtual set, must be appropriate and natural for the Selected locations and their surrounding environments, whether face to face or remote.

Aside from the many practical and logistical factors to be taken into consideration when choosing locations for a live brand experience, there is the pressing fifth factor: cost. Space hire can vary from free to extremely expensive, and can be the make-or-break factor when it comes to the ROI and LROI from a live brand experience. The cost should be directly in line with the location's footfall (or visitor traffic), ambience, physical space and positioning.

For example, a high-footfall location might cost more to hire than a low-footfall location, but if you compare the cost per thousand people visiting both locations, then you may find that the space with the lower price is far more expensive when it is related back to the volume of interaction opportunities that it provides. In this respect, looking at the cost of hiring live brand experience space is similar to looking at the cost of hiring media space. Placing an experience in the right physical or virtual space is similar to scheduling an advert in the right media space. Some owners are aware that their space is very valuable from an ambience or positioning (how it is perceived by its visitors) perspective and take advantage of this by charging high rates to those who wish to hire space. Other space owners (from event promoters to property tycoons, and website entrepreneurs) haven't taken the financial opportunity of hiring space for live brand experiences into consideration; when this is the case, they will usually be willing to provide good rates or contra deals, so sometimes it is good to be creative and think 'out of the box' when scouting or on reconnaissance. Think of places that other brands may not have used for this purpose in the past, in order to maximize the value of the space you can get in return for your investment.

Every element that has been covered thus far in the SET MESSAGE planning system will come into play when selecting the right locations for the brand experience. Therefore, you should keep in mind the Situation and background, the Experiential objectives, the Target audience, the Message – key communication, and the Experiential strategy when considering the space hire options that you have available.

Bear in mind that any location with people in (or on) it could be a potential locations for live brand experiences, from cinemas, to television channels, to gyms, to Second Life, to libraries and many,

many more. Below are some examples of locations that have been used for live brand experiences.

Examples of live brand experience locations

An in-store live brand experience

Harry is a marketing manager for a market-leading brand of PCs and printers. When his experiential marketing agency was tasked with the brief of increasing sales and bringing to life the stylish Brand personality of an expensive new printer it was launching, the agency decided that the right locations would be in-store. The printer, which has a premium price and targets affluent dads, required an experience that both added value to the participant and drove sales. The experiential marketing agency designed an experience held in the stores where the printers were sold. The experience invited participants (dads with their kids) to have their photos taken in front of a branded backdrop. Their photos were printed out on the spot and given to the participants. Those who chose to buy the printer also received a high-quality, sterling silver frame for their photo.

Live brand experiences at events

Events-based experiences can be wholly or partly organized by brands, and provide the opportunity to create a large-scale environment with plenty of chances to add value and bring the Brand personality to life. In Britain, Ben & Jerry's organizes an annual music festival 'Ice Cream Sundae', while Innocent Smoothies organizes an annual organic-themed festival 'Village Fete'. Both of these attract thousands of avid participants, who interact with these brands while they makeover large parks in the summer.

Even though it can be successful to organize a large-scale event, existing events can also be fantastic settings for live brand experiences. They are especially effective for achieving objectives such as 'position the brand as x' or 'gain credibility with y'. By positioning a live brand experience at an existing event, you affiliate with the event's values and the aspirational lifestyle it represents for its guests, in much the same way as sponsoring such an event. The visitors' perceptions of the event instantly 'rub off' onto their perceptions of the brand, and vice versa. Though live brand experiences enable deep and relevant two-way interactions that sponsorship can't achieve alone, the branding opportunities that sponsorship deals provide can be complementary to the live brand experience, reinforcing awareness and strengthening the impact of the live brand experience channel. Sometimes, good package deals that include both live brand experience space and sponsorship branding can be negotiated at events.

A live brand experience at a sports match/game

The founder of a poker website wanted to bring to life the brand's 'Living the dream' message while driving membership sign-ups. The experience he designed with his experiential marketing agency involved a branded stretch Hummer limo with external plasma screens. The Hummer parked outside sporting events and a team of Las Vegas-style female Brand ambassadors, the 'Living the dream girls' exited the Hummer, which had a casino-themed interior, and they invited the male sports fans to have their photos taken with them. The sports fans sat in the Hummer and felt like they were 'living the dream'. The team of glamorous Brand ambassadors also distributed scratch-cards to passers-by, encouraging them to scratch off the printed poker card design and win 'free money' (online gambling credit). The sports fans who had their photos taken with the girls were invited to log on to a micro-site and download their photos, whilst being entered into a competition to win prizes such as trips to Las Vegas, and a VIP night out with the 'Living the dream girls'.

A live brand experience at an exhibition

A brand of premium gin that targets fashionable females aged 18–30, wanted to create a live brand experience that brought its Eskimo-themed Brand personality to life, drove product trial and captured participant data. The data would enable continued communication with the participants, allowing the brand to invite them to exclusive gin events that they planned to organize in the future. Sandy, the marketing director for the brand, hired an experiential marketing agency to deliver the live brand experience on a trial basis, prior to shifting more resources and investing in the ongoing live brand experience programme. For the trial, the agency hired space at a fashion exhibition, knowing that the Target audience was the primary demographic of the exhibition's guests. It would be the only gin brand to exhibit at this show, which would be saturated by clothing and cosmetics brands.

The set was a super-cold igloo-style stand, which was very realistic and even featured real ice and real-looking snow. The participants were invited to put on branded Eskimo coats and go into the two-degree igloo, enter a competition to win a fashion-filled party holiday to Iceland and receive a shot of gin. The Brand ambassadors were fashion models dressed as Eskimos who engaged the participants and appealed to their aspirational lifestyle. By positioning the brand experience at a fashion exhibition, the brand gained credibility with a hard-to-impress audience, and the experience was 'the talk of the show'. By capturing data through the competition entries, the brand succeeded in building a database of participants who would soon become brand evangelists and spread word-of-mouth – especially after being invited to exclusive invite-only fashion events.

An online live brand experience

Live brand experiences are not only suitable for face-to-face locations; you can deliver a great live brand experience online or in any remote environment that facilitates two-way interactions in real time. In recent years, a well-known brand of iced tea wanted to reach large numbers with a limited budget. It decided to save money on logistics and space hire by holding its live brand experiences on the internet. The iced tea brand had a sexy and refreshing Brand personality, and the objective of the live brand experience was to drive word-of-web.

The brand worked with a digital agency to develop a micro-site featuring a flash game. The game featured a beach setting and showed lots of animated 3D sexy people sunbathing, surfing, walking around and playing volleyball. The game challenged participants to refresh the beachgoers before they became dehydrated and dropped to the floor. To rehydrate the beachgoers, participants had to drag-and-drop cans of iced tea from a branded cooler, quickly enough to fill up the 'refresh-o-meter' on the side of the screen. The fun and addictive game had the exponential element of a score board with the option to send a 'challenge invite' to a friend, and as a result its hits grew exponentially. High scorers on the game received a month's supply of the iced tea and all participants had the opportunity to order a free branded T-shirt, thus becoming walking adverts for the brand.

A live brand experience outside stores

A marketing manager at a mobile phone manufacturer wanted to drive footfall into the stores that were selling an innovative new phone. She designed a simple live brand experience held on the street outside the

stores. The experience involved a team of Brand ambassadors wearing Adscreens on their backs. The Adscreens were connected to the phones, and the Brand ambassadors demonstrated the unique features of the phone to passers-by. During this time they were able to communicate key messages and ask participants about how they organize their social life, demonstrating how the phone's features could facilitate socializing. This interactive demo brought to life the phone's Brand personality, which focused on the 'business of socializing', whilst driving footfall into the stores and thereby increasing sales.

A live brand experience in shopping malls

A clothing catalogue that targets busy women aged 25–50 has a fashionable and relaxing Brand personality. The Message – key communication was that with the catalogue, busy women can shop easily and conveniently from home without the stress of shopping malls. Grace, its brand manager, wanted to encourage consumers who were in shopping malls to relax and shop from home using the catalogue. Her objectives were to promote the catalogue's new cosmetics offering and sign people up for catalogue subscription.

She worked with an experiential marketing agency and created a live brand experience that toured 12 shopping malls (with a high percentage of the target demographic) with a weekend at each. The experience invited visitors to be pampered in a branded relaxation set. The participants received a relaxing pedicure and foot massage, relieving their tired 'shopping feet'. While they were enjoying this treat, they were given copies of the catalogue by the Brand ambassadors, who encouraged them to browse through the cosmetics and fashion items on offer. Grace succeeded in driving catalogue subscriptions by making subscription a prerequisite for participating in the live brand experience. After being pampered, participants were given goody bags by the Brand ambassadors that included a copy of the catalogue, make-up samples from the catalogue's cosmetics range, and a discount voucher for their first/next purchase.

A live brand experience in offices

An upmarket credit card brand that targets affluent professionals wanted to communicate its Message – key communication, that it goes 'the extra mile' for consumers and has a helpful, concierge-style Brand personality. The credit card brand gained permission for its Brand ambassadors (who were dressed as concierges) to enter the office blocks of large, successful organizations and offer executives the chance to have their suit jackets dry-cleaned and returned by the end of the day. The Brand ambassadors returned the pristinely dry-cleaned blazers in a protective branded wrap. Then, they communicated the message: when the professionals signed up with the card, they could call and ask for advice on anything, from dry cleaning services and hard-to-find sports tickets, to restaurant reservations and movies. This office-based live brand experience succeeded in engaging the right demographic while communicating the brand's message and bringing to life the credit card's concierge-style Brand personality.

A live brand experience at skiing /snowboarding slopes

Marko, a brand manager for a manufacturer of gadgets and MP3 players, wanted to bring to life the funky, trendy Brand personality of its latest MP3 player and recorder. Marko secured a partnership with a funky skiwear shop for the live brand experience. He organized skiwear fashion shows with popular DJs and stylish light displays at snowboarding and skiing competitions. Brand ambassadors invited participants to watch the skiwear fashion show, gave out PDAs that were pre-loaded with multiple-choice questions and encouraged participants to identify which brands of clothing each model was wearing. The models on the catwalk had numbers on their backs, and participants logged their guesses (along with providing their contact data). The top 10 scorers won MP3 players, whilst all participants received earmuffs featuring the logo of the player.

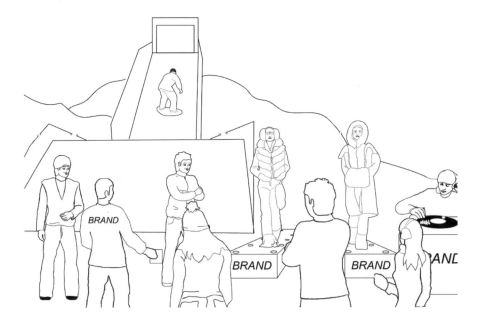

A live brand experience on the beach

Greg, the owner of a restaurant chain located in tourist resorts, targets families on holiday. The restaurant chain's Brand personality was 'fun' and 'kid friendly'. Greg had not seen a good return on investment from his previous marketing and advertising campaigns and wanted to try an experiential marketing approach with live brand experience at its core. He hired an experiential marketing manager to organize an interactive live brand experience targeting families at the beaches near his restaurants. Jackie, his new employee, carefully followed the SET MESSAGE system and designed a live brand experience that invited beach-going kids to enter the 'Sandcastle Challenge', a sandcastle-making competition. She asked kids from families who already ate at the restaurants to use the crayons provided and draw pictures of themselves on the beach making sandcastles. The best drawings were adapted to form adverts promoting the 'Sandcastle challenge'. The ads that served as an amplification channel were printed in tourist guides, shown as banner ads on resort websites, and even used to make flyers that were displayed in branded dispensers at reception desks in local hotels. She hired and trained bubbly children's entertainers, forming teams of Brand ambassadors. The teams were deployed at beaches and gave out sandcastle-making kits that featured the restaurant chain's branding. The Brand ambassadors encouraged kids to participate and make impressive sandcastles in the hope of winning a free meal for their whole family. All participating children received branded caps to wear when making their sandcastles, while the mums and dads received flyers featuring the restaurant's menu and a buy-one-get-one-free offer.

On the selected beaches, the 'Sandcastle Challenge' (and therefore the chain of restaurants) became the main topic of conversation for every family with kids. Jackie also used PR as an amplification channel by giving local newspaper editors free dining passes in return for them featuring photos of the competition winners on the front pages of their publications. Photos of the kids making the sandcastles were even featured on a hall-of-fame board inside the restaurants, further enforcing the restaurant's fun and kid friendly brand personality.

Live brand experiences are like theatre productions

A live brand experience is like a theatre production, where the Brand ambassadors can need as much training and rehearsal as actors on a stage. The cast, the lighting, the rigging and the audience are all key factors in the smooth delivery of a successful performance. This is not to say that the Brand ambassadors should not believe what they are saying; that would be far from ideal. In fact, a vital factor in the success of a live brand experience is that the Brand ambassadors have an opportunity to experience the product themselves, like becoming method actors who truly feel that they are the character they are playing.

If the Brand ambassadors are given the opportunity to trial the product or service prior to the live brand experience going 'live', they will always be able to speak from the position of a genuine personal recommendation when communicating with participants. The personal recommendation and word-of-mouth, as previously discussed, are the ultimate marketing tools that create the golden bonds between consumers and brands.

The reason it is important to draw a parallel between actors and Brand ambassadors is that they need to be carefully trained on the brand, product and Experiential objectives, but most important, truly believe in the brand, similar to the way in which actors must get into their role, fully rehearse their lines and movements, and truly believe that they are the character. The Brand ambassadors should be as rehearsed and genuine as actors, and the behind-the-scenes cast of a live brand experience need to work together as a team, just like the behind-the-scenes cast of a theatre production. There must be a strict schedule, highly organized production managers and contingencies in place across every element of both types of production because, as with theatre, live brand experiences are executed in real time. There is no time to edit later or cut out the bad bits.

Brand ambassador selection

Proper selection of Brand ambassadors is of ultimate importance to the success of live brand experiences. When your agency is selecting Brand ambassadors, there are three key factors to be taken into consideration:

1. Matching the Brand ambassadors to the Target audience and/or their aspirational lifestyle.
2. Selecting Brand ambassadors who are suited to the brand and the Experiential objectives.
3. Contingencies need to be put in place when hiring Brand ambassadors.

1. Matching the Brand ambassadors to the Target audience and/or their aspirational lifestyle

The first key factor is deciding when it is appropriate to match the Brand ambassadors with the Target audience themselves (so that participants can relate to the Brand ambassadors), and when it is preferential to match the Brand ambassadors to individuals that reflect the Target audience's aspirational lifestyle (so that the participants look up to the Brand ambassadors).

A nappy brand

For example, a popular brand of nappies uses an integrated experiential marketing strategy and places live brand experiences at the core of its campaigns. If it hired glamorous young models to become its Brand ambassadors while promoting its brand of nappies to mothers at supermarkets, it is unlikely that the mothers would have been able to relate to the Brand ambassadors, or that a genuine relationship between the two groups would have formed. Young Brand ambassadors of this type are unlikely to be running a family of their own, and therefore would not have been able to relate to the concerns and considerations that the mothers have when they are purchasing nappies.

The nappy brand knows that it is best to match the Brand ambassadors to the Target audience, which is why when briefing its staffing agency, it clearly specifies that its highest priority in Brand ambassador selection is that the Brand ambassadors are mothers with young children themselves, and it is compulsory that they receive nappies to trial before they are able to work on the live brand experience.

A tanning product

In contrast, a brand of tanning products targets women who aspire to be glamorous and sun-kissed, and it is correct in encouraging its agency to select the aforementioned variety of model-like Brand ambassadors. The brand knows that its customers purchase tanning products because using them makes them feel closer to achieving their aspirational lifestyle.

During its last campaign, tanned and beautiful Brand ambassadors engaged women and encouraged them to participate in the tanning product's live brand experience. As a result, the participants made the connection between the beautiful Brand ambassadors and the tanning product, which led them to associate the outcome of using the product with their desired physical appearance. Therefore in this brand's live brand experience programme it was more appropriate that the Brand ambassadors matched the aspirational lifestyle of the Target audience, rather than if they had been selected to match the Target audience themselves.

A nicotine patch

When a brand of patches that help people quit smoking designed a live brand experience to promote the patch, it ensured that the Brand ambassadors were non-smokers who at some point in their lives had smoked but succeeded in quitting. The reason for this choice was that during the Target audience part of SET MESSAGE, Tom, the patch's brand manager, had identified a key insight while he studied the Target audience's aspirational lifestyle (smokers who want to quit). He found that the Target audience aspired to be like people they knew who had previously smoked and succeeded in quitting. The Brand ambassadors were able to encourage many of the live brand experience's participants to try the patch because they had inspired them with their stories of having previously achieved quitting smoking themselves.

Just imagine the consequences if the brand hadn't taken any precautions, and Brand ambassadors wearing anti smoking T-shirts were seen smoking cigarettes on their lunch breaks!

Life insurance

Recently, a financial services company launched a live brand experience that targeted one of its life insurance products at men and women aged 55 to 70. The Selected locations were bingo halls and golf clubs frequented by the Target audience. The day-in-the-life analysis and aspirational lifestyle research conducted by the company's experiential marketing agency showed that the 55–70-year olds considered their 40s to have been the time of their lives that were most enjoyable, and they often aspired to recapture the way they looked and felt during that time. Some additional supporting research also provided an important insight: the Target audience didn't consider young people to be credible sources for information on important financial matters such as life insurance.

The agency had an in-house staffing division and strategically selected Brand ambassadors who were mainly in their 40s because they were old enough for the Target audience to relate to while still young enough to represent the Target audience's aspirational lifestyle. As a result, the Brand ambassadors were able to successfully connect with the participants, strengthening the relationship between the brand and its Target audience whilst selling the life insurance product to a record percentage of participants.

2. Selecting Brand ambassadors who are suited to the brand and the Experiential objectives

It is important that the Brand ambassadors are reflective of the brand personality and are suited to the campaign's Experiential objectives. Some Brand ambassadors are good at driving sales; they have the qualities required, including persistence, charm and stamina.

Brand ambassadors need to be carefully selected to reflect the brand personality and bring it to life. If a brand is sophisticated, its Brand ambassadors must be the epitome of sophistication. On the other hand, if a brand personality is fun and comical, so must be the Brand ambassadors.

A brand of streetwear

A brand of hooded sweatshirts, hats and jackets had the Experiential objective of positioning itself as a preferred choice of funky streetwear, and gaining credibility with a funky youth audience. The brand manager, Laura, hired a promotional staffing agency to provide Brand ambassadors who were skateboarders and graffiti artists with progressive looks such as funky hairstyles, tattoos and piercings. The skateboarders and graffiti artists who were selected locally were well-known on the streets in their areas, and once they interacted with the Target audience through a street art competition, the results were exceptional.

The experience invited the Target audience to participate in spray-painting the purpose-built walls surrounding the stores, as well as the skateboarding ramp inside the store, giving them a chance to win concert tickets and other youth-oriented prizes. The brand gained the same respect and credibility that the skateboarders and graffiti artists had to begin with.

3. Contingencies need to be put in place when hiring Brand ambassadors

The third and most important factor to remember when you or your agency are selecting part-time Brand ambassadors is that many of them have other commitments that they may see as a higher priority than being a Brand ambassador.

Many Brand ambassadors are out-of-work actors, models, singers or dancers who are well suited to live brand experiences because of their bubbly, performance-oriented nature. Though these types of people can be very good choices on many occasions, and the work suits them because they need to maintain flexible employment to enable them to go to castings, auditions and performances when necessary, they may be liable to cancel at the last-minute due to 'call-backs', or bookings for their 'real careers'.

Some Brand ambassadors are housewives, or students who again have other commitments such as children or degrees, which they are likely to see as higher priorities than your campaign, and if they need to attend to their existing commitments due to an unexpected occurrence, they are liable to let you down. Additionally, there are also many genuine reasons why Brand ambassadors might let down their agencies and their agencies' clients. They might pull out at the last minute due to sickness, car breakdowns, deaths of relatives, along with a multitude of other unpredictable emergencies.

These apparently devastating and unavoidable occurrences need not jeopardize the success of the live brand experience. If Brand ambassador contingencies are adequately planned and prepared, and a 'problem solving in advance' approach is employed, then these types of cancellations will not cause major problems.

No matter how friendly, well-meaning or committed your Brand ambassadors are, difficult things will happen and in a live marketing environment, there needs to be a Plan B for every scenario. By having additional Brand ambassadors trained and on standby, or present during the live brand experience as 'reserves', a full team headcount can usually be achieved.

Reserve Brand ambassadors are crucial to the success of the live brand experience. Most good experiential marketing agencies have an in-house staffing division, because the agency will know the importance of the Brand ambassadors to the success of the live brand experience (especially when it is executed face to face).

It can be highly detrimental to attempt to book, train and manage Brand ambassadors yourself if you don't have the proper resources to do so. This is a full-time activity and requires a lot of patience, skill and experience. Therefore, it is best for clients not to attempt to manage Brand ambassadors and leave this task to a specialist agency (or an agency that will effectively outsource to one).

The extensive experience that is required for this type of problem solving and trouble shooting strengthens the argument for not attempting to bring staffing in-house. It must also be remembered that experiential marketing agencies or staffing agencies provide their Brand ambassadors with regular work, and they maintain a certain level of loyalty as a result. The relationship between an agency and its Brand ambassadors (and event managers) is extremely valuable, and its importance should not be underestimated.

Recruiting Brand ambassadors

It is good to try and gain an understanding of your experiential marketing agency's recruitment strategies and policies, because its approach to recruitment can make a difference to the performance and success of the Brand ambassadors in your live brand experience.

There are two different approaches to recruiting Brand ambassadors: either they are recruited specifically for a one-off live brand experience, or they are recruited to join a general database where they can be booked for lots of jobs, and then selected from that database for specific live brand experiences. Brand ambassador recruitment ads can be placed online on relevant websites and forums or offline, for example posters in independent shops or face to face at events.

Word-of-mouth is also a common recruitment driver. Once an agency gives lots of fun work to its Brand ambassadors, they often tell their friends and colleagues about that agency and many Brand ambassadors start applying to join their books. Word-of-mouth recruitment can be encouraged by the use of 'Refer a friend' schemes, where Brand ambassadors are incentivized to recommend others to join the agency's books. There can be downsides to such schemes. For example, if a team of friends are booked to work together as Brand ambassadors, and one cancels, the others are more likely to cancel too. A social attitude to work can develop that is unprofessional; it can create a situation where Brand ambassadors spend too much time chatting and not enough time engaging with participants.

With that said, there are some advantages. Small or remote geographic areas can be hard to recruit in, and in these cases 'Refer a friend' schemes can be successful as long as relevant precautions are taken, such as not booking friends to work together and ensuring that only experienced Brand ambassadors are able to work. In addition, good Brand ambassadors who have worked in live brand experiences for years, tend to know other good Brand ambassadors from past live brand experiences. This is a definite advantage and can mean that when Brand ambassadors try and join an agency's books, another member of staff can vouch for them. The Brand ambassador who vouches for them is unlikely to put his or her own reputation on the line to get work for a friend, so this can usually be trusted.

Important points that an experiential marketing agency's staffing division should review when selecting and recruiting Brand ambassadors are as follows.

Selecting Brand ambassadors

- The Target audience and their aspirational lifestyle.
- The Brand personality and the Experiential objectives.
- Contingency Brand ambassadors.

Recruiting Brand ambassadors

- The communication skills of the individual.
- Their experience.

- The geographic locations that they cover.
- Their willingness to travel.
- References from other agencies.
- Their availability.
- Their tax status (self-employed or otherwise).
- Whether they drive or own a vehicle.
- Whether they own a camera.
- Whether they have internet access.
- How easy they are to get hold of (do they usually answer the phone straight away?).

Briefing Brand ambassadors

The agency should always send a briefing manual or document to the Brand ambassadors prior to their attending or participating in the training. The briefing manual should cover:

- legal issues;
- code of conduct;
- background information on the brand;
- the live brand experience's objectives;
- a description of their role and what is expected from them;
- the elements of the Message – key communication they should say;
- the Target audience;
- practical information such as times, dates, locations, routes or transport schedules;
- their rate of pay;
- a summary of any bonus scheme or fines;
- the agency's terms and conditions;
- rules prohibiting Brand ambassadors from poor conduct or last-minute cancellations;
- contact information;
- a confidentiality agreement (to ensure that information about a launch or live brand experience does not leak to the public prior to the intended date).

Training Brand ambassadors

Training Brand ambassadors and event managers prior to a live brand experience going live is extremely important and usually a necessity. In some cases, face-to-face training is not feasible due to budgetary restrictions. Though this is not ideal, in this instance I highly recommend intensive remote training. Remote training should include online webinars, teleconferences and one-to-one phone training, supported by an automated quiz. It is important to remember to train the reserves and back-up staff as well as the main team, so that if somebody cancels, the replacement is of an equivalent standard.

A key part of training is that the Brand ambassadors have the opportunity to trial the product or service sufficiently. This ensures that their positive attitude towards a brand is genuine, and participants will be able to 'buy into' the real enthusiasm that the Brand ambassadors have for the product.

When holding a face-to-face training session, there is a format that has proved highly successful. It should be conducted only after the Brand ambassadors have received and had a chance to study their briefing manuals. The face-to-face training format should include:

- Brand information (an overview provided by a member of the client team).
- Demonstration or trial if relevant.
- Message – key communication training by a representative of the agency.
- Role-play. The Brand ambassadors are split into small groups, some taking on the role of the consumer and others taking on their actual role as Brand ambassadors. This should be supported by constructive feedback provided by at least one agency representative.
- A mini-performance from each of the small teams to the larger group. The team should swap so that everyone has a chance to perform as a consumer and as a Brand ambassador.
- A quiz game with a prize for the highest-scoring Brand ambassador.
- A question-and-answer session where a member of the client team and a member of the agency team address any queries from the Brand ambassadors.
- The trying on of uniforms to ensure good fit.
- A brief lecture from the agency member on the code of conduct and physical appearance.

Managing Brand ambassadors

When a live brand experience is active, Brand ambassadors will need an experienced event manager to oversee them. The role of the event manager can be varied but usually includes:

- Rating brand ambassadors' performance.
- Giving constructive feedback and on-location coaching.
- Positioning the team-members strategically in high-footfall positions, and away from each other to prevent chatter.
- Managing the budget and expenses.
- Giving a briefing and pep-talk prior to each shift.
- Managing the uniforms and stock control.
- Monitoring distribution data and data capture.
- Noting results, consumer feedback and qualitative surveys.
- Taking photos and video footage.
- Filling in reports and feedback forms.
- Driving vehicles or rigging sets.

Event managers are usually paid around double the rate that the Brand ambassadors are. Team leaders, who are like senior Brand ambassadors, are a good idea for most live brand experiences. They support the event manager and act as motivators for team spirit and positive moral, and they usually get paid 50 per cent more than the Brand ambassadors.

A loyalty scheme on each live brand experience, to incentivize successful individuals, is a big motivator. Points should be given to reliable, punctual and high-performing Brand ambassadors, team leaders and event managers. This can be very effective at encouraging loyalty among a live brand experience team. Inside an agency, the bonuses of its staff bookers and staffing managers can also be linked to the positive performance of the Brand ambassadors.

Summary

In summary, Brand ambassadors are like the face or identity of the brand during the live brand experience, especially when it is executed face to face. Their attitude, communication, appearance and morals represent your brand to your Target audience. Adequate selection, product trial, briefing, training and management are all important phases in ensuring the right human touch for your live brand experience. Brand ambassadors are a very important consideration when selecting an agency, whose approach to this matter should be a major consideration. By applying the best practice guidelines detailed in this chapter, you will be doing everything possible towards achieving the ultimate goal: that the Brand ambassadors speak from a perspective of personal recommendation, form a genuine connection with your Target audience, and inspire the participants to become brand advocates who spread positive word-of-mouth.

As well as providing an exceptional face for your live brand experiences, this part of your SET MESSAGE plan will ensure that the Selected locations (whether face to face or remote) are ideal in regard to the Target audience, their state of mind, practical considerations, and the reach of your live brand experience. This chapter will have guided you in planning a live brand experience that achieves 'the right experience for the right people'.

11 Systems and mechanisms for measurement

As detailed in Chapter 1, live brand experiences are seen as a relatively new marketing discipline and have been the subject of heavy criticism regarding the metrics used to measure their success. Marketing channels all tend to have metrics, which can be applied to benchmark and cross-reference campaigns against each other. Because these industry-wide metrics are generic, they provide a standard way to gather and compare results.

The instinctive approach of many traditional marketers, when venturing into live brand experiences and attempting to measure their success, is to try to apply the same metrics that are used to evaluate other channels. In fact, live brand experiences lend themselves perfectly to cost-effective, qualitative and quantitative measurement of success in regard to their capacity to meet their Experiential objectives. This is because of the interactive nature of the discipline. While a brand is interacting with consumers during an experience, the consumer is usually benefiting and receiving to one degree or another, and is therefore very likely and willing to give back. This can take the form of answering questions, on-the-spot reactions, or agreeing to future communication.

This chapter is about how to build Systems and mechanisms that facilitate measuring how successfully a campaign has achieved, or is achieving, its Experiential objectives into your experiential marketing plan. Because each live brand experience can differ greatly from the next, it is important to tailor these systems to the activity itself (the location, the time, the people) and ensure that from a practical perspective it is feasible to implement these systems with the resources allocated to the live brand experience.

In Chapter 6 we looked at different options for Experiential objectives. At this stage in SET MESSAGE you will be building into the plan several Systems and mechanisms that are specific to the Experiential objectives as defined earlier in your plan. This stage of your plan is not to be confused with the Evaluation stage, which will look at every aspect of your live brand experience, focusing on what will happen after the campaign. This chapter and part of your plan purely concerns the measurement of your live brand experience's objectives, and the results will contribute to the overall evaluation of the experiential marketing campaign as a whole (which will consist of the live brand experience channel and possibly other amplification channels). The amplification channels should still be measured using the standard metrics of each channel respectively.

In addition, different live brand experiences require different degrees of research. Some situations require an in-depth level of insight and analysis, such as cases when a live brand experience is a pilot that has the possibility of a large-scale roll out. In this instance, anything that can be learnt from the successes and failures of the live brand experience will be valuable when planning the larger-scale strategy.

This in-depth analysis looks at why each specific element worked or did not, and creates insights into what can be changed or expanded. In this case, it is worth investing more significantly in good Systems and mechanisms for measurement. When a multi-million budget is being invested in the larger-scale activity there is little margin for error. Therefore, the pilot should serve as a learning experience that helps perfect the broader plan.

How much to spend on measurement

There are varying degrees of resources that can be applied to the Systems and mechanisms for measurement, and depending on how high evaluation is on your list of priorities, you will spend a relative amount. The good thing about the nature of live brand experiences is that successful and valuable Systems and mechanisms can be implemented without any significant or additional investment to your existing budget. Many of the Systems and mechanisms detailed in this chapter can be built into the SET MESSAGE plan without any financial implications.

Table 11.1   Experiential objectives and KPIs

Code	Experiential objective	System or mechanism for measurement
A	Conduct market research (eg, gain understanding of consumer opinions about the brand and product, and competitive brands and products)	1. Note relevant consumer feedback, questions, etc) 2. Administer surveys with participants, with relevant questions (qualitative and quantitative)
B	Drive word-of-mouth	Number of interactions (Y)
C	Raise awareness	1. OTS 2. Distribution data
D	Drive product trial	Number of product trials
E	Demonstrate a product's features and benefits	Number of product demonstrations
F	Capture data	Number of data entries captured
G	Drive word-of-mouth	1. Word-of-mouth reach $(Y \times 17) + Y$ 2. Monitor number of referrals from any 'Refer-a-friend' schemes initiated by the experiential live brand experience
H	Drive traffic to website	1. Number of hits to website (compare to previous hits) 2. Number of hits to micro-site, and from micro-site to main site
I	Drive word-of-web	Number of people forwarding the online experiential element to a friend
J	Increase sales	1. Number of items sold (compare to control groups)

Table 11.1 *(Continued)*

Code	Experiential objective	System or mechanism for measurement
		2. Number of sales promotion vouchers/codes redeemed
K	Increase footfall into store	Compare activity with footfall into store during and after activity
L	Increase customer loyalty/strengthen brand relationships with target audience	1. Monitor consumer behaviour long-term through loyalty schemes 2. Contact participants subsequently
M	Create a long-lasting, memorable experience	1. Monitor consumer behaviour long-term through loyalty schemes 2. Contact participants subsequently
N	Bring the brand personality to life	Survey non-participants and compare results with participants
O	Communicate complex brand messages	Survey non-participants and compare results with participants
P	Gain credibility with target audience x	1. Survey non-participants and compare results with participants 2. Analyse customer demographics prior to live brand experiences activity and then at specific intervals during and after ongoing activity, and note a shift in customer demographic long term
Q	Position the brand as x	Survey non-participants and compare results with participants

Qualitative data can be gathered by Brand ambassadors easily while they are engaging with and talking to participating members of the target audience, and quantitative data can be a combination of survey results, numbers, and the quantification of qualitative responses. Quantitative data gives hard facts and numbers, which are always valuable and appreciated because they enable easy comparison. Qualitative data can help to analyse why you got the results that you did, as well as achieving market research objectives during the live brand experience.

Quantitative data can include hard numbers that are figures-based and can be calculated. It can also include the number of specific and similar responses to a qualitative survey question. You need to have a combination of both quantitative 'counting' mechanisms (eg how long people stayed in a shop, how many items were sold, how many products were trialled, and how many people interacted with the experience) and qualitative open question-type mechanisms (eg what does brand x represent to you?). Then, by grouping and analysing qualitative 'open question' responses, and correlating answers for similarities, you can extract hard numbers and data from apparently 'woolly/fluffy' questions, therefore enabling factual measurement of 'fluffy' objectives, and the conversion of qualitative data into quantitative data.

Table 11.1 lists many common Experiential objectives and then aligns Systems or mechanisms that measure if these objectives have been achieved. Each System or mechanism for measurement should be tailored to the live brand experience, and its available resources and technology, to enable them to be built in seamlessly without interrupting the natural flow of the live brand experience.

When you arrive at this stage in the planning, you can cross-reference your Experiential objectives against those in Table 11.1, and then assign the most relevant systems. Once you have allocated the Systems and mechanisms, you can create your own table that demonstrates in more detail exactly which questions you will ask, or exactly what data you will capture. For example, if your Experiential objectives for a live brand experience (promoting a drink outside 50 of the stores that sell it) are to increase sales, drive footfall into store and bring the energetic brand personality to life, your objectives and measurements could look similar to Table 11.2.

Whichever Experiential objectives you have chosen from Table 11.1, you will be able to measure them by thinking carefully about how you will go about building the Systems and mechanisms for measurement that are recommended for your objectives into your live brand experience. The example in Table 11.3 demonstrates that this approach works with any combination of Experiential objectives. If your live brand experience promotes a retail website at shopping centres, and your

Table 11.2 Objectives and measurements

Experiential objective	System or mechanism for measurement
Increase sales across the 50 main stores during experiential live brand experience	We will ask the store managers to provide data that show the sales of this product in each of the 50 participating stores for one month prior to the experiential live brand experience.
	We will then ask the store managers to provide the same data and monitor sales volumes of the product in the same participating stores during the experiential live brand experience.
	By comparing these results, we will measure any direct increase in sales that the experiential live brand experience made while it was live.
	Note: If sales-tracking technology is not built into a store's cashier system, then the above data will also be collected by the Brand ambassadors. They will count stock at the beginning and end of every day, noting the percentage of stock that was sold.
We will also want to gauge whether the increase in sales volume is temporary or has longevity	To do this, we will monitor the product sales at the stores that participated, for one month after the live brand experience is finished.
	We will then compare these sales volumes with those of the same stores in the one month prior to the live brand experience going live.
Drive footfall into store	We will note the data on the stores' electronic footfall tracker prior to the live brand experience.
	These data will be compared to the data on the electronic footfall tracker during the live brand experience.
	Any increase in footfall will be noted as a percentage (when comparing, ensure that factors such as days of the week are kept consistent between control data and live brand experience data).

Table 11.2 *(Continued)*

Experiential objective	System or mechanism for measurement
Bring the energetic brand personality to life	We will create a brief survey application to be loaded onto the Brand ambassadors' PDAs.
	At the beginning of each live brand experience, they will come in 30 minutes early, and without wearing their uniform or being in close proximity of the set, they will ask passers by a brief question about the brand.
	The question will be: What do you think of when you think of brand x?
	a) being energized; b) being relaxed; c) being happy; d) being trendy.
	The Brand ambassadors will ask the same question of consumers during their participation in the brand experience.
	An increase in the target audience choosing the correct answer (a) will be measured as a percentage increase in recognition and understanding of the brand personality.

Experiential objectives are to drive traffic to the website, spread word-of-web and capture data for future marketing purposes, your table could look similar to Table 11.3.

Summary

The level of investment you wish to put into understanding how the experiential marketing campaign, and specifically the live brand experience channel, are impacting the Target audience's behaviour and opinions is a decision that you will need to make in advance. Experiential marketing can include simple, cost-effective Systems and mechanisms for measurement which when built into the live brand experience channel

Table 11.3 Objectives and measurements – website

Experiential objective	System or mechanism for measurement
Drive traffic to website	We will compare the number of hits we are getting to the website (and their geographic location) prior to the live brand experience against the number of hits (and their geographic location) we are getting during and after the live brand experience.
	The increase will be noted as a percentage, which will allow us to benchmark the success the live brand experience's channel had in achieving this objective against the percentage increase we had in web traffic from previously implemented forms of marketing communications.
Spread word-of-web	When (as per the Experiential strategy) consumers download the photos (which are loaded into a gallery on the site) of themselves participating in the live brand experience, they have the opportunity to forward their photo (which arrives in a branded e-mail) to 10 friends and receive a free T-shirt.
	To measure word-of-mouth driven as a direct result of this strategy, we will monitor the number of times this offer form is completed, and with each time counting for 10 recipients of the key communication message, we will easily be able to quantify the word-of-web.
Capture data for future marketing purposes	Prior to entering the photo gallery on the website to download their photos, consumers will be required to fill in a quick form that captures their contact data. The form will feature an opt-in tick-box stating that they are willing to receive future brand communications.

during the planning stages will enable you to evaluate the success of the live brand experience (as well as the amplification channels) and gauge whether it has achieved its predefined objectives.

In many instances, marketers and agencies overlook this crucial stage of experiential marketing planning. As a result, live brand experiences have been subject to the criticism that it is 'difficult to measure whether a live brand experience has done the job it set out to do'. Many people will argue that when you know how to achieve something, it is no longer difficult (like a dish that appears hard to cook, but which is easy once the recipe is followed step by step). It is not a particularly time-consuming process to build in Systems and mechanisms for measurement, compared to the value of doing so. By integrating the guidelines in this chapter into your SET MESSAGE plan and implementation, your live brand experiences can be fully accounted for, and you will be able to evaluate their long-term return on investment (LROI) and make it easier to demonstrate to stakeholders the results of your overall experiential marketing programme.

12 Action

It is time to instigate all aspects of planning the delivery of your live brand experience. This part of the plan is of utmost importance. You, or your agencies, can come up with the most innovative and groundbreaking concepts and strategies, but if your campaign activation and project management are flawed, then it was all a waste of time and money. The execution of a successful experiential marketing campaign, especially the live brand experience, is not an easy task, and should be regarded as being like the production of a movie, but without the opportunity to edit later.

This would be a good place to reinforce an earlier recommendation: employ a specialist experiential marketing agency for the execution of your campaign. Some experiential marketing agencies have a stronger background in strategy, while others are more experienced in activation. This is an important distinction to make when choosing an agency to activate the campaign. In fact, some experiential marketing agencies outsource the Action part to other more action-oriented experiential marketing agencies. The ideal situation is to work with a fully integrated experiential marketing agency that has expert strategy/planning/ creative and activation/logistics/staffing in-house. The reason is that communication between planners and activators needs to be clear, with great attention to detail. Without this communication, what is promised to a client may be very different to what is delivered. In addition, the more attention to detail and experienced thinking that goes into the Action plans, the higher the chances that those following it will succeed.

This chapter should prove useful whether you are a traditional agency that is outsourcing to an experiential marketing agency, or a client working directly with the experiential marketing agency. From a client perspective, this chapter can provide a guide that will help when discerning between a good detailed activation plan and a poor one. Obviously, different agencies may be inclined to involve their clients in the small details of the Action plan to a greater or lesser degree. However, most will aim to accommodate a client's request to see any of the planning. Even if you are an experiential marketing practitioner yourself, this chapter will provide an outline for best practice for the Action part of your campaign planning.

Contents of the Action plan

The action part of your SET MESSAGE plan should include the following sections:

1. Recipe (how the experience will actually happen from a consumer perspective).
2. Budgets.
3. Project plans (WBS, Gantt chart, critical path analysis, schedules, risk analysis, checklists and external analysis).
4. Communication and collaboration.
5. Suppliers and third parties.
6. Approvals schedule.

1. The recipe

Every live brand experience has behind-the-scenes activity and a great deal of careful coordination, and it is important not to lose sight of consumer perspective. The Target audience, and participants' experience, is extremely important. The Action plan starts with a breakdown of what happens if you are looking at it from the perspective of the Target audience. This part comes first in Action planning because it will keep the rest of the plan grounded; it is a blueprint summary of what will happen 'live'.

The best way to write the recipe is to think of it as similar to a good cake recipe. It should start with a paragraph stating the ingredients (including quantities) that will be in place, and specifying where the experience will be positioned (whilst naming the set, the campaign and the team). This introductory paragraph creates a still photographic image in the mind of the reader of your plan. For example:

The 106.9 Radio Experience is positioned outside a surfing festival and includes: the Radio Experience Zone (one giant radio set, two branded DJ Hummers, two sampling trolleys, one branded reception counter, lots of branded tables and chairs), and the '106.9 Team' (a team of 10 Brand ambassadors, one DJ and one event manager).

This paragraph sets the scene of the plan in the mind of the reader, because it allows him or her to correctly visualize the physical elements that will be in place. This is a vital step, as it provides clarity to both the people who are buying the campaign, and the people who are executing it.

After the summary paragraph, the recipe continues in a similar manner to that of a cake, by breaking down systematically what will happen and what actions are involved in the experience itself. This should be formatted as a numbered list of summarized steps. For example:

a. The DJ is playing funky music and hosting on the microphone.
b. The 106.9 Brand ambassadors approach the target audience and invite them to participate in the experience.
c. The target audience signs in at the front counter.
d. The target audience is greeted by Brand ambassadors that bring them into the Radio Zone.
e. Once inside the Radio Zone, consumers can make their own compilation CDs.
f. As the consumers leave the Zone, they receive branded goody bags containing a branded iPod case, a free concert ticket and stickers.

As you can see, this numbered list allows a moving image to be visualized in the mind of the reader, or executor, which is key in creating a framework and story for the experience. This step should also facilitate estimating the duration of the experience, as well as the maximum number of participants at any one time. This is highly important because it will then allow you to calculate how many consumers can potentially participate in the experience per day and location. By multiplying these figures by the number of live days and locations, you will get the number of interactions. This, as previously mentioned, is a crucial common metric when measuring live brand experiences and justifying the cost, because the number of interactions will enable a prediction of the word-of-mouth reach and the long-term return on investment (LROI).

Finally, to finish off the recipe, you should write a paragraph that summarizes what the outcome of these steps will be. For example:

By participating in the 106.9 Radio Experience, the target audience of alternative music fans will feel satisfied after enjoying the process of compiling their own customized CDs. They will be pleased to receive the goody bag, whose contents will act as memorabilia for their positive brand experience.

This stage is equivalent to answering questions like 'And why is this happening, again?' or 'Remind me, what will this achieve?' Your response is the same as it would have been, except for the fact that you're still wearing a consumer hat, rather than a marketing hat. By placing yourself in the shoes of the consumer, you maintain an objective outlook, with your number one priority being the participant experience. With this approach, you will be more likely to spot any flaws in the plan or story.

When you think of a cake recipe, it starts with the ingredients, then it lists the method, then it clarifies the desired outcome. By following the recipe formula in the introduction of the action part of your SET MESSAGE plan, you will crystallize the experience story, ensuring ultimate clarity.

2. Budgets

The next part of the plan is the all-important budget. Obviously, there will be two budgets; one is the internal (agency) budget and the other is the external (client) budget. The internal budget should state the maximum amount that everything should cost the agency. This will be used for agency purposes only, and will allow the project management, or activation team, to adhere to clear guidelines on how much they can spend. This part may also elaborate on certain internal costs that are not to be passed on to the client (to provide added value), such as staff incentives or any anticipated increase in overheads (such as large calling or texting volumes, etc).

The client budget will be presented to the client and should already include agency mark-ups, margins and fees. If a traditional agency is outsourcing to an experiential marketing agency, then partner agency commissions will need to be built in (by either party, depending on their policies). There are certain broad generic cost categories that can be looked to for structure when considering all possible costs of experiential marketing. These categories are as follows for a live brand experience channel.

Production

- set/branded roadshow vehicles/audio and lighting or other equipment and wiring;
- merchandise (goodies, gifts, vouchers, giveaways, flyers, etc);
- uniforms.

Staff costs

- front-of-house team;
- Brand ambassadors;
- speciality staff;
- event managers;
- team leaders.

Behind-the-scenes crew

- riggers and production crew;
- photographers/videographers;
- drivers.

Face-to-face training

- venue hire;
- staff (payment for their time and expenses for attending);
- refreshments and snacks;
- equipment (PA/projector, etc);
- training session administrators (may be agency staff);
- assistants (meet and greet, registration, etc);
- campaign manuals/other printing or documentation.

Remote training

- webinars;
- staff (payment for participation – less than face to face);
- teleconferencing;
- automated quizzes and surveys.

Logistics and transport

- vehicle hire;
- petrol (calculate as cost-per-mile × estimated mileage);
- parking;
- travel time (calculate by mileage).

Stock control

- storage/warehousing (calculated by space, remembering that storage will be required for promotional merchandise, sample stock, the set, vehicles, and uniforms – possibly in several locations, either simultaneously or consecutively);
- couriers (to deliver stock to the team and crew, either hired directly by the experiential marketing agency or outsourced to a courier company such as UPS);
- temperature control (refrigeration or freezing when and if the campaign involves samples of food, drink, ice-cream, etc).

Space hire

- venue/space-owner hire fees;
- intermediary fees if applicable (if space is booked through a specialist broker or agent);
- administration, for the time and service of the completion of space hire-related paperwork (such as set maps and dimensions, risk assessment, portable appliance testing, fire safety documents, method statements, hire forms, contracts, health and safety certificates, criminal record bureau checks, public liability insurance, etc).

Staff/crew expenses

- travel fares/petrol;
- travel time;
- phone (for event managers and other managerial activation team members);
- hotel (when travelling);
- food (when travelling);
- parking (for team and crew members).

The amplification channels

The cost sections below can vary greatly depending on whether they are implemented by the experiential marketing agency, outsourced to third parties, or executed in collaboration with the client's existing agencies:

- ads (used before experience to drive participants and generate awareness);
- broadcast media slots, live or recorded (to expand the reach of the experience);
- PR prior to live date (to drive participants and generate awareness);

- PR at or post the campaign (to expand the reach of the experience and create interest);
- digital (to generate pre- and post-campaign interest or to broadcast the experience, live or otherwise);
- buzz, word-of-mouth or word-of-web (whispering campaigns, either online or offline, deigned to create an interest prior to the experience, and drive traffic).

Management

This cost category is usually presented as one item and calculated as a percentage of totals, or by the estimate of time that will be spent, plus expenses:

- research and idea testing;
- planning;
- activation management;
- evaluation.

Reporting

- technology (PDAs, web surveys, telephone surveys, etc);
- campaign audit (an audit, either internal or by an external research agency, to measure outputs using the systems and mechanisms for measurement);
- administration (updating online client access pages, data entry, etc);
- visual reports (editing of video footage and preparing presentations).

While building (transparently or not), contingencies should equal around 5 per cent of the campaign total; and agency commissions, usually between 10 and 25 per cent depending on the number of partner agencies.

The budget should be prepared in a spreadsheet and is usually broken down to include unit costs, descriptions, quantities, duration of time, and totals. Table 12.1 is a sample bolt-on budget, which is designed to show what a small budget presented to a client could look like. This budget relates specifically to the costs of booking additional elements (staff and extra venues) as an add-on to an existing live brand experience for a brand of juice.

It is widely accepted that some of the categories listed are not applicable across every experiential marketing campaign, and there will doubtless be unaccountable elements that will arise in specific situations. The most important thing when budgeting is to include contingencies

Table 12.1 Sample budget

Additional budget 'Juice April 2'	NOTE: This budget is for additional items as requested by client 'Fresh Juice' to supplement existing April budget				
Staff costs					
Item	Description	Unit cost	#	Days	Total
Brand ambassador	Will activate the interactive juice game + engage consumers	£119	4	12	£5,712
Event manager	Will manage team, take photos, and feedback data	£213	1	7	£1,491
Event manager (on travelling days)	Will manage team, take photos, and feedback data	£213	1	5	£1,065
				Total	£8,268
Transport					
Item	Description	Unit cost	#	Days	Total
Travel expenses when travelling	Plane ticket return to Town x	£80	1	1	£80
Travel expenses when inside local area	To and from event 1	£20	1	5	£26
Parking	Parking budget for van to park outside locations for the day	£20	1	12	£240
Food	Food budget per day for event manager	£30	1	7	£210
Hotel	Hotel for event manager	£80	1	7	£560
				Total	£1,116
Space hire					
Item	Description	Unit cost	#	Days	Total
Event 1 space hire	Space hire 4mx4m	£5,500	1	7	£5,500
Event 2 space hire	Space hire 4mx3m + additional branding	£5,940	1	5	£5,940
				Total	£11,440

Client totals	
Subtotal	£20,824
10% mgmt fee	£2,082.40
Grand total	£22,906.40

and to remember to think about each and every cost, however small. Sometimes, clients who are used to planning only media campaigns or more predictable forms of marketing, will find it hard to accept that their experiential marketing agency is billing them for contingencies. Therefore, it is not uncommon for experiential marketing agencies to build a contingency margin of around 5 per cent into all the unit costs rather than itemizing it as an independent cost category.

Whichever way a contingency is built into a campaign budget, it is crucial that it is not neglected, because to successfully and flawlessly activate an experiential marketing campaign including a live brand experience, an attitude of predicting potential problems and preparing contingency solutions in advance is vital. An 'It'll be alright on the night' attitude is the worst approach to this stage in your planning.

At the end of the budget, a proposed payment schedule should be detailed. This usually would require several upfront costs to be paid to the agency in advance, with ongoing or running costs paid at regular intervals or immediately after the campaign. Sometimes, clients buying experiential marketing services for the first time may have unrealistic expectations about payment terms, such as a desire to receive 100 per cent credit until up to 30–45 days after the campaign ends. This is not because they are crazy or wish to exploit their agency, but they simply require some additional knowledge and understanding. This is why it is important for their agency to explain to them that there are many upfront set-up costs involved in live brand experiences, which is something that everyone can appreciate. Clearly no client would expect their experiential marketing agency to provide them with a loan, which is exactly what they would be doing if they agreed to payment terms akin to those that are commonplace when buying some traditional media.

3. Project plans

The project plans should include a combination of both the top-line and detailed blueprints that will guide the project management team in their step-by-step preparation and implementation of the campaign Remember, 'If you fail to plan, you plan to fail.' This could not be closer to the truth in the case of detailed live brand experience project plans.

When there is a short timescale involved, some say they do not have time to plan carefully, but they might as well not take on the project in the first place if that is the case. If you are a client considering live brand experiences, keep in mind that though an agency may accept a short lead time, the more time that you allow them for careful project planning, the better the execution will be.

The project plan section should include the following elements (or equivalents): WBS, a Gantt chart, a critical path analysis, a schedule, a risk analysis, checklists (for staffing, production and logistics) and an external analysis (PESTEL 'Problem and solution' table).

The work breakdown structure

Start by creating a work breakdown structure (WBS) for the project. A WBS is an important element that you will need to develop your Action plan. It lists all of the categories and sub-elements that you will use to achieve and deliver the project. A tree structure of Post-it Notes can be a great help in developing your WBS.

Gantt chart

The Gantt chart is a table; a simple example is shown in Table 12.2. The first column features task categories with each individual small-detailed task appearing in the rows under each category header. These will be extracted straight from the WBS. The Gantt chart organizes the items on the work breakdown structure against a timeline. The titles across each column are dates, months or weeks. After creating this table, the next step is colour coding each person who is part of the project activation team. Then, simply highlight each square of the table in a colour that is affiliated with the individual due to complete it, as well as the number of hours required for its completion.

According to the PMBOK Guide,[1] it is absolutely crucial that you include '100 per cent of the work defined by the project scope and

Table 12.2 Sample GANTT chart

	Person
	Sandra
	Bob
	Lisa
	Matt
	Galila
	Ramez

21–26th 07/09	21/07/2009	22/07/2009	23/07/2009	24/07/2009	25/07/2009	26/07/2009
PRODUCTION						
Complete set build	■					
Take client to visit set		■				
Make any changes			■	■		
Conduct safety testing					■	
Deconstruct the set for transport						■
SPACE HIRE						
Finalize rate negotiations	■					
Complete paperwork		■				
Pay deposit			■			
Sign contract				■		
Review site maps						■
STAFFING						
Check availability of relevant people	■					
Shortlist staff		■				
Send shortlist to client		■				
Receive input/preferences from client			■			
Book the selected staff				■		
Book reserves and backups				■		
Send briefs, manuals and contracts				■		
TRAINING						
Provide venue options to client						
Book selected venue						
Create agenda for training						
Ensure appropriate equipment is in place						
Create training presentation						
LOGISTICS						
Package kits for each staff member					■	
Arrange kits to be couriered to staff					■	
Ensure staff have received packages						■
Hire a lorry		■				
Hire a van			■			
Plan route for event manager and driver					■	

capture all deliverables – internal, external, and interim – in terms of the work to be completed, including project management'. The best way to define tasks is to state the deliverable outcome or result, rather than the actions required to achieve that outcome, ensuring that defined outcomes are bite-sized, and not too broad. It is also important to remember not to allow any overlap between tasks, as this causes confusion and potentially repeated work. The total number of hours in each colour will indicate the estimated workload of each member of the project team. This will allow the manager to assess whether the tasks they have allocated to each individual are feasible. Again, a time-based contingency will need to be applied, which should be around 10 per cent of total project hours.

Critical path analysis

A critical path analysis is also a great way to manage the project activation milestones. It maps milestones onto a timeline, and then an arrow starting from a milestone branches off to show tasks that cannot start until that milestone is complete. The relationships between interdependent tasks and task categories are therefore clearly defined. This process helps to ensure that a project, in this case a live brand experience, can be delivered on time. Many different project management programmes are available, allowing the easy creation of a critical path analysis and Gantt chart.

Figure 12.1 shows a sample critical path analysis. It was set up to manage the timeline of a staff booker who was booking some Brand ambassadors and an event manager for a live brand experience at short notice.

The project manager who leads the activation team will now be able to closely monitor progress and identify any potential consequences for other deliverables following a delay in the completion of an individual task. If the individual task is interlinked with other tasks that depend on the completion of the original task, then it is crucial that it is achieved on time.

As per Figure 12.1, if the staff booker delayed steps 7 or 9 (confirming that shortlisted applicants are still available), then he or she wouldn't be able to send the shortlist to the client. If he or she did send the shortlist to the client without ensuring that all the people on it were available, and the client chose someone who was in fact unavailable, then the client would be disappointed.

Schedules

A schedule in calendar format is an essential part of the project plan; see the example in Figure 12.2. It is quite an obvious and basic tool, but

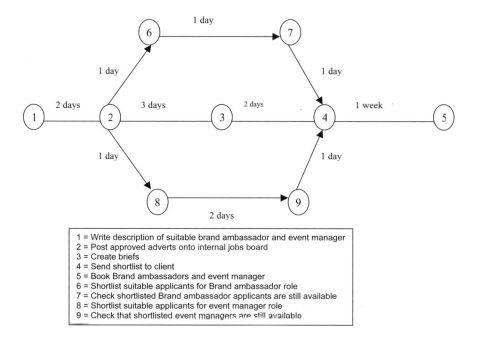

Figure 12.1 Sample critical path analysis

without one an activation team or client could feel lost. The schedule should map out which parts of the experiential marketing campaign are happening on certain dates, at certain locations. The agency that is responsible for activating the campaign, and the client, should put the campaign schedules up on a wall or somewhere visible, for easy reference.

Risk analysis

Arguably one of the most important parts of the project plan is the risk analysis. With live brand experiences, many factors contribute to the success of each and every element of the campaign. If one cog in the campaign wheel is missing or jeopardized, then it is highly probable that a chain of undesirable events will occur.

For example, Frank was the account handler at an experiential marketing agency. He didn't have much on, so when he was approached by a client to run a live brand experience roadshow for a sports channel on TV at short notice, he quickly took it on board. The sports channel usually advertised on television and it was the first time that it was running a live brand experience tour, hence the fact that it expected it

Monday	Tuesday	Wednesday	Thursday	Friday	Sat/Sun
27 April	28	29	30	1 May	2
					3
4 FRUIT JUICE CAMPAIGN AT EVENT 1	5 FRUIT JUICE CAMPAIGN AT EVENT 1	6 FRUIT JUICE CAMPAIGN AT EVENT 1	7 FRUIT JUICE CAMPAIGN AT FESTIVAL	8	9
					10
11	12	13	14 FRUIT JUICE CAMPAIGN AT EVENT 2	15 FRUIT JUICE CAMPAIGN AT EVENT 2	16
					17
18 FRUIT JUICE CAMPAIGN AT MALL 1	19 FRUIT JUICE CAMPAIGN AT MALL 1	20 FRUIT JUICE CAMPAIGN AT MALL 1	21 FRUIT JUICE CAMPAIGN AT MALL 1	22 FRUIT JUICE CAMPAIGN AT MALL 1	23 FRUIT JUICE CAMPAIGN AT MALL 1
					24 FRUIT JUICE CAMPAIGN AT MALL 1
25	26	27 FRUIT JUICE CAMPAIGN AT BEACH	28 FRUIT JUICE CAMPAIGN AT BEACH	29	30
					31

Figure 12.2 Example of a schedule

to be turned around in under two weeks' planning. The concept, which was designed by the TV channel's PR agency, involved a giant-sized interactive 'spot the ball' game, featuring a large set that looked like a real football pitch with grass and a goal. The live brand experience was scheduled to tour around many different shopping malls, for one day at each mall.

There was a short lead-time for the campaign, and some things in the Action planning were rushed. As a result, an inexperienced driver was mistakenly hired without reference checks. He filled the van that was transporting the set with petrol instead of diesel. The van broke down late on a Friday evening, with the campaign due to be live in another city the following morning. As a result, every step of the plan, scheduled to occur directly after he picked up the set with the van, was considerably delayed. Consequently, the live brand experience was a disaster and the client was devastated. All the Brand ambassadors, event managers, venues, suppliers and the experiential marketing agency suffered too, both financially and emotionally.

The reason that the inexperienced driver was hired in the first place was that the original driver had existing commitments with his church that Sunday. When he had been booked for the campaign, he was unaware that he would not be able to return in time for his commitments. This confusion was due to lack of proper communication from Jane (the staff booker) and the driver. When he cancelled at short notice, Jane panicked because there was no back-up plan, and no contingency in place. This left Jane desperate, and so she sacrificed the quality of the replacement driver to try and lessen the impact of her original communication error by rebooking the position as quickly as possible.

Sometimes these types of problems can occur without anyone being at fault, and without communication errors. The moral of this story is that it is the project manager's responsibility to carefully conduct a risk analysis during the Action planning stages, and then ensure that each team member (such as a staff booker) has appropriate contingencies in place early on. Something will always go wrong and someone will usually let you down, even if it is due to a genuine emergency, a weather issue or a legal factor. No client is interested when their agency's driver has existing commitments to his church, or that a team leader's grandmother has died, or that their experiential set was not waterproof when it rained, because their branding, and potentially their campaign, is in jeopardy. Therefore, the only way to ensure flawless execution and client satisfaction is to check well in advance that all bases are covered, and that contingencies are in place at no additional cost.

By conducting a risk analysis through a lengthy brainstorm between the activation team, and then filling in a risk analysis form, some of these types of things may still happen, but there will be an effective solution, ready and on standby. In addition, many potential problems can be predicted with some careful thought and lots of experience. This process will shape the strategic creation of many elements of the campaign, aiming to prevent unnecessary problems and risks from occurring. The risk analysis form in Table 12.3 factors in both the likelihood and the impact that a problem can have, therefore showing the risk score. Risks with higher scores will need to be prioritized, though all risks will require a contingency plan and a person who is accountable and responsible for that contingency.

The form was completed for a live brand experience for a brand of designer clothing. The campaign, featuring an interactive catwalk and models, was positioned outside 18 fashion stores and had the experiential objectives of bringing the clothing brand to life, driving footfall into the retail store and thereby increasing sales. Once each contingency element has been allocated to an activation team member, their responsibilities will need to be added to the campaigns' Gantt chart and critical path analysis.

Table 12.3 Risk analysis form

Likelihood and Impact: High = 3, Medium = 2, Low = 1

Nature of risk or uncertainty	Likelihood high/ medium/ low	Impact high/ medium/ low	Likelihood × impact [score]	Contingency required and who will take responsibility to manage the risk and backup plan
Rain	3	3	9	Order branded umbrellas or a canopy (Sam)
Vehicle breakdown	1	3	3	Have the vehicle checked out thoroughly prior to the campaign (Robert)
Staff 'no shows'	3	3	9	Ensure that reserves are at the location, and the back-ups are on standby (Christina)
Staff lateness	3	2	6	Book the staff to be at location 1 hour prior to campaign start time (Christina)
Low footfall on the street outside the shops	1	3	3	Ask the client for the footfall data of each store to ensure there is a benchmark point (Matt)
Uniforms not fitting	2	3	6	Order spare uniforms in every size (Sam)
Running out of merchandise	1	3	3	Ensure that there is 50% more merchandise than anticipated distribution estimates (Sam)
Client not liking the appearance of the set	1	3	3	Build in enough time for the client to view the set and potentially suggest changes prior to the campaign going live (Matt)
Event Manager mobile phone out of battery	3	2	6	Provide the event manager with two spare batteries (Christina)
Traffic on the route to location	3	2	6	Ensure that the Event Manager and driver arrive 1 to 2 hours early to allow for traffic (Christina)
Store managers not fully understanding when/if the campaign is happening	3	2	6	Ask the client for permission to contact store managers directly to liaise and ensure they are 'in the loop' (Matt)

Checklists

Checklists are a great way of managing small daily tasks. A good project manager should ensure that every team member is working from a comprehensive checklist that includes every task allocated to them on the Gantt chart. Each day, or week, the checklist should be handed in to the project manager for review, and the completed tasks should be 'scratched out' or changed colour (to the colour that represents a completed task) on the Gantt chart. It is advisable to create a checklist template for each team member, containing tasks that reoccur with the majority of live brand experiences, then add to it and adapt it on a campaign-by-campaign basis.

External analysis: PESTEL factors

PESTEL stands for Political, Economic, Social, Technological, Environmental and Legal analysis, and describes a framework of macro-environmental factors. This acronym is usually used for a different purpose early on in marketing planning, but it lends itself very nicely to this stage of the project plan. At the end of the action part of SET MESSAGE it is important to state any legal, social (this includes health and safety, employment, public liability and insurance), environmental, economic and technological issues, and precautions for any such factors that the client or stakeholders should be aware of (including how these issues are addressed and covered). This external analysis should be formatted as a 'potential PESTEL problem and solution' table; an example is shown in Table 12.4.

Table 12.4   PESTEL problem and solution

Potential PESTEL problem	Solution
Environmental problem: Unwanted environmental waste	• Build in a 'litter pick' at the end of each day
Social problem: Noise pollution and disturbance of local residents	• Ask residents' permission before holding a music-based experiential event in a nearby park
Legal problem: Injury of small children	• Ensure that the set is appropriately designed for small children and made from soft materials with no hard corners or edges. Also have a health and safety officer present

The external analysis is the final part of the project plans within the Action stage in SET MESSAGE.

4. Communication and collaboration

After the project plans, the communication and collaboration plan comes next. One of the most important rules in successful activation is not forgetting to plan the communication methods and review points between the agency, client and stakeholders into the action stage. Include, in the Action part of SET MESSAGE, a clear outline of when and where client/agency meetings will occur and how information will be passed between relevant parties, and ensure that everything that is agreed is confirmed in writing or by e-mail to avoid people forgetting or being confused about what they, or others, did and didn't agree to.

Part of good communication is the ability to share information and documents with ease. There are many ways to enable this, both within an agency activation team and between the activation team and the client. There are plenty of open-source file-sharing applications available, such as Google's web-based file-sharing application. Alternatively, remote networking can also be a good approach. Rather than constantly e-mailing revised spreadsheets and risking the chance that someone will still be working from a wrong version, work on one collaborative spreadsheet online. If you can create a system that enables seamless communication and easy access to current versions of plans and documents, then the chances of communication problems occurring will be minimized.

5. Suppliers and third parties

Suppliers are a key part of the success of a campaign. Even if you are a client outsourcing to a specialist experiential marketing agency, it is likely that not every single part of the campaign will be managed by the agency in-house. Even fully integrated experiential marketing agencies will still outsource some things, for example venue, space hire, props, uniforms and merchandise printing.

It is good to know that you can trust the suppliers involved in your live brand experience, and it is worth checking their references and making sure the agency that appoints them involves the client in the process. From an agency perspective, when planning the outsourced elements of a campaign, there are eight key steps to the process. These should be addressed in this part of the plan:

1. Identify the different types of suppliers you will need and your exact requirements.
2. Consider if you want to outsource to a company that will manage big chunks or small elements (for example, hiring one company for the truck and another company for the branding on the truck).
3. Identify two or three existing suppliers that you could potentially appoint each outsourced element to, and score the anticipated pros and cons, based on past experience, of outsourcing to each one.
4. Send highly detailed briefs that specify the exact requirement, the budget and the deadline for production, as well as the preferred format and deadline for bids and proposals.
5. Carefully evaluate each supplier's bid and proposal, checking references and considering both the anticipated pros and cons, and scoring the pros and cons of each proposal.
6. Appoint a main supplier for each element and appoint a second supplier to be on standby for each element, in case you are let down or unhappy with the result and need to change supplier.
7. Allow enough time for unexpected delays, for switching suppliers if necessary, or for requesting changes to anything that is unsatisfactory.
8. Ensure that you have everything that is agreed in writing, and that the payment schedule with the supplier fits within the payment schedule agreed with the client.

6. Approvals schedule

In this stage of the plan, there should be a clear approvals schedule stating dates and deadlines for approvals that the client needs to make. It is important to any brand that the client has the opportunity to approve anything that goes to print with their logo, or approve any experiential set or individual that represents the brand. To avoid any delays in the approvals process, clients should request any artwork components in the correct resolutions and formats from their creative agency well in advance and at the beginning of the planning process. The agency needs to be very clear about when they will be sending proofs or samples, or when the client can visit the set. That way, the client can inform any relevant stakeholders or decision makers that they will need to be available for approval on certain days. Also, the agency will not be stressed by worries that the schedule will be thrown off track due to the client not approving things on time or not providing the relevant artwork components. Time should also be factored in for the client not approving something and wanting it changed. Some things that will need client approval are:

- branded vehicles;
- branded merchandise or giveaways;
- branded uniforms;
- the set;
- the experience team (Brand ambassadors, speciality staff, team leaders, event managers);
- the space hire locations;
- competition prizes;
- a micro-site and any other online elements;
- any ads, press releases or amplification elements;
- the briefs given to the experience team;
- the training (the approach, venue, presentation and agenda);
- anything else that features the client's brand.

Another thing that should be considered in the approvals schedule is that some of the printing may be in a much larger format than the client is used to, and therefore the clients' creative agency may require additional time for reformatting. For example, a giant logo that needs to be printed onto vinyl to wrap a 40-foot trailer is not something that will necessarily already be on file. In addition, sometimes there will be elements that need to be approved by external or third parties, such as any partner logos or space hire applications. These third-party approvals should also be factored into the timeline, as always, allowing for contingencies.

It is crucial to include notes on this schedule that clearly describe any negative implications of any delays. This timeline can alternatively be formatted as a critical path analysis.

Summary

In summary, the Action part of SET MESSAGE is of ultimate importance because there is no point in creating the most innovative and revolutionary experiential strategy, or in booking the highest footfall venues or designing the best amplification plan for the live brand experience, if the execution is going to be flawed. The statement 'If you fail to plan, you plan to fail' is most apt at this stage, and is something that nobody would choose to learn the hard way.

If the Action part of your SET MESSAGE plan contains a recipe, budgets, project plans (WBS, Gantt chart, critical path analysis, schedules, risk analysis, checklists and external analysis), a communication and collaboration plan, a suppliers and third-parties plan and an approvals schedule, then you have covered all the bases. Your SET MESSAGE plan is almost ready for activation, with only the Gauging effectiveness and Evaluation stages to come.

Note

1. Project Management Institute (2004) *A Guide to the Project Management Body of Knowledge,* PMBOK Guides, Project Management Institute, Newtown Square, PA

13 Gauging effectiveness

As we have seen, there are many unpredictable events and variables that can contribute to the success or failure of a live brand experience. If you plan a TV advertising campaign, once the advert has been created, approved and scheduled there is not much that can come in the way of it being aired as planned. It is pre-recorded, controllable and reliable. A live brand experience, on the other hand, has people's free will (along with all the previously discussed risks and external factors) to contend with. Methods that allow you to gauge the effectiveness of the live brand experience part of the experiential marketing campaign during its progress are of ultimate importance, and allow you to monitor the results of the experience and react accordingly. Even though careful action planning and contingencies can contribute greatly to the success of the activation of this plan, there will always be some completely unpredictable dynamics. Sometimes these dynamics are positive and sometimes they are negative. Gauging effectiveness is about telling the difference and reacting appropriately; this is achieved by reviewing the results of the systems and mechanisms for measurement and ensuring flexibility options are in place.

Live brand experiences, especially when implemented face to face, can require a certain amount of improvisation. Because things can go wrong, and many unpredictable positive opportunities can also be created during the process, it is wise to be mentally and emotionally prepared. If you are on the agency side, it is your duty to ensure that the client is also prepared for the unpredictable.

It is true that the more careful action planning you do, the more you will be in control. But because so many factors come into play and relate to each other in a multitude of combinations, there will be things that are out of your control when you are action planning and that will only be discovered during the live brand experience.

The Gauging effectiveness stage will ensure that not only do you plan methods that allow you to react quickly to the fluid reality of your live brand experience, but that you have a way to monitor the campaign while it is live, using those methods. Such methods include real-time reporting of results from the live experience team (Brand ambassadors, team leaders and event managers) to the experiential marketing agency, and online real-time reporting from the experiential marketing agency to the client. Flexibility options are important and allow you to adapt to the findings, such as ensuring scalability in terms of staff and locations. The systems and mechanisms for measurement that you built into the plan already will ensure that the people who are present at the live brand experience are feeding back all the relevant data. During the evaluation stage you will be estimating the outputs of those systems and mechanisms. When you are gauging the effectiveness of the live brand experience during its progress, you will compare the data that is fed back with the estimates in the plan. This way, if something turns out better than expected, the insights and learning that can be gained will be available instantly to leverage the results of the rest of the campaign. Likewise, if something is working less well than expected, or if unpredictable circumstances arise, then instant changes can be made and damage is minimized.

Systems and mechanisms for measurement and how they enable Gauging effectiveness

For a system or mechanism for measurement to be of any value, there must be a way to accurately define and measure it. After you complete the evaluation scorecard, which will be covered in the evaluation stage of the plan (see Chapter 14), quantifiable estimates will be associated with each of the mechanisms for measurement that you have built in to your plan already (each corresponding with an experiential objective), as discussed in Chapter 11. The quantifiable estimates will act as targets and will allow continuous Gauging effectiveness of the live brand experience during its progress. For example, a live brand experience for a washing powder, held in shopping malls across Europe, had a mechanism for measuring word-of-mouth that was based on the number of interactions.

The estimated number was 2,000 participant interactions per location, per day. This was calculated by dividing the total number of interactions (as logged in the experiential scorecard during the completion of the evaluation stage) by the number of locations and days. In this case the estimate of 2,000 participant interactions per location, per day became a target. The event managers at all the locations would fill in a PDA survey every few hours, each day, and part of that survey involved logging the number of participant interactions. When the number of interactions was far higher or lower than expected, the agency and client would know immediately, get to the bottom of why there had been a dramatic variation, and be able to react fast.

As previously discussed, the Systems or mechanisms for measurement relate to the Experiential objectives. In some instances two of those systems are linked to each other. For example, the System for measuring the word-of-mouth reach (multiplying the number of interactions by 17 and then adding the initial number of interactions) is interlinked with the System for measuring the participation of the live brand experience (counting the number of interactions). Therefore, since the word-of-mouth reach cannot be estimated or measured without the number of interactions, it would be useless to set the Experiential objective of driving word-of-mouth without following through by gauging the effectiveness of the live brand experience in that respect (using the System or mechanism for measurement data).

Deciding in advance how the data gathered from the Systems or mechanisms for measurement will be communicated quickly, and establishing what percentage of positive or negative variation is considered to be poor, acceptable or exceptional, is crucial. Defining how far above or below the estimate you should go before adapting the live brand experience is very important. The experiential scorecard will provide the estimate across the whole campaign, and you will need to divide that estimate by the number of locations and days to get the unit estimates (which act as targets); then during the actual campaign, you will need to know how the real results compare to those targets.

Whether these targets are to be measured qualitatively or quantitatively should have already been specified during the Systems and mechanisms for measurement part of the plan. Moreover, it is important that the experiential marketing agency and client stick to these definitions and acceptable or not acceptable variations during all ongoing live brand experiences from month to month, or year to year, to allow for benchmarking and realistic comparisons. Likewise, if a client is switching experiential marketing agencies, it should ensure that the new agency applies the same systems or mechanisms for measurement to its plans that the previous agency did, to allow easy gauging of effectiveness during a campaign and to enable clear understanding of what is a positive or negative result. If the actual results of several Systems or mechanisms for measurement on a specific day or location of a campaign are poor, then the agency should quickly try and gauge why and, if relevant, propose adequate changes to the client. Changing and adapting quickly is essential to the positive outcome of a live brand experience programme.

Real-time reporting and online client access pages

By monitoring the results of your live brand experience in real time, you can continuously aim to improve and adapt it by learning from the variations between the actual outputs of the Systems or mechanisms for measurement (such as consumer feedback and data collected) and the estimated outputs. You can also learn from the event manager's feedback. The Brand ambassadors and team leaders should feed back the data to the event managers, who should regularly and systematically communicate back to the experiential marketing agency. There are several ways that technology can enable this process to happen efficiently and reliably. One option is that the event managers report the feedback and data into survey forms on their smart phones (such as a palm pilot or BlackBerry) or PDAs, and instantly transmit from the devices to the online client access page, which should be on the experiential marketing agency's website. Another option is that a telephone survey line is set up with multiple-choice and qualitative answer options and that the event managers and Brand ambassadors call the line at regular intervals, and their responses are automatically processed and accessible on the experiential marketing agency's online client access pages.

It is important that the internal agency team, the client and its stakeholders are able to view the results of the Systems or mechanisms for measurement with ease throughout the live brand experience's progress. This is why it is important that the experiential marketing agency designs bespoke online client access pages on their website, and tailors them for each individual campaign's reporting needs. That will allow the internal agency staff and the client to log on to the campaigns page, and gauge the effectiveness of the campaign during progress, reacting and adapting as necessary.

There are many types of online client access pages, but all should allow users to log on with a unique password and view web-based or telephone-based survey results, which can include distribution data, interaction figures, consumer feedback, and all the results from Systems or mechanisms for measurements. Any other change requests, issues or information that the client should know about should also be posted manually onto the client access page by the internal agency staff responsible for doing so. The experiential marketing agency should have the facilities to upload results in real time so that the client is always up-to-date. As well as results in real time, the experiential marketing agency should be able to upload visual evidence (such as photos and video clips) onto the same client access page within 48 hours of a campaign going live and any other documents or files that they want the client to download.

Flexibility and change management solutions

There may be areas that need quick adaptation, scaling up, down or amending, depending on the variations between actual results (discovered through the real-time reporting) and estimated results (calculated by dividing the broader estimates in the experiential scorecard). If the experiential marketing agency notices a variation that is either a problem or opportunity, and wants to propose a change to the client, then there needs to be a planned and agreed procedure for doing so. At this point in the plan, it is important to include procedures for approving changes during a live brand experience's progress. The recommended method of doing this is to create forms like those shown in this chapter and to ensure that all relevant members of the client decision-making team are aware of the possibility of a change request during the campaign. A sample change request form is shown in Table 13.1.

The change request form can be uploaded onto the client access page or e-mailed, as long as it is sent in a way that allows quick decision making and reaction. The chances of the live brand experience succeeding can directly relate to the speed with which the results and any corresponding change requests are shared (by the agency) and the speed with which the receivers can react (the client).

Once a change request form has been approved, there will need to be a log of that change and any other changes that are requested and approved. These changes can easily be logged in a form such as the change control log shown in Table 13.2, which will prove useful when conducting the final Evaluation of the campaign.

Table 13.1 Change request form

CHANGE REQUEST FORM		
Live brand experience name:		
Project manager name:		
Live brand experience location:		
Agency originator name and phone:	Date of request:	Change request no.: *allocated by Change controller*
Items to be changed:		Reference(s):
Description of change (reasons for change, benefits, date required):		
Estimated cost and time to implement (quotation attached? Yes/No):		
Will this cost be additional, or part of existing contingencies?		
Priority/constraints (impact on other deliverables, implications of not proceeding, risks)		

CHANGE EVALUATION			
What is affected:		Work required (resources, costs, dates):	
Related change requests:			
Name of evaluator:		Date evaluated:	Signature:
CLIENT CHANGE APPROVAL			
Accepted/Rejected/Deferred	Name:	Signed:	Date:
Comments:			

CHANGE IMPLEMENTATION			
Asset:	Implementer:	Date completed:	Signature:

Table 13.2 Change control log

CHANGE CONTROL LOG					
Live brand experience:		Date (from/to)			
Project manager:		Client:			
Change number	Description of change	Date Received	Date Evaluated	Date Approved	Date Completed

Summary

In summary, the ever-changing environment of the real world and the force of individual free will are bound to create unexpected circumstances. Just imagine if, during a live brand experience that was being executed face to face, a group of radical political protestors decided to march with picket boards in the same location. Would the client be happy to be affiliated with this radical cause? Would the experience's Brand ambassadors and participants be safe in such as volatile environment? The answers are 'probably not'. Though the client is likely to want to move the campaign, they would not be happy if they were not informed of what was going on, and they didn't have the opportunity to participate in deciding on the solution. If the proposed solution were to change locations, they surely would want to be involved in that decision.

If a client hoped that their live brand experience channel, with the objective of increasing sales, would result in a big sales uplift in the stores where the experience was positioned, and some of those stores ran out of stock during the first hour of the experience, the client would want to know about the problem and decide on an appropriate solution. Depending on circumstances, they might want to attempt to transport stock from other stores to the affected stores, relocate the experience to a store that had sufficient stock, or postpone the experience to another day. Regardless of which solution they would have preferred, the client would not have been happy if their experiential marketing agency hadn't informed them of the problem until it was too late to react. If the experiential marketing agency didn't have real-time reporting in place, then it is not likely that the client would be informed in time.

There are plenty of examples of unpredictable circumstances which, when addressed swiftly, can be dealt with in a manner that optimizes the results of the live brand experience and ensures maximum achievement of Experiential objectives. By building Systems or mechanisms for measurement in the plan, completing the experiential scorecard in the evaluation stage, and Gauging effectiveness of the campaign by comparing actual outputs with estimated targets and using a combination of real-time reporting facilities and change management solutions to adapt and react, optimum results can be achieved. The Gauging effectiveness part of the SET MESSAGE plan will enable you to create a smooth and clear process for optimizing the live brand experience part of your experiential marketing campaign for best results.

14 Evaluation

Introduction

The Evaluation stage, which begins during the SET MESSAGE planning process and is completed after the experiential marketing campaign is implemented, is arguably one of the most important stages of the campaign cycle (which are: planning, activation and evaluation), because even if your strategy was fabulous and your activation was flawless, if you don't effectively evaluate the campaign results then there is nothing tangible indicating that the campaign was successful.

It is very important to remain results-oriented when planning, activating and evaluating experiential marketing campaigns. It is true that there are many 'fluffy' benefits to experiential marketing, but, as previously discussed, there are also many tangible and quantitative benefits to be gained. By using the same metrics and Evaluation approaches across all your experiential marketing campaigns, you will enable benchmarking and comparison, and LROI measurement, not only in regard to comparing one experiential marketing campaign with another, but also in terms of comparing an experiential marketing campaign with a previous marketing communications campaign run without an experiential approach.

As previously discussed, live brand experiences should be placed at the core of experiential marketing campaigns. The unfounded myth that they cannot be evaluated properly arose for a number of reasons, including the fact that non-experiential marketing specialists are a popular choice for clients that want to plan and activate high-profile live brand experiences. Some of these campaigns have been managed by full-service agencies for big clients without thinking about how to evaluate until after the campaign is finished. Essentially experiential marketing can include any marketing channel as long as the live brand experience is at its core, and the other selected channels are designed to amplify the live brand experience. The traditional channels can still be measured and evaluated using the common metrics that are accepted across the industry, while the live brand experience channel lends itself especially well to easy and comprehensive Evaluation, due to the two-way interaction with consumers. The human interface, direct engagement and relationship building with participants that characterize live brand experiences are all reasons why they are in fact often easier to measure than many other channels. However, it is true that there is not one consistent method used by all experiential marketing agencies for measuring and evaluating live brand experiences. As a result, it makes it harder to benchmark the results of a live brand experience implemented by one agency against the results of a similar live brand experience implemented by a different agency.

It should be acknowledged that this lack of a widely accepted Evaluation approach does contribute to a difficulty in comparison and benchmarking of live brand experience results. Hopefully this phenomenon is only temporary and is a symptom of the fact that live brand experiences and the experiential marketing methodology as a whole are part of a relatively new approach to marketing communications. In time there will be more consistency in the metrics. This SET MESSAGE planning system aims to unify the ways in which experiential marketers evaluate their experiential marketing campaigns, with a strong emphasis on how to evaluate live brand experiences.

This chapter covers two different steps, the first being how to complete the Evaluation part of your SET MESSAGE plan, where you will plan and summarize the ways that you will evaluate during the campaign (the Gauging effectiveness stage) and the second the actual Evaluation stage, which is how you will evaluate the experiential marketing campaign once it is over.

It is hoped that from reading previous chapters you have already built in Systems and mechanisms for measurement into your plan, and already know how you will go about Gauging effectiveness during the campaign's progress. Therefore, by the time that you come to evaluate the campaign post-activation, you will have acquired plenty of qualitative and quantitative data for you to format and analyse. If the experiential marketing campaign is ongoing, then you may want to break it up into chunks and complete the Evaluation stage at the end of each chunk.

After the campaign is over, the results from the amplification channels should be straightforward as those channels have common metrics. The results from the live brand experience channel that were collected in real time when you gauged the effectiveness of the activity should be combined into a report that includes the results of the amplification channels. The two sets of data form the body of information and intelligence that you will then dissect to evaluate the experiential marketing campaign as a whole.

Your Systems and mechanisms for measurement should have been built into the live brand experience, and the Gauging effectiveness stage should have been completed during the campaigns process. Even if this is all handled by an experiential marketing agency and their live brand experience team, you may want an external market research agency to complete a formal independent audit. The combined results should form the basis of information and data that you (or your experiential marketing agency) will work with when evaluating the campaign.

The written Evaluation section

This section of the SET MESSAGE plan should outline the ways in which you will evaluate the campaign once it is over. If you refer back to Chapter 11, you checked which Systems and mechanisms for measurement corresponded with your selected Experiential objectives (by checking the table provided), then you prepared your own table detailing the Systems and mechanisms that you would use for measurement. That table acts as the basis for the experiential scorecard.

The experiential scorecard will be featured in the Evaluation part of the SET MESSAGE plan. It is a table that acts as a quantitative measure of both quantitative and qualitative Systems and mechanisms for measurement. It should be formatted as a table that shows the appropriate measurement mechanism or system and its corresponding objectives, the estimated results (which you will fill in at this stage of planning), and two blank columns for the actual results and comments, detailing theories on why any positive or negative variation occurred, which will both be filled in during the Gauging effectiveness stage; see the example in Table 14.1. After completing the written Evaluation part of your SET MESSAGE plan, your experiential scorecard should therefore include estimates that show the anticipated results.

These estimates should be completed based on past experience and should always be realistic. The locations of the live brand experience (whether it is face to face or remote) should be able to provide footfall or visitor data that can help in determining how many people will be at the live brand experience. If the live brand experience invites people to it, then the number of people who have confirmed attendance should also be able to guide these estimates. It is important to factor in the length

Table 14.1 Experiential scorecard

Car X Experiential Campaign Q2			
Measurement mechanism + corresponding objective	Estimate	Actual	Comments
OTS (opportunity to see) [Objective: Raise awareness]	658,000		
Word-of-mouth reach[i] [Objective: Drive word-of-mouth]	2.56 million		
Number of interactions [Objective: Drive word-of-mouth]	150,000		
Increase in awareness of key communication message (survey Q1) [Objective: Communicate complex brand messages]	30%		
Increase in perception of Car X as a stylish as well as capable vehicle (survey Q2) [Objective: Position the brand as x]	65%		
Number of visitors to Car X website that clicked from micro-site [Objective: Drive traffic to website]	40,000		

[i] Jack Morton studies show that each person who interacts in an experiential campaign tells an average of 17 people (source: Kevin Jackson, at Jack Morton).

of time that its takes for participants to complete their interaction in the live brand experience, as well as the maximum number of participants that can be involved at any one time. Other things to factor in when estimating are the number of Brand ambassadors, the number of locations in which the brand experience is occurring, and the number of days that the experience is taking place; also include the estimates for the results of the amplification channels.

The Evaluation part of the plan should also list and describe the documents or presentations that will be shown to the client at the end of the campaign for review, from either the experiential marketing agency or other agency partners to the client, or from an in-house team directly to internal and external stakeholders.

The campaign Evaluation (post-campaign)

The Evaluation packet will be prepared after the campaign and should be presented in the agreed format that was specified when you completed the written Evaluation part of the SET MESSAGE plan. It is likely to contain:

- the completed experiential scorecard;
- an ROI and LROI analysis;
- a change analysis;
- visual evidence review (video edits and photos);
- an SW+I report (strengths, weaknesses and insights).

All of the above will be explained in detail in the course of this chapter.

The order that the elements above are listed in is a recommended order in which to conduct the post-campaign Evaluation process. The rest of this chapter will explain how to perform each step.

Experiential scorecard

The experiential scorecard is based on the same table that you created when you completed the written Evaluation part of the SET MESSAGE plan, but at this stage should also show the completed 'actual results' and 'comments' columns. An example is shown in Table 14.2.

Table 14.2 Experiential scorecard post-campaign

Car X Experiential Campaign Q2			
Measurement mechanism + corresponding objective	**Estimate**	**Actual**	**Comments**
OTS (opportunity to see) [Objective: Raise awareness]	658,000	700,000	Based on mall footfall data.
Word-of-mouth reach[i] [Objective: Drive word-of-mouth]	2.56m	3.15m	Higher than planned, due to a higher number of interactions than anticipated.
Number of interactions [Objective: Drive word-of-mouth]	150,000	175,000	It was higher than anticipated due to a higher footfall than usual.
Increase in awareness of key communication message (survey Q1) [Objective: Communicate complex brand messages]	30%	50%	Survey results showed a 50% increase in awareness of the key communication, when participant data were compared to non-participant data, collected during the campaign.
Increase in perception of Car X as a stylish as well as capable vehicle (survey Q2) [Objective: Position the brand as x]	65%	40%	The increase in perception was not as big as anticipated due to Car X's existing positioning as capable, along with a common view among is both participants and non-participants that the car was stylish.
Number of visitors to Car X website that clicked from micro-site [Objective: Drive traffic to website]	40,000	72,650	The number of hits to the micro-site was higher due to the number of participants and word-of-mouth reach being higher.

[i] Jack Morton studies show that each person who interacts in an experiential campaign tells an average of 17 people (source: Kevin Jackson, at Jack Morton).

The experiential scorecard's purpose is outputs; even qualitative questions have been quantified to show an increase or decrease in a common response. As long as the previously defined Systems and mechanisms for measurement were chosen in line with the Experiential objectives (using the chart provided in Chapter 11), then the experiential scorecard should facilitate easy Evaluation of whether those objectives and their targets were met. The comments should throw some light on why a positive or negative variation occurred between estimated and actual results.

The experiential scorecard quantifies results in a tangible way that can justify the spend on experiential marketing initiatives. The process of tailoring the metrics to the Experiential objectives during the Systems and mechanisms for measurement stage, then Gauging the effectiveness of the campaign in relation to the metrics, and finally formatting the results in the experiential scorecard during Evaluation, is a full circle of measuring the desired outcomes against the actual outcomes while learning from any variations.

ROI and LROI

'Return on investment' originated as an accounting term but is usually regarded as a grey area in marketing, often being loosely referred to as what results are generated from a campaign. The term 'ROI' can be used as a financial measure of the actual percentage of profit made, as a direct measurable result of a campaign. For that to be instantly possible in the case of a live brand experience, the experience would need to be either near to a store that sold the product being promoted, or there would need to be a traceable mechanism and incentive in place, such as redeemable sales promotion vouchers or online promotional codes. All this clearly points towards short-term thinking. This also implies that the goal of the investment is an instant sales uplift and suggests that it is necessary for sales promotion to be involved.

Another way to look at the return is in the context of a long-term experiential marketing strategy, where the ultimate objective of the live brand experience channel is to convert participants into loyal customers, then into brand advocates, and finally into brand evangelists. In this case, the return can be measured by how far the live brand experience succeeds in moving the consumer through the advocacy pipeline.

With that said, it is clear in business that good healthy sales and market share are the ultimate goals. There is no reason to think that the goalpost is moving, in fact far from it. The value of a customer who talks about your brand as if it were a trusted friend, and considers his or her relationship with your brand to be a two-way street, is priceless. People trust people, and there is nothing that could be more desirable from a business perspective than your target audience spreading positive word-of-mouth about your product to their peers. It is proven that personal recommendations are the most likely factor to influence purchase consideration, and the lifetime value of the customer is far greater than the value that any instant sales uplift campaign could generate.

The impact of a positive live brand experience can be so great that a participant can move through the advocacy stages very quickly, but to make a long-lasting impact across a whole target audience, those reached by the word-of-mouth and amplification channels of the experiential marketing campaign should be factored in to the equation. For long-term return on investment (LROI), a long-term experiential marketing strategy is required. The interactive, two-way communication (the live brand experience) should be at the core of the overall marketing strategy, thus allowing all the marketing communications channels to work in alliance with each other and amplify the live brand experience. This amplification approach can be applied in many ways. Whether the amplification is in the form of branded content on TV, through an interactive call to action on a billboard, or through a radio broadcast of a live brand experience, the unified channels work together to create the complete experiential marketing campaign that builds long-lasting relationships with the members of the brand's Target audience whom it reached. The aim is that those Target audience members then become brand advocates and evangelists who proceed to take the positive brand Message and Key communication to the masses, increasing awareness and sales in the process.

Calculating LROI for live brand experiences

The sales generated from a live brand experience should be seen to be symptomatic of the word-of-mouth reach generated from that positive, two-way, brand-relevant interaction. By creating a link between the number of interactions of the live brand experience and the long-term word-of-mouth reach, while taking into account, that word-of-mouth generates sales; we get closer to correlating the number of interactions generated from the live brand experience with the number of sales generated. The ultimate aim is to estimate the long-term return on investment (LROI) of live brand experiences.

It is proven that the long-term effect that word-of-mouth has on sales is greater than with any other approach. This is why, by using a model that calculates LROI, which factors in the word-of-mouth reach of a live brand experience, we can quantify the impact that the live brand experience has on sales (which should be at the core of the integrated experiential campaign and combined with the ROI results of the amplification channels).

The steps involved in calculating the LROI for live brand experiences formula are:

Step 1. Each person who interacts in a live brand experience is likely to tell 17 others. Therefore, the word-of-mouth Reach can be calculated as the number of interactions multiplied by 17, plus the number of interactions[1].

Step 2. The Number of Sales (estimate)can be calculated as 2.6 per cent of the word-of-mouth Reach of the live brand experience (this percentage is based on the average number of sales from direct mail campaigns[2], even though it is proven that word-of-mouth is more likely to generate purchase consideration than any other marketing)[3], [4], [5], [6].

Step 3. The profit generated from the live brand experience can be calculated by multiplying the profit per sale by the number of sales (estimate). Then subtracting the cost of the live brand experience.

Step 4. In order to calculate the LROI you divide the profit generated, by the cost of the live brand experience and multiply by 100.

Therefore, the formula is:
LROI = (X ÷C) x100
(This is the profit divided by the cost, multiplied by 100)
S = number of sales based on 2.6 per cent of W (word-of-mouth reach)
P = profit per sale
X = the profit generated from the live brand experience, based on S (number of sales) x P (profit per sale)
C = cost of the live brand experience
N = the number of consumer interactions with the live brand experience
W = the word-of-mouth reach, based on 17N +N.

A small-scale example

Hamed is the marketing manager for a website selling customized greeting cards that can be ordered online. His cards sell at £4 and his profit per greeting cards is £1.50. He approached an experiential agency to create an integrated experiential campaign, featuring an interactive greeting card road-show and amplification of the activity using PR and digital advertising. The live brand experience channel's total cost was £50,000 and generated 115,000 interactions. He wanted to measure the LROI and used this model to estimate what his long-term return on investment would be.

Step 1. He multiplies the number of interactions in the live brand experience (115,000) by 17 (the number of people that each participant will tell about the experience on average) and then adds the original number of interactions to get the word-of-mouth reach (2.07 million).

Step 2. To get the estimated number of sales resulting from the word-of-mouth reach, he calculates 2.6 per cent of 2.07 million (the word-of-mouth reach). This produces 53,820 sales.

Step 3. To get the profit generated from the live brand experience, he multiplies the profit per greeting card, which is £1.50, by the number of sales (53,820) to get £80,730. Then he subtracts the cost of the campaign, (£50,000) to get the profit generated of £30,730.

Step 4. He calculates the LROI of 161 per cent by dividing the profit generated from the live brand experience by the cost of the live brand experience, and multiplies the result by 100.

The formula is:
LROI = 161 %, based on $(X \div C) \times 100$
S = 53,820 number of sales (estimate) based on 2.6 per cent of W (word-of-mouth reach)
P = £1.50 (profit per sale)
X = £80,730 the profit generated, based on S (number of sales) x P (profit per sale)
C = £50,000 (cost of the live brand experience)
N = 115,000 (the number of consumer interactions with the live brand experience)
W = 2.07m (17N +N, the word-of-mouth reach)

In this case, Hamed can predict that 161 per cent will be the LROI from the live brand experience activity, because he used the formula that factors in the long-term effect of the campaign, taking into consideration the estimated word-of-mouth reach.

Actually, this is a very conservative estimate because the 2.6 per cent return is based on an average return from a direct mail campaign, while **word-of-mouth has been proven to be around ten times more effective**, and also has been voted above traditional media as **most likely to drive purchase consideration**.

To calculate the return on investment of the integrated experiential marketing campaign in full, it is important to include measurement of the amplification channels.

The other marketing communication channels that Hamed used to amplify the live brand experience for his online greeting cards were interactive online ads and PR. The interactive online ads featured slideshows showing some of the cards made by consumers who had participated, and an invitation to submit a card design to be shown on future ads. The amount of people who clicked on an online advert and then purchased a card measured the success of the online channel. The PR channel was based on a photocall of all the Brand ambassadors and consumers engaging in the live brand experience, which went on to feature in a number of national and local newspapers and magazines. The PR channel was measured by column inches (how much the space would have cost if it were paid advertising space). The online and PR metric he used are commonly-used measures, though obviously approaches vary. Hamed combined the LROI generated from the live brand experience with the generic measures that he placed on the PR and online advertising channels, allowing him to evaluate the success of the integrated experiential marketing campaign as a whole.

Another example (larger scale)

Jane is a senior planner at an experiential marketing agency. Her client is a high-end white goods manufacturer. When the client approached Jane with the task of launching a new brand of luxury energy-saving washer-dryers, Jane designed an strategy that featured a six-month live brand experience tour. The tour involved an energy home, which toured around the United States. Consumers were then invited to walk around the energy home, and learn how to save energy in their own homes, while creating their own energy-saving binder and having their 'aura photo' taken. The aura photo, which mapped out the energy around their head and shoulders, was slotted into the front cover of their energy-saving binder as a souvenir. The live experiential marketing strategy was a major hit amongst the target audience of affluent housewives.

Jane's client was over the moon, but wanted Jane to provide a method of showing her bosses that the constant rise in sales since the start of the experiential marketing campaign was directly linked to the activity. Jane proposed looking at the LROI of the live brand experience, and calculated it using the same formula.

The formula is:
LROI = 1800 %, based on (X ÷C) x100
(This is the profit generated from the live brand experience divided by the cost of the live brand experience, multiplied by 100)
S = 140,000 estimated number of sales based on 2.6 per cent of W (word-of-mouth reach)
P = £450 (profit per sale)
X = 63m is the profit generated based on S (number of sales) x P (profit per sale)
C = £2m (cost of the live brand experience)
N = 300,000 (number of consumer interactions with live brand experience)
W = 5.4m (17N +N, the word-of-mouth reach)

As you can see, whether the investment is small or large and whether the product is a high involvement purchase like an energy-saving washer-dryer or a low involvement purchase like a personalized greeting card, live brand experiences can generate a high long-term return on investment. By aiming to also combine the ROI of each amplification channel, you can endeavour to evaluate the complete integrated experiential marketing campaign.

The LROI gives you the figure for the longer-term financial return you can expect to gain from the live brand experience. Depending on whether it is a high involvement purchase (like a car) or a low involvement purchase (like a candy bar), the timeframe can vary from 1 day, to 1 week, to 5 years. By using the LROI formula, it is easy to evaluate and estimate the long-term effect that the live brand experience part of the experiential marketing campaign will have.

By combining the LROI of the live brand experience (using the formula) and the ROI of the amplification channels (using standard metrics) for the evaluation, we can begin to predict the combined effects of the complete campaign. It is important to also factor in the CLV (the lifetime value of the customer), especially in specific industries where the long-term profit to be gained from each customer is greater down the line. One example is the gaming industry, where the profit margin on a console is far lower than the profit margin on the consumer buying video games on an ongoing basis.

If you would like to generate long-term return on investment from experiential marketing, you must invest in a long-term experiential marketing strategy. By placing live brand experiences and the experiential philosophy at the core of your long-term marketing strategy, the long-term return on investment will be far greater than if you approach it as a tactic for a quick sales uplift.

The change analysis

The next part of the Evaluation stage is the change analysis. This is a careful examination of what differed between the original plan and the delivered plan. This should encompass changes in timing, cost and outputs. The data that should form the basis of this will have already been collected during the Gauging effectiveness stage using the change control log. The purpose of the change analysis (see Table 14.3) at this stage is to determine the reasons behind any changes and to gather any insights, useful in future planning.

Note: The change number should correlate with the change number on the change control log that was used during the Gauging effectiveness stage.

Table 14.3 Change analysis

Live brand experience:			Date (from/to):		
Project manager:			Client:		
Change number	Description of change		Reason	Impact	Comments

Visual evidence review

Visual evidence is a crucial part of ensuring stakeholders internalize the positive results of an experiential campaign. The live brand experience should be captured in both moving and still pictures, which should be edited and presented in a concise, attractive format for all to see exactly how it worked and, most important, how consumers reacted and participated in the brand-relevant interaction. From a marketing perspective, there is nothing more fulfilling than to see the Target audiences' faces lighting up with happiness and appreciation for your brand. One minute of edited video footage and a slide show of photos taken from a live brand experience can say more than a thousand words' worth of data and analysis. The visual evidence from the live brand experience (assuming that it was executed face to face) can also be used to amplify the campaign – forming content for TV adverts, digital messages and a platform for future relationship-building. The participants themselves usually love to receive a letter or e-mail showing them clips of the experience that they so much enjoyed. This is even more effective when the process is handled with enough sophistication to enable the matching up of sections of the visual evidence with the details of the consumers who are featured in it.

Along with the edited live brand experience footage and images, there should be visual evidence of the amplification channels as well. For example, if part of the experiential marketing campaign featured a TV show that was branded and based on interactive audience participation and audience-generated content, then an edited 'best bits' from the show would be great to use in the Evaluation report. In another example, the PR amplification channel invited consumers to attempt to break a world record. A compilation of the consumers' competition entries and the news coverage was included in the visual evidence part of the Evaluation packet. No matter which amplification channels you used, or whether the live brand experience was online, in person or through some other method of remote communication technology, the visual images and footage that capture it present a much more vivid picture and understanding of what happened than any black and white data can. The visual evidence of the experiential marketing campaign provides a souvenir that reminds the participants and/or stakeholders of the experience, thus keeping the vivid memories of the campaign alive for far longer than in the mind alone.

Strengths, weaknesses and insights

The strengths, weakness and insights report is the final part of the post-campaign Evaluation. The body of this report should be formatted as a table, with two columns, one for strengths and one for weaknesses. It should be split into three sections: planning, implementation and results. Following the table, there should be a summary of insight for the future.

The purpose of the report is to summarize everything that was good, bad, adequate and outstanding about each of the three stages, as well as how these stages could be improved. This will facilitate better performance when conducting the next stage of the experiential marketing programme. It should take into consideration all data gathered during Gauging effectiveness including a careful analysis of if and why the targets affiliated with the Systems and mechanisms for measurement were met or exceeded.

Summary

In summary, it is important to outline exactly how the experiential marketing campaign is going to be evaluated during the planning stages. Then during the Evaluation stage, post-campaign, a detailed Evaluation packet should be prepared. It is obvious that every client and brand is different and obviously different people and budgets demand different levels of Evaluation. A fully comprehensive Evaluation packet should contain:

- The completed experiential scorecard.
- An LROI and/or ROI analysis that takes into account both the live brand experience and any other amplification channels that comprised the experiential marketing campaign, taking into consideration the CLV (customer lifetime value).
- A change analysis.
- Visual evidence (combining edited video footage and photos).
- A strengths, weaknesses and insights report that elaborates on the positives and negatives from both the client and agency perspectives during the planning, implementation and results, and looking at what can be learnt from them.

Notes

1. Jack Morton studies show that each person who interacts in an experiential campaign tells an average of 17 people (source: Kevin Jackson, at Jack Morton). Jack Morton Worldwide. An executive summary of this survey is available online at www.JackMorton.com
2. The DMA analysed 1,122 industry-specific campaigns and determined that the average response rate for direct mail was 2.61 per cent (source: *The DMA 2003 Response Rate Study*)
3. A 2004 UK survey by CIA:MediaEdge of 10,000 consumers found that 76 per cent cite word-of-mouth as the main influence on purchasing decisions, compared to traditional advertising which comes in at 15 per cent (source: cited in *Connected Marketing* by Justin Kirby and Paul Marsden published by Butterworth Heinemann)
4. Euro RSCG has found that when it comes to generating excitement about products, word-of-mouth is 10 times more effective than TV or print advertising (source: Euro RSCG survey 'Wired and Wireless: High-tech capitals now and next' archived at http://www.eurorscg.com/starview/doc/ww_summary.pdf)
5. 'The one thing known to drive business growth; word-of-mouth advocacy' (source: Reicheld, F (2003) 'The one number you need to grow, *Harvard Business Review*, **81**, Nov/Dec, pp 1–11
6. Ninety-one per cent of people would be likely to use a brand recommended by someone who has used it themselves (source: Keller, E (2005) The state of word-of-mouth, 2005: the consumer perspective, conference paper presented at the Word-of-mouth Marketing Association Summit, Chicago, 29–30 March)

15 Interviews

Here is a series of interviews with some of the leading experts in experiential marketing worldwide:

David Polinchock CXO, Brand Experience Lab, Global (DP)
Richard Norby and Kirsten, Live Marketing, Chicago, United States (RN)
Erik Hauser, Founder of IXMA (International Experiential Marketing Association) and EMF (Experiential Marketing Forum), Global (EH)
Kevin Jackson, Jack Morton Worldwide, United Kingdom (KJ)
Justin Singh, One Partners, Australia (JS)
Spero Patricios, Launch Factory, South Africa (SP)
Ian Whiteling, Events Review, Global (IW)
Paul Ephremsen, ID, United Kingdom (PE)

How would you define experiential marketing?

DP: We define it as the sum of everything you do. The experience has to represent what you say you stand for.

RN: Many people have started to think of it as a marketing channel, equating it to marketing in face-to-face or live environments. I think of it differently, I think of experiential marketing as a technique that can be applied to any channel. The key points are to involve the audience intellectually, physically and emotionally. As long as you have those three types, you have experiential marketing. It allows you to create a deeper connection with them and a more memorable meaningful experience.

EH: It is a more holistic approach to marketing, it's a marketing methodology. It's not a catch phrase, buzzword or tactic. A methodology that appeals to both the rational and emotional side of the consumer mind. Previously traditional marketing was a monologue, through mediums such as TV – they said 'Here it is'. Now it's turning into a conversation. It allows brands the opportunity for people to tinker around with their brand and make things the way they want it. It's really the methodology that's customer-centric instead of product-centric.

KJ: Experiential marketing is any communication that has an emotional richness, and that allows for some connection that isn't there by the mere fact of communicating. Experiential marketing involves changing beliefs and behaviours. Unless you engage the communication with an emotional trigger, it won't work. It must bring you into the message.

JS: The way we define it as a company is 'We are not purely an experiential live agency, we are the antithesis of advertising.' We create experiences where people choose to engage, which is the opposite of big traditional advertising agency models.

SP: It is an interaction between the brand and consumer on a physical, one-to-one level. The key thing is that it must be an interaction.

IW: Communication or engagement of an audience using as many senses as possible.

PE: Experiential involves live interactions with brands and consumers. Memorable interactions that involve the senses and a degree of creativity, that allows the brand to create emotions that a consumer can relate to.

How do you see the evolution of live marketing?

DP: In an ultra-marketed world, one of the best ways to break through the clutter is to engage in one-on-one interaction.

RN: Part of the evolution comes out of two big influences: one is the collapse of mass media and as it becomes fragmented – things have to become specific to each type of people. If you combine this with another influence, which is the internet and web 2.0 – which is creating richer experiences for people on the web, providing them with opportunities for them to interact, it's a multi-way communication between companies and their customers. The web development companies have also begun to blur the lines between people's professional persona and their private personas. It's within that context that we see it becoming more effective to create experiences for people so that they can connect in this rich and meaningful manner.

Because there are so many marketing messages, its crucial for them to have these relevant meaningful experiences – that's why participants understanding what the product, the brand is really is so much more beneficial, not only to the company but also to the end user.

EH: Experiential is a methodology that can be applied equally across any media: there are some great experiential TV commercials that are not simply about the product. There is a misconception in the market that it has to be tactile in nature; that you have to physically touch it. You do not have to touch to feel it. You can move people just using sight and sound, not just with a live event. Having said that, the live event is one of the better media to yield experiential methodologies, as it is multi-sensory.

Going back to television or print, to say that experiential marketing cannot be on a print ad is like saying that a picture could never make you cry. There are several memories of adverts that when you look back to your childhood, you never forget, and you remember the brand. It's about connected meaning and relevance between the product and the audience. If you can achieve that, then you wind up with these campaigns that are timeless and unforgettable. That is the ultimate win. Sometimes people put together campaigns that are funny just for the sake of being funny, but not connected back to the brand. In that case, you can forget whom the ad was for. Experiential marketing is about being authentic and genuine, as consumers can see right through brand pretences.

KJ: I think the evolution of live marketing has already started. It's human nature to want to belong to something. It allows audiences to join into the communication; that's one of the most important aspects, being part of something. Everyone is on a journey, and the brand journey and consumer journey are joining together in this thing called live marketing. That's why it's so important; it's the live part, the growing part of the communication mix. People want to connect to something, that's why they go to festivals.

JS: I think the one thing that is certain is that the live marketing-based opportunities will increase. The proportion of budgets invested by clients is increasing. Live event marketing has been planned separately, and now it is being integrated into the broader communications plan and the overall strategy. I also believe that experiential-based communication is the future for lots of smaller, more targeted programmes.

SP: A lot of brands are still doing it on a promotional level, but to make it a conversation and an interaction we must come up with creative ways to make it interactive. Sampling is not experiential. There is still quite a way to go because people view it in a different light, and it's executed in different ways.

IW: It came about due to necessity, essentially within the last five years, with the opening of more global markets. This means increased competition for every single business, along with fragmentation of media, which has meant that companies can no longer mass communicate through one channel such as TV.

On top of that, there has also been an increased awareness amongst business and consumer audiences, which means that they've become wise to the traditional forms of marketing. One of the best ways of getting around this is to create a unique experience that communicates brand and product messages directly to the consumer or the target business.

PE: It went through a confused stage with no central body in the UK, and definitions were blurry. People who were doing sampling and roadshows were talking about it, and a division started forming between the field marketing agencies and the experiential agencies. ID's view involves the commonality in the use of people on the field, and that's where the similarity stops. Experiential is about creativity and creating an 'on-brand moment'. Field is about a functional service that facilitates sales. Originally the term didn't exist; activities in the field with live scenarios were there, but what has evolved is the discipline itself. Creative people have jumped on the bandwagon and realized that if this is creative, we should be involved. More traditional media are realizing that consumers are being bombarded with messages, and therefore the marketing environment is playing into the hands of the experiential discipline. More agencies are trying to get into this space.

How would you compare live brand experiences to other marketing channels?

DP: Live brand experiences as a marketing channel have great power because you are engaging the audience. It is an opportunity to bring the brand to life. Hamley's is a store with products on the shelf, everyone including employees and guests acting as friends – the store has such a life and vibrancy. Also the Apple store – it's alive, you're excited and enthusiastic. These are as opposed to other stores that don't stand out that have no engagement experience at all. I am giving cash, so they have to give something back tangibly. Experiential marketing is that heart and soul of the consumer experience.

RN: I think that there's a fundamental shift away from 'one size fits all' marketing. Experiential marketing plays well in this one-to-one, or one-to-few kind of world that we are transitioning to. It's not so much that it's a new channel; we have to look at all the channels and see how they can be more experiential. It's not just your live strategy, it's about engaging people physically and emotionally, more than ever before across every channel.

EH: It's not one tactic, but rather a methodology that can be utilized across any media. It's not just live events, but much more.

KJ: The thing I've always loved about brand experience since 1998, the thing that brand experience does that no one else does, is it's aware of the context in which you are exposed to it. If you're at home watching TV there's no contextual relevance. DM is the same. Live marketing makes you ready for the message, gives you the message, and gives you a way to behave and believe. That's the important thing.

JS: I think that it almost speaks for itself. At One Partners it's about people actively choosing to engage with the experience, rather than the traditional model of trying to ambush people while they are unaware.

SP: I don't say that we should do away with other channels where experiential has an upper hand. Where people are bombarding consumers with messages, the consumer is starting to fight against that. Experiential has an advantage because we can start interacting with consumers and they will want to interact back. The other mediums will never go away, and experiential should be used with them, even though it does have the upper hand.

IW: I think it is more holistic, and it also gives something back to the target audience which no other medium achieves with credibility.

PE: It's more interesting. Consumers seem to enjoy and want it, and there are stats here to back that up. It's more memorable and directors have voted it the most memorable medium. It's obviously an opportunity for consumers to touch, taste, feel and interact with your product or brand. It's a good way of conveying complex information that couldn't be placed in a product or advert because it allows explanation. It has the ability to generate word-of-mouth and it can increase sales. It's direct, and therefore you can choose who speaks, and log who you've spoken to.

The greyest area is that it's potentially easy to measure, but in reality it seems difficult to get an industry norm to what you would expect results to be. On paper of course you know who you are talking to. You could then, in theory, contact that person in 12 months' time and find out what effect you had on them. The difficulty in doing that is it's not a broadcast media, volumes are lower, and it's difficult to isolate the effect of the medium when that same consumer has been exposed to other media. It's also relatively high for the cost per interaction compared to other media. The challenge is to talk about the effect per interaction, in which case it would be far higher.

How do think things have changed or are changing regarding marketing budgets and what portion goes to experiential marketing or live brand experiences?

DP: We are seeing big changes. Traditional marketing approaches are being seen as less effective. The challenge in trying to figure out where the budget lies is that there are many categories: for example outdoor in the United States is one of the largest categories. This could include an ad in the background or an experiential campaign. Therefore it's hard to measure exactly, and soon the challenge will be for companies to create an experience across all their advertising and marketing channels.

RN: It's a little bit scattered right now. Obviously there's been a move of money away from mass media, with a lot of it going to digital and live events. Within live events, we've seen people going to more experiential approaches. With a technology brand, instead of giving people 100 demos, they are getting away from that; they'll do fewer demos but they'll make the demos experiences where people can see how the applications can work in their daily lives. Companies are shifting away from older traditional approaches to things that are more experiential.

EH: Again, running under the assumption that experiential is a methodology, companies are starting to realize that they need to utilize that methodology. The minute it becomes about product, it becomes about price, and that's a deadly spiral. You need to form a bond beyond price with the customer. You need to appeal to the emotional side; you need to tug on the heartstrings a little bit. It's about forming a connection but not quite falling in love. You're not going to get that deep with most of your customers.

KJ: First, there is no such thing as an experiential marketing budget. It is a new thing. The recognition is that it needs to be done.

JS: I think, first, there's no general rule of thumb in terms of what the proportion of budget is spent on experiential. We work with clients on an individual project-by-project basis, though other brands, such as Nokia, have a set portion that always goes to experiential marketing. Budgets are increasing. We work with Unilever, Electrolux, the big banks, Samsung, and more – all of them have increased their budgets over the last few years. In terms of what they spend with us, they have at least doubled in the last couple of years. There's also more scope for revenue for agencies like us; we are the lead agency for the Unilever deodorant project. Specifically in terms of channels, a big component of what we do is digital or we guide the media, working with the media agency. More and more clients are looking to their media agencies and asking them to allocate money to experiential marketing without knowing what it costs. We create branded experiences that people choose to engage with in any interactive medium, such as digital, mobile or live.

SP: I believe that they are changing. It's hard to measure though. The traditional mediums have measurement tools, but in experiential you can't measure what your competitors are doing. In regard to our clients, there has been a 25 to 35 per cent shift from traditional to non-traditional media in a 24–36 month period.

IW: It's no secret that companies are dedicating more resources to live marketing in all its forms, from internal to external on the internal side, in response to a skills gap that many developed countries are facing, and a need to retain and motivate their staff. There's also been a shift in talent from traditional media to experiential marketing. Classic examples include the Peter Cowey move within Fitch from advertising to live medium. It will be interesting to find out his next appointment. More interestingly, Larry Deutch recently moved from Ogilvy in the United States to Jack Morton Worldwide. This move is particularly noteworthy because Deutch was working on the experiential side of Ogilvy. He wanted to move to a company that specialized in experiential. Furthermore, experiential activity is increasingly forming a focus of marketing campaigns from which other disciplines such as DM and digital are spinning off.

PE: It all depends how far up the organizational food chain your client is. Some clients have an allocated budget for experiential (clients that spend more than 2 million pounds per year). With clients that spend

100,000 or 200,000 per year, it's unclear where the budget came from. It's still rare to deal with marketing directors; most are still dealing with brand managers or events teams. Procurement is signing the deals. Signing deals with multi-brand clients is the future, and historically it's been very tactical. People will start doing it through procurement and then becoming the 'official preferred supplier'. Changes include predicting the majority of turnover for the year, not just as and when stuff comes in. The knock-on effect of this is that only the strongest agency will survive. Roster, etc, will make it harder for smaller agencies. This will lead to more mergers and acquisitions, and consolidation.

Is experiential marketing effective across different sectors?

DP: From pharmaceutical to automobile and packaged goods, it has to be executed effectively for the audience, but yes, it is effective.

RN: Yes. Because, if you involve people emotionally, intellectually and physically – this is something you want, no matter what product you have. You are going to make an impression on people and move them further down the sales tunnel.

EH: I believe yes, if done appropriately. No matter whether you're in the business of widgets or software, it's the most effective methodology out there. Especially all this talk about dollars, especially in the recession in the United States. Even a brand like Wal-Mart who are subject to great commoditization says 'Save money, live better' instead of what it used to say, which was just 'Save money'. It's about what they are going to do for the consumer in terms of experience. It's a major shift in how they speak with their consumers, to shift from saving money to focusing on the customer experience in a Wal-Mart.

KJ: Yes, absolutely. I don't know of a sector where we wouldn't be able to do something (at Jack Morton), eg B2B, consumer, stakeholders, shareholders, etc.

JS: Yes, absolutely. It's a philosophy, relating to any brand or target audience. People appreciate experiences that are targeted towards them. Five years ago it was mainly used to target youth-based brands, but that's no longer the case.

SP: Yes. It is definitely effective across any brand.

IW: Due to the flexible nature of experiential marketing, I'd have to say yes.

PE: Interestingly, most of the business is FMCG (low-ticket items), food and drink, etc. On paper, you would think brands that are big-ticket items would be more into it, because there's more space to demo features and benefits. Also, the cost of acquisition, ie if you were selling a car it would be more cost-effective. It's therefore easier to justify the fact that it costs, for example, £1.50 per consumer when then they go on to buy an expensive vehicle. Maybe it's different for other agencies and their clients.

What are the pros and cons for a brand to outsource or keep an experiential campaign in-house?

DP: Experiential agencies have the experience, they bring to the process a route map of how to miss all the missiles, they know what tools and skill sets you need, they know how to activate an audience. The potential downside is that if it is not connected with the brand in an intrinsic way, then it becomes insincere and inauthentic.

RN: It's fine to do it in-house if your internal resources have the expertise and the depth of resources to do it. Most companies find themselves in a position where they don't have the internal resources to develop it, or they become too inbred either creatively or otherwise and need an outside view. This is especially relevant in challenging economic times where they might want to keep their internal headcount lean. One other advantage in turning to outside practitioners is that they are continually exposed to ideas and fresh thinking, and constantly exposed to things that are going on across the board.

EH: No brand should ever do their own marketing internally; they are too close to the brand to be objective. There always needs to be a third party, because if you work for a brand day in and day out then you loose objectivity. If you have problems in life you bring in a friend; if you have a problem in business you bring in a consultant. You cannot see it from an external perspective because you are way too close to it. There should be a position inside the company called an experiential marketing manager or department who manages the relationship between the agency and the brand.

KJ: Experiential marketing is just like any other marketing in some respects. You have brands and clients who try and cobble together their own team, and others who say they need an agency to do it for them. The beauty of an agency is that they tend to be very experienced. One of my old bosses said that the agencies are like bees that pollinate ideas. They work with so many different clients and environments, and they understand the relationship and leverage for the good of the client. This is why you employ an agency of any type.

JS: I'm not sure, but it's a natural evolution. Look at clients that brought advertising in-house. Clients actively outsource it now so it will be the same. It's very hard for people inside a brand to see best practice across the board. If you want to save money then bring it in-house, but you might not get the best results. A specialist is needed. Customer experience management is something that should be brought in-house also, because it's important to maintain this throughout the whole organization.

SP: The age-old saying of 'You need to use experts in their field' is true. You need a lot more experience. Experiential companies can work on any brand and still have a project team, an infrastructure, that can focus on the cause. With in-house the skill set is wrong. It's simply not high enough. It's like when clients bring advertising in-house, they outsource again later on. To do real experiential, not just promotional marketing, you need to outsource because the creative process requires more, such as art directors, etc.

IW: Deutch was quoted as saying businesses are moving away from being attracted to integrated agencies, seeing a need for specific talent that relates to each discipline. The key factor of experiential is that it is very difficult for an agency to simply add it to their spread of expertise, because experiential requires not only creative, but also logistical and organizational skills that are generally only found amongst individuals who have direct experience organizing events. Although companies often have internal marketing teams, and occasionally specific event organizing teams, they rarely combine the two disciplines.

PE: It's about expertise; from venue strategies to understanding the idiosyncrasies, logistics, production, insurance, staffing, recruitment and training. It's all about specialist training now, and it's taken us 14 years to build what we see as a suitable infrastructure. It's not something that someone can do instantly. That's another difference between this and other mediums. With a poster or an ad it's an idea, but then it doesn't require a similar level of management once it goes live. There is a much more sophisticated level of infrastructure required to make things go smoothly. This is even good protection against agencies that come in and want to become this type of agency overnight. Speciality staffing databases can't be built overnight.

How should creatives come up with the big idea (the live brand experience)?

DP: Again our approach is a story-telling approach at the heart of everything we are talking about. We are trying to tell a compelling story; we approach it from a theatrical perspective. Write the right script; produce the right show for the right audience. Some people come up to us and want us to have a tactical perspective, such as 'bring our numbers up'. What they should do is say 'What is our story, how will we tell it effectively and therefore how will we execute that?'

RN: This is an excellent question, because most people start in the opposite of the right place: they start by thinking about the product. The first place to look at is the target audience, who they are, what their persona is, what are their key wants, desires, visions. Then you look the qualities or unique things about the product, you look to match them up. Then you have the material that you need to start brainstorming creative ideas. You need to thoroughly understand the target audience.

KJ: Well, to go back to an earlier point about budgets, there was a time when experiential was based on a creative, wacky 'let's just do this' method. Now creative has to be based on audience insight. It's no different to a TV campaign: understand the audience through planning, research, audience insight and creative platform, and translate it to creative wow.

JS: There are numerous models. There should be individual people who are responsible for this such as creative directors. We work collaboratively, but there are numerous methods, such as brainstorming. We think holistically about people. We think about what the target audience enjoys and what they're into rather than their media habits.

SP: The LORERIES are the South African Creative and Advertising Awards, and I head up their experiential ideas. When we measure creativity, we put the ideas up and they are ranked from 1 to 10. That's how we measure creativity on experiential.

IW: As in every single marketing campaign, it is essential to carry out extensive research before the creative process event starts and the main key areas are objectives, and audience. We have said before creativity alone will not produce a viable experiential campaign.

PE: We get an in-depth understanding of the brand and the brand cues, then we try our best to come up with something that brings that to life, making it clear what product it is. With Crofts we wanted to educate consumers about 'the drinking occasion', changing perceptions of when alcohol should be consumed – moving it from a brand that people assumed was drunk occasionally (ie Christmas) to a drink that can be chilled over a summer evening. So we created an experiential environment Croft spot, hired a famous designer-gardener to create an area which we placed at places like Hampton Court, and then a scaled-down version which we took to places like Fireworks in the Park. It was a relaxing environment where consumers could enjoy it, and sample the product. It's not a product-oriented event, it's an emotional experience. That's the type of thinking that would go into most campaigns.

What's most important when planning experiential marketing?

DP: First and foremost today is utmost respect for the audience, who they are and what motivates them. Be respectful of their time in delivering that experience. A brand has a personality just like everyone on this planet; you have to be respectful of the brand story so that it's authentic. Otherwise, it is just tactical.

RN: There are a number of things; first, I want to reiterate understanding the target audience. Probably equally important is be very clear on your objectives. Also take into account the resources – what are you going to have available to execute this? People come to us and say we want the best programme ever, but they have a tiny budget. At the end of the day the two don't go together. Also be realistic of the timeline.

EH: Make sure first and foremost that you set up the proper metrics and proper objectives, make sure that the client buys into it and that they are very clear and not subject to change. State that we are going to measure it by x.

JS: The most important thing when planning is an audit: consumer, product, retail, getting relevant information and being able to derive the right insights that will drive the strategy. We have got planners who are from a traditional agency background and it can be quite similar.

SP: It's a process. The big idea always has to come across.

IW: A key part of the planning process is making sure that every aspect of the experiential activity matches both objectives and is also effective with the target audience. Key elements would include engaging content, venue or location of the activity, and appropriate methods of delivery. If all elements can be satisfied, you will be well on the way to planning a successful campaign.

PE: Considering the consumers' mindset is important, and also the relationship between volume expectations from the client against the depth of the experience. Remember your consumer profile in detail.

What's important about the situation and background of a brand when they approach you for experiential marketing?

DP: We use a softer language. When I talk about the brand story, it's an understanding of the brand objectives and what they have been doing.

If you copy what BMW does, it will not work because the experiential campaign was designed to be relevant to BMW. If a new technology is brought in and used incorrectly, people do not say 'I didn't use it right', they say 'It doesn't work'. People are very critical in the United States.

RN: The key things we look for about the situation of a brand are: what do people think of it currently? What is the competitive landscape, how do they position themselves? Also, is the brand authentic? It has to be real, you have to say what the brand really is. We do an analysis of these things; we will definitely get into the perception, the competitive landscape and the market share too.

KJ: Situation analysis is very important in its entirety in the experiential context. In an experiential planning model, the brand/company journey runs parallel to the consumer/internal journey.

JS: Again it depends on the brand. Some brands are suffering with cut-through and engagement, or if you have a product in a low-interest category, this might cause an opportunity to engage. We will do a situation analysis, and we also get briefs. Most clients don't look to their experiential agency to undertake situation analysis in terms of a broader strategy. We work with some clients across their whole organization, looking at all experiential touch points.

SP: We have a strategist on our team. We look at what the client has done, and we also look at their competitors. We access their adverts and advertorial, we analyse them and their competitors, and then come up with the concept in line with the client's marketing strategy. That's why it's not just promotion. It's more strategic.

IW: It's essential, because experiential is all about experience as a result of any preconceptions that the audience may have. Often the aim of experiential campaigns is to actually change perceptions, or develop perception of the brand.

What role should live brand experiences play in the overall marketing communication strategy?

DP: It should play a much bigger role than it's currently playing today. It is at the heart of who you are and what you deliver; it needs to be in-depth across every channel. It should not be a tactical afterthought or add on. When Volvo launched the XC70 in the UK, the tagline was 'Life: Live Better Together' – all about people doing things together. We created an experience where the whole movie theatre moved the car together by moving at the same time in seats, the only way to play the game was to do it together, bringing the message to life. People said it was cool because the experience was relevant to the brand message.

RN: I think that it's important to make everything that you can as experiential as possible. When you think about the various ways that you are going to touch people, you want to create experiences in as many ways as possible. Therefore, the theming of your media, DM, live events is the same.

  This is an area where very creative agencies or clients sometimes fail because they get bored of doing the same things. It's the constant reinforcement that works, to connect with the potential customers.

JS: It depends on the brand, the situation, and the brief. It shouldn't be preached to all clients and sometimes it isn't relevant to the brief.

SP: If brands don't include it in their strategies today, they will have a big threat from competitors in their category. Experiential must be part of the overall strategy. It is vital.

What should marketers think about when deciding on experiential objectives?

DP: They should think about what impact it's going to have on the audience. We create a report card about the audience, including things like 'Is it going to tell my story in a positive way?' Is there some kind of measurement (doesn't have to be financial) so that at the end of this you can say it was or wasn't successful?

RN: You want to think about a couple of different types of objectives. Think about soft objectives like, did we create a buzz? Were people excited about it?

You can measure these things by surveying people and getting answers to questions, you can design questions to capture the emotional response. Then you also need to measure the business result by doing market studies that track purchase or questions such as 'How has this experience influenced the likelihood that you will buy this product?' Questions that say are they going to take action, as well as softer questions. Think of what type of results you want to see out of it before implementing it, so that you can put these measurements in place to allow you to demonstrate the value of these campaigns to stakeholders.

EH. They should think about sales, that's obvious, to build a programme that is sustainable and wrapped around one big idea. That one big idea will manifest itself across different media. Once you have reached the maximum point of sales then it's all about getting people to continue perceiving the brand in the way that they already do.

KJ: I think this is a real point of difference. There is real opportunity for marketers to be smart about where experiential objectives are. You can quantify down to how many leads it generated, what was the word-of-mouth generated, but they must have a very short, focused list of three objectives that are quantifiable. Experiential could step up to the plate and deliver similarly to DM. You can measure what we did.

JS: Experiential marketing today is looked at by clients and brands as a channel in the broader communications mix. If that's someone like Nokia, this might be to get the handsets into consumers' hands so that they are exposed to the functionality of the handset. There are broader opportunities which are more holistic. Brand experience should be managed across the whole organization. Every company should have CEM happening across their organizations, and if you really want to develop relationships with consumers, then you need to orchestrate the touch points that consumers have with their brand throughout the experience.

SP: You can't be all things to all people. You need a single-minded message. What is the product and who is buying the service. Clear goals. All campaigns are quite different, so it's good to know exactly what a client wants to achieve.

IW: I think experiential can be used to deliver on more objectives than any other single discipline. There is a tendency to perhaps set too many objectives due to the flexibility of live marketing, but focusing on no more than three is the key to delivering a successful campaign.

Every single experiential campaign should these days have an element of data capture because the information produced is invaluable and the technology is now available to delivery. It is particularly useful because every single experiential campaign should aim to deliver value, not only to the target audience, but also to the client.

There is a campaign by Haygarth which used classic live activity integrated within a digital mobile technology to deliver a truly interactive campaign with huge amounts of data.

'Rock up and play' for Nokia was basically when they were trying to reach the under-24 age group, and they found the best way to do this was to use festivals and music events.

PE: Short-term vs long-term. Is it just about trying to drive sales at the cost of the experience, or is it about changing people's long-term perceptions? Think about the length of time you want to commit to with your experiential agency. Measure changes over time. Don't appoint an agency for three months and expect to achieve long-term objectives.

Is experiential marketing especially effective for specific target audiences?

DP: It's hugely effective for all target audiences: my 70-year old mother will get equally excited about an experience as my 7-year old daughter.

The great thing about experiences is that they are not culturally or economically limited. I can be rich or poor and enjoy an experience. I can be Catholic or Muslim. They transcend all the traditional limitations.

RN: That's another interesting question. It's effective for all audiences, but the form it takes will differ depending on the audience. You will create a different experience for, say, young consumers than, for example, doctors. Even if you are appealing to both doctors and nurses, the experience for the nurses will be different than for the doctor's because what is emotionally impacting will be different to the two groups within one market.

KJ: Yes, absolutely. Even with the great things that people are doing with seeding brands, and seeding with hard-to-reach groups, it's experiential that can change people's beliefs. I'm not saying that experiential is the answer to every problem, though maybe it is with all those tough audience groups such as youth and high net worth individuals. It's experiential that will change those people's beliefs.

SP: You have to know who they are because the campaign will vary. What is effective for one target market is not necessarily going to be effective for another. You must design something specific to that market.

IW: Experiential can work across a variety of different audiences but it can be especially effective at reaching those who are harder to engage with, such as the 18 to 24 age group. Once again, it depends on creating the right experience for the right people.

PE: We did a survey on that last year. Older people are relatively less open-minded about participating. Youths are always willing to participate as long as the activity is credible. More important is the profile of the person – is the activity in relation to the environment that you're doing it? If you're at a festival they are there to enjoy themselves, so don't try and sell them a credit card. If you were at an airport then maybe a credit card is more interesting than doing nothing.

Is there an experiential marketing mix, and if so what is it?

DP: I don't think there is, everything should be reinvented. Because the experiential marketing programme needs to match who you are as a brand, each brand should look at the set of tools available to them based on who they are and who their audience is.

RN: You should be as experiential as possible across all of the marketing mix. As much as you can, try and connect emotionally, physically and intellectually; it's about looking for ways to experientialize all elements as much as possible.

EH: The mix is bringing the brand together; it's spending the client's money where the audience is. That's the mix. If the audience is online, go heavy online. I see ads sometimes and think, there's no chance that the audience is in the place I saw the ad.

KJ: Look at what we at Jack Morton call a 'touch point map'. Where does the consumer come into contact with the brand, and what is it that we can do experientially to support those touch points? They can record the totality of a brand's interaction when, for example, a consumer buys an airline ticket. Getting on the flight can be a touch point journey, or we might have to communicate with employees about a new company direction. The touch point audit is an interesting way to look at it.

JS: It depends on if it's seen as a channel or as an approach.

SP: I do think that it depends on the campaign. We would include radio, TV, print and all the mediums. It must be carefully designed so that one drives you into the next. For example, the TV drives you to the mall, the mall drives you online, and then online drives you to the store.

IW: It all depends how broadly you want to view experiential. If experiential is a technique, then every marketing discipline should try and embrace the experiential concept which can bring the target audience closer to the campaign, such as building interactive elements into a DM campaign. If you look at it as a technique, then it could be argued that this is how every other discipline should aspire to be like.

PE: It's a specialist service, so that's a dangerous outlook from the perspective of an experiential marketing practitioner. Maybe from a marketer's view that's OK. From an experiential point of view we need to specialize; we must be in a specific box, otherwise you compete with people like large communications agencies for business, and you will never win. Experiential marketing is one channel.

Why integrate amplification channels?

DP: That's where the experience conversation comes in. If I do something at events or something at retail, but it's not integral to who I am, they may enjoy the tactic but they don't connect with my brand. Once you start talking integration, you need to deliver that message across every single thing you do. If we are the car dealership that is friendly, then everything we do needs to be friendly, from the sales people to the website and the ads.

I have many choices as a consumer and the minute you let me down as brand I can go to another brand. Also as a consumer I have instant communication ability with the world, I can tell everyone about it from numerous different means of communication and technology.

EH: Again, it is about the great idea, and that idea will manifest itself differently across all media.

KJ: I think clients are doing that for themselves. Both within agency networks, or even independent agencies, clients are saying 'I don't care who's coming up with the idea, or even how you deliver it, but here's the objective – how do you deliver it?' It doesn't matter whether it's an ATL, experiential, DM or brand ambassador amplifier programme. The client is the leader or conductor, in that more and more we are working with other marketing disciplines across multiple agencies.

JS: From a messaging perspective, if you can have one consistent message to your market, it is best practice. Again it doesn't matter what the channel is, it's always good to integrate. It's part of a total message that a brand is communicating.

SP: You cannot look at one thing in isolation. That's how successful marketing works; every channel is entrenched. You just use a variety of integrated mediums, especially as a big brand. It's not an easy process, but if you understand the strategy well enough, and you understand what the client wants to achieve, with good strategy and creatives you can then implement in line with the overall plan.

IW: It's dangerous to assume that every campaign needs an experiential element because then there is a danger that it will be carried out gratuitously. However, if after analysing the audience and objectives experiential is chosen as the right way to deliver a campaign, it would make sense to base it at the core of the campaign because of its cross-disciplinary nature. Once the form of the experiential campaign has been planned, other disciplines can be looked at with respect to how best they can support and enhance the core strategy, such as building in a digital or DM element. Other elements can spin off the core element.

PE: You should be integrated where possible. The reason is that you make the most effective use of the live space and broadcast. My favourite experience is a campaign called 'Living by the book' by BT. There was a new phonebook being launched, and if you had this book you could live your life by it. They found some live space, and they created a Perspex box. They also ran radio promotions which gave it broadcast elements. People were offered a chance to live in the box with £1,000, the book and a phone. Then, rather than getting just the people who passed the site, they got 22 million exposures. What a great opportunity to take a boring product and make it an exciting experience. By using other media in an integrated way you make it massive. They got lots of PR as a result as well.

What is the importance of brand ambassadors in live brand experiences?

DP: Utmost importance because what makes me connect to the brand is the person with it. Everyone under your employment is your brand ambassador. When you are staffing your company you should think,

'Is this person a brand ambassador?' We have all been to a restaurant where a mediocre food experience is fantastic because of the people serving and greeting you.

RN: They are critically important because people relate to other people, and they experience those people as your brand – this is another mistake that I see clients make. They think 'I can go to this agency and get college students or stay-at-home people who will come and work as temps' – you are taking pot luck, some may be great and some may be miserable. You save $2 but you can do untold damage because people are representing your brand. We look for people who are professional, who relate well with the target audience and are capable of communicating the company's message.

Sometimes programmes fail and they (clients) don't realize it because that's how they staffed it. A brand ambassador is the living embodiment of how a brand represents itself. In the mind of the target audience, the experience they have with the staff reflects on the brand; they need to have all those characteristics because that is the overall experience with the brands.

EH: You can have the best strategy in the world and if the brand ambassadors do not represent the brand then you flush the money down the toilet. It really boils down to something that I found out, that we hire people not CVs. I hire people who have relevant experience but it is not all about the résumé.

KJ: I think that whatever you call them, brand amplifiers are about how experiential marketing drives word-of-mouth. While only a certain number of people can experience the experiential campaign, it's the word-of-mouth that will drive the large numbers, resulting in a significant number of people being exposed to it. Brand ambassadors are all crucial in the word-of-mouth programme.

JS: In terms of live experiential marketing where you are physically engaging people in the real world, they offer a human face. For some brands, especially Telco, it's a great way to humanize the brand. It offers flexibility of message, so whatever people ask, there is a specific response that a brand can give instantly, while in other communications the message is not responsive or flexible.

SP: Depending on the campaign, brand ambassadors are a vital part. They must be trained correctly, understand the brand, and understand the objectives. They are a major cog in your experiential wheel.

IW: Brand ambassadors are key, as they create an important human element with which to communicate with the target audience and can significantly boost engagement levels. It is vital that brand ambassadors are well briefed and trained, otherwise they can undermine any experiential activity.

PE: Hugely important. You could do the best planning, creative, etc, then if the person who has the final interaction with the consumer is poorly briefed, off brand, or doesn't create a positive interaction, it is pointless. It's all about the personal touch with human beings. That's the biggest risk the sector faces, employing a sub-standard staffing agency which doesn't select, train or pay staff well enough. The barriers to entry to starting a staffing agency aren't big enough. Many brands have been bitten by that and are starting to use credible, sophisticated staffing agencies.

Scrutinize the agency in terms of their recruitment agency. Do they distinguish between booking and recruitment? How up to date are their records and employment laws? What training programmes do they have in place? Are they operating legally regarding taxation on staff? Can you get references with staff in the field? How long have they been working with their clients? What do industry forums say about that agency? How regularly and on time do they pay their staff, and at what rates? How do they motivate them? How do they train event mangers? There should be generic training, and each job should be training face to face if possible. If not, there should still be remote training.

What are the pros and cons of placing live brand experiences in different locations and environments?

DP: The first factor in choosing is the target audience; is my target audience there? Is it so far away from where they can actually experience the product and brand that the memory is lost between store and location of the event?

RN: This is very similar to the approach with different target audiences. It's not so much that there are pros and cons to the different locations, it's that they have to be treated differently.

There has to be an appropriate level of engagement and it cannot be overly intrusive. In an exhibit or store you can be more aggressive with it because people expect that in that environment. On a shopping street people aren't looking for people to come up to them; in those environments it has to be very attractive but not aggressive or intrusive. It's about changing the approach depending on the location or environment.

EH: An agency can miss the mark and come off as being non-authentic or having relevant meaning to the brand by choosing the wrong environment.

If all goes well in the media, it is signed off and it is done, live events are fluid and you deal with a lot of people and things go wrong. You need a contingency plan for everything and there need to be fail-safes for every individual element of the campaign. If it goes horribly wrong, it lacks appropriate planning.

KJ: I would have to answer that with the Jack Morton 'flawless, faultless' delivery mantra. If the experience is about the brand, if your actions say more about your brand than your words, then the experience has to be superb. That's why we are obsessive about delivery. It's not like a TV commercial where you can reach out to 34 markets around the world with the same ad. An experience has to be delivered within the confines of the facilities that you're working in, so we are driven by our flawless, faultless delivery because we don't allow it to go wrong. This is vital.

JS: It's primarily about logistical issues. With live marketing in an uncontrolled environment you must have weather contingencies.

SP: A brand often says 'It's expensive to talk with low numbers', but reach is very important to clients who are used to reaching people in large numbers through adverts. In regard to different locations, if executed well, it has to be an interaction and not an interruption. The campaign has to be skilfully created and carefully designed so that it interacts successfully with the consumers, in any one of those environments.

IW: Used appropriately, experiential can be effective in any environment, from classic product sampling in retail locations through to a business conference. Location is always vital.

PE: Top-end grocers are great because they are by the POS. People are in shopping mode. If FMCG were in shopping malls, the same could be applied. Additionally, people are potentially more in leisure mode and have more of a time frame to talk to people. Brands that require more in-depth description would be perfect, for example technology brands. Other environments are good because of volume, such as train stations. Things that require basic communication such as sampling would be good for this. Offices are very expensive in terms of cost per contact, but highly impactful and valuable (though logistically difficult). Festivals have a specific target audience, but it has to be a more impacting experience. Also, it's not near a POS, so sales are irrelevant unless it's drink or food. But there is a big plus in terms of gaining credibility.

What do you think about measuring and evaluating experiential marketing campaigns?

DP: You absolutely have to, but we have to understand that they have to be measured differently from traditional campaigns. We shouldn't let our fear of measurement prevent us from doing these programmes. Television ads have a cost per thousand; but I am not creating a real impact so much as esoteric awareness.

What we should do as an industry is figure out a standard measurement system. Something needs to happen because each agency creates different metrics and they are not aligned between providers of different parts of experiential marketing. We need to learn from the positive aspects of television measurement such as Neilson, because on the positive side, buyers like that security of comparison. At the moment the buyers don't know how to compare our measurements.

RN: It's very important to ensure you formulate your metrics at the beginning of the planning process. Some people wait until they are well into the planning process but you need to have them upfront. And then you can say 'is this going to help me achieve my objectives?' If it's not, let's change the course of action in the plan to something else that *is* going to achieve the objectives.

EH: With live there are a myriad of techniques. If the client wants to drive purchase then we measure sales. If I'm looking to change perception then that's the programme we build. I tend to break stuff down to the lowest level: what is the purpose of the programme?

KJ: Every client, every brand, and every product has to measure the effectiveness of their programmes. Jack Morton has spent the last 14 months developing their proprietary measurement tool, which is called Engage. It's unique and makes a real difference. You need to predict outcomes. I mean, look at TV; you can run an ad at a certain time and know how many people are going to see it, and clients need that confidence. Justify expenditure; that's the world in which we live.

JS: This is a hot topic. There are various levels of measurement and evaluation. We have to get really good at establishing objectives and KPIs. In terms of measurement we would measure on a number of levels. If there is an experience at the point of retail you can track sales and scores in terms of the objectives.

An example is the Electrolux campaign in shopping malls. We tracked key scores because what they were trying to do was (they had just launched cooking products) get them to believe that they had good cooking credentials despite the background in vacuum cleaners. We tracked various shifts in key brands scores, ie 'Do you believe that Electrolux has good credentials in cooking products?' We also generated measurable sales leads. But was what great was that we had measurable results on brand perception that showed shifts. This can happen instantly, not just long term. It's part of the power and appeal of brand experience. We do a lot of music festivals for Nokia, and in post-event research we have tangible shifts in consideration of purchase. This is independent research.

SP: We haven't found definitive ways to measure. There are a few things that we can measure; how many people arrive, how many interactions, and how many calls to action. We haven't found a definitive easy way to measure similarly with television.

IW: Measuring and evaluating experiential campaigns is often said to be very difficult. Indicators and strategy must be worked out from the start. Evaluation is as important as creativity, logistics and organization.

Should marketers expect good ROI from experiential marketing campaigns?

DP: Absolutely, but they should see it as return on expectations, because right now the word 'investment' refers to dollar for dollar return. Not everything should directly be measured financially on that basis.

Again an example: when we did the Volvo experience, we knew it was a $60,000 car. Can you measure by people buying the car? We looked at media mentions, how bloggers responded to it, people in the audience, we talked to the audience after the movie. We did things so that the client could look at what happened and say 'that really kicked ass' and they loved what we were doing.

RN: Absolutely but with a caveat: people use the term ROI very loosely. It is really an accounting term saying how much money I get back for the money spend. It is impossible to do that accurately for any element of the marketing mix, because there are too many elements that influence the sale.

If you go to an exhibition and they bought the products, how can you definitely attribute that sale to the exhibition? They may have seen an advert on the way or receive a recommendation.

You have to try and measure value – sometimes it's immediate and translates into sales; other times it's less instant, like awareness or brand perception. It should accomplish something in the sales pipeline, either increasing awareness or moving people towards a preference.

EH: Taking into consideration the lifetime value of the customer, then the only way to engage them for long periods of time is through experiential marketing. You get a higher CLV (customer lifetime value). It's going to make them want to keep coming back for more.

KJ: Yes, because experiential is not just the 2,000 or the 40,000 that see the thing. The numbers we've got is that that 40,000 tell 17.5 people and then that group tells a further 1.65.

Say we've got 40,000 who experience the experiential campaign. They tell 17.5 people on average; that's 700,000 people. They then tell another 1.65 in a second wave, which is 1,155,000. So, in two waves, your 40,000 is multiplied. That's only two steps. That's the passion and engagement that experiential evokes. Those are the industry numbers. That's the ROI moving that number of people.

JS: Yes. If you're not expecting good returns, why do it? There's always a learning curve if you're a brand newly entering the discipline, so learn on the job. Advertising has been here for decades and lots of clients still don't know which of the ad channels works and which don't.

SP: Yes. If it's cleverly crafted, and the campaign is executed by a professional experiential marketing agency, they will get a brilliant return. It cannot just be placing individuals in a location to hand out products.

IW: Arguably, experiential campaigns can not only deliver effective ROI, but should also be able to measure in detail the key areas where the return has been generated. Return on investment is about measuring effectiveness, and how this is calculated is personal between agency and client. The actual means by which it's measured is immaterial.

PE: Every campaign should have some KPIs in terms of expected reach, interactions, OTS, data capture, voucher redemptions, instant sales if appropriate, hits to website, staff compliance, samples distributed and third-party evaluation or research. A company should evaluate things like changing brand perception, and have a budget to measure over time.

The industry still doesn't have a magic number at the end of it. You are painting a picture of all the things that you are expecting to change. I don't believe the other mediums do that either. It's hard to attribute success specifically to the experiential, because the cost of the other mediums is much higher. It's also harder to know where the regulars came from.

Anything else you want to say on experiential marketing?

DP: There is nothing better than watching people enjoying a great experience. Brands adding fun to people's lives makes this world a better place.

RN: People fall in love with the creative side and the fun of the experience and the edginess or the excitement. That's all well and good but you can't do that to the exclusion of looking for positive business results.

It has to be directed at moving the target audience closer to achieving sales and achieving a business result. Otherwise it doesn't matter how great the creative idea, it was a waste of time and money for the company.

EH: Yes, live events are a great place for experiential, but not all live events are experiential, about connected meaning and relevance for the brand. Make sure yours is.

KJ: It will kick the ass of any other discipline. What I want to say is that it's sort of common sense. You would never go to a plumber from an ad rather than a recommendation. Look at Expedia, or eBay. You go onto the votes and reviews and you see what other people have done with it. Word-of-mouth, word-of-mouth, word-of-mouth. There's some great marketing through ads, but experiential fuels conversation, person-to-person.

Even TV like 'Lost', 'Dexter', etc is all about word-of-mouth. My personal opinion is that even kids are saying it's an advert. They're trying to sell us something. If you're 35 and under you've grown up discounting ads, because the whole cult of youth marketing, the guys that started it were 16, and now they're 35 they're still discounting them. Part of your own personal growth as a teenager is to find the brands you like; you want your mates to tell you 'go there'. That's why Playstation spends so much on skate parks, because the attributes of the brand match the attributes of the activity.

If you're a client and you go to an ad agency you get advertising; if you go to a fish shop you get fish. They won't say the meat at the butcher down the road is great. We, as experiential practitioners, can only do it through proof points. At Nike and Playstation, they've got that. Enough brands are doing it. Nobody wants to do it first. It's still working, it's still delivering.

JS: It's definitely an area that more and more people are extremely passionate about. From a client perspective, the response that we get from a consumer instantly is great and refreshing. It's great that it's professionalizing the medium. We are very strategic, and coming to an area that is traditionally executed, it's great that it's starting to gain a seat at the table and becoming more planned.

SP: Just do it!

16 International case studies

The agency: VIP Ideas

The country: Ireland
The brand: Danone Essensis

The brief

When Danone set out to launch its new Essensis brand, the first ever mainstream dairy product formulated to nourish one's skin from within, it required a commercial launch like no other. The launch team was formed of one of the top PR agencies in Dublin (Kennedy PR), an action marketing and experiential marketing agency (VIP Ideas), and one of most respected event design companies in Dublin (Catapult).

It was set to be one of the most successful commercial launches ever to happen in Ireland, an explosion of ideas, media coverage and interactive and experiential marketing concepts. Danone Essensis Beauty Bar was a live brand experience at the core of the commercial launch strategy of Danone Essensis in Ireland.

The aims were:

- to communicate the message to consumers that Essensis was a fresh dairy product designed to nourish the skin from the inside;
- to promote to women that within six weeks of daily consumption you could find a noticeable improvement in your skin's health;
- to allow consumers to taste the Essensis range of drinks.

The live brand experience

To bring to life the product, a specially designed set allowed luxury pampering experiences to be given to every woman entering the zone. VIP Ideas implemented and coordinated the features that were included within the zone and liaised with Centre management and retailers within the shopping mall to create a hugely successful launch.

On arriving at the custom-built Beauty Bar, the public were greeted by Danone Essensis brand ambassadors and offered a complimentary sample of Essensis. Visitors to the zone were invited to book in with a Danone Essensis consultant at the custom-built Beauty Bar to have a luxury treatment with one of 16 beauty therapists and consultants and to avail themselves of the many complimentary treatments, ranging from mini-manicures to nail care, hand treatments and make-up applications or massage.

The Danone Essensis 'celebrity expert area' was also set up, providing participants with expert advice from top beauty, hair and fashion consultants on site over the three days to provide hints and tips.

The amplification channels

POS and in-store promotions invited shoppers to sample the product and invitations for female shoppers to attend the Danone Beauty Bar were distributed within the shopping centre. Live radio competitions and Danone Hamper giveaways offered consumers a chance to win fantastic Danone prizes and pampering gifts from Dundrum retailers.

Dundrum TV ads ran during the promotion, promoting the new product and the live brand experience, featuring the large POS stands positioned around the malls. The ads invited women to come and experience the Danone Beauty Bar.

The results

Around 10,000 guests received free beauty treatments during each weekend of the live brand experience.

Testimonial

Damian Hughes, Senior Brand Manager, Danone Ireland:

> The experience was one of the key launch pillars for the brand and helped to cement its place in both the beauty and nutrition worlds. Visitors to the Danone Essensis Beauty Bar had the opportunity to taste the product, experience an array of mini beauty treatments and request advice from an

on-hand team of expert advisers. The experience exceeded my expectations and delighted the public.

The agency: Blazinstar Experiential

The country: England
The brand: Gordon Ramsay's Cookalong LIVE

The brief

MandB, a strategic media agency approached Blazinstar Experiential on behalf of the British TV channel Channel 4, with a brief to engage supermarket shoppers in a creative way that encourages them to participate in a one-off live brand experience on Channel 4. 'Cookalong LIVE' was a live brand experience on Channel 4 that starred Gordon Ramsay, the renowned celebrity chef. Gordon challenged the British public to cook a three-course meal in one hour, from the comfort of their homes, while he showed them how to do it and cooked with them on live television. The show also featured TV screens on the set, which were broadcasting live from the homes of many of those participating.

On the day before the Cookalong LIVE, Blazinstar Experiential implemented a large-scale nationwide activity to support the live brand experience. The objective behind the activity was to encourage purchase of the required ingredients and to promote participation in the Cookalong LIVE, amplifying the live brand experience.

The activity

Staff Warehouse (Blazinstar Experiential's staffing division) provided 200 brand ambassadors who wore Gordon Ramsay masks and chef uniforms and became Gordon Ramsay clones. Each of the 'Gordons' who were positioned at 50 major supermarkets around the United Kingdom pretended that they were Gordon himself doing the food shopping for the following night's show.

Each Gordon had a wicker basket and was purchasing the required ingredients while engaging consumers by speaking in first person and inviting the supermarket shoppers to 'Cookalong LIVE with me tomorrow night'. The Gordons helped supermarket shoppers purchase the required ingredients that they needed to participate in the following night's live brand experience. They also gave out invitations that featured the Cookalong LIVE ingredients.

The amplification channels

Blazinstar Experiential played a key part in the integrated amplification of the TV-based live brand experience. Other amplification channels included TV ads, radio mentions, and intensive print advertising, all promoting the Cookalong LIVE.

The results

As a direct result, the main ingredients that were required for the tantalizing cooking challenge (including scallops and steak) sold out in an overwhelming number of supermarkets nationwide, following a reported 'shopping frenzy' in national newspapers.

Needless to say, the viewing figures that resulted were far above average, totalling 4.4 million viewers, which is unheard of for a Friday night slot. A first in interactive live brand experience TV for Channel 4, though judging by the success of Gordon's Cookalong and the enthused client feedback, it won't be the last.

The agency: 5ive Senses

The country: Australia
The brand: LG Viewty camera phone

The brief

LG appointed 5iveSenses Experiential to work with it in creating an experiential marketing campaign that would engage executives in premium office buildings in Sydney and Melbourne. The target audience for the phone was predominately affluent males.

The activity

The live brand experience was crafted around the idea of offering busy executives a free shoe shine whilst receiving a free demonstration of the phone and a chance to win a trip for two around the world by 'Viewing the World with Viewty'.

Peter Wales, business development manager at 5iveSenses, said it was the first time an experiential campaign had been conducted on such a scale in premium office towers, activating in 12 premium office towers in Sydney and Melbourne. 5ive Senses designed an experiential activation that offered the building owners, managers and tenants a value-add service that was relevant to their environment and space. Premium office towers are traditionally resistant to live brand experiences unless you offer a programme of relevance.

The amplification channels

5ive Senses worked with Inlink Elevator screen media to organize a comprehensive and integrated campaign that worked on a number of levels. Inlink negotiated the promotional space and ran both a branding campaign on the lift screens and a building-specific campaign to pre-promote each event. 5ive Senses also conducted a pre-promotion viral campaign by e-mailing the tenants in all the buildings to inform them of the LG Viewty shoe shine activation taking place in their workplace.

The results

Mr Wales said: 'The average amount of time these busy A/B executives spent with the LG Viewty phone was 5 minutes; you just can't buy that level of engagement using traditional media to target these time-poor executives.'

Throughout the activation 90 per cent of the LG Viewty phone demonstrations were to males, while 10 per cent were to females, making it a very efficient and targeted experiential activation. The results speak for themselves: over 47,100 business executives were reached in 385 companies across 12 buildings, resulting in 5,269 direct consumer connections and 2,375 5-minute shoe shines, each resulting in a five minute engagement with the LG Viewty mobile handset. The campaign was deemed a real success by all involved.

The agency: Out of the Blue Communications (OOTB)

The country: United Kingdom
The brand: (Unilever) Persil

The brief

To deliver widespread excitement about Persil's 'Dirt is Good' above-the-line campaign, drive additional exposure for the activity via a large-scale live brand experience and bring the advert to life with innovative ideas.

The activity

Out of the Blue formed a valuable partnership with the Forestry Commission to take Persil directly to the target audience, involving the first ever sponsorship property with the Forestry Commission.

Persil sponsored playgrounds in 15 UK parks. The sponsorship allowed OOTB to give the playgrounds a complete Persil makeover, and deliver key campaign messages to the target audience in a non-intrusive, sympathetic and genuinely credible way while the kids enjoyed themselves on the playground equipment.

The results

The activity targeted 650,000 children and 320,000 adults in 15 locations over a six-month period.

The agency: Onepartners Brand Experience Group

The country: Australia
The brand: Vodafone Australia

The brief

The brief was to help ensure that Vodafone live! 2.5G customers migrated to Vodafone's new 3G service rather than to competitors, whilst also attracting new customers. Because Vodafone had fewer customers and perceived credentials in the 3G market, the campaign needed to establish a greater emotional connection with the audience. The decision was made early on that an experiential marketing strategy was required to complement a very experiential-based product offering. People needed to 'experience' Vodafone live! with 3G for themselves as it was difficult to articulate what 3G was through traditional advertising. Vodafone wanted to get handsets into people's hands to get them talking about Vodafone live! with 3G.

The activity

The mobile 'play time' phenomenon was identified as a time when people were more likely to play with their mobile phones, usually during downtime moments. We all know them well, when you're waiting at a bus stop, or waiting for a friend in a pub. The engagement strategy was planned to target these moments of play time as a perfect opportunity to trial Vodafone live! with 3G.

Most of the younger target audience travel on public transport, high reach during peak commuter hours, and catching the bus and train most popular. However, there are currently no media opportunities that allow the required access to their 'down time', ie on the *real* bus or train platform. Therefore the perfect medium was created.

Two buses were 'stripped' with their interiors designed to form sets that reflected the vibrant red and white identity of Vodafone stores, including red upholstered seats and white shag pile cushions, complete with AV entertainment and PA systems. With 18 handset 'pods' fitted on board each bus, a free charter service was provided along major target hot spot commuter zones, offering a lift to work across the summer.

Weekends focused on recreational activities – beach, sport and music events and Vodafone sponsored assets. Participants were aided by brand ambassadors, who manned the exciting, interactive environment in which they stimulated and engaged participants. Other Vodafone collateral included 3G brochures and $100 off in-store vouchers to drive store traffic.

The amplification channels

A consumer promotion on radio was developed featuring Merrick and Rosso, who randomly called installed handsets on the buses, to encourage people to pick up and interact with them.

Airports are a rich environment to target business people and the more affluent early adopters. The member lounges offer a great opportunity to engage people with the product, with the average dwell time around 30 minutes. Once the lounges were identified as a connection point, an engagement strategy was developed centred on the provision of a full-time professional barista making espresso coffee. People who approached to get a free coffee were asked to watch a 30-second product demonstration first.

Many different, innovative and interactive experiences were developed from agency partners – from holograms to interactive audio walls. Other campaign components included radio partnerships, 15-second idents directly after the 'South Park' credits, and product placement on STV channels, which demonstrated Vodafone Live!'s content offerings.

The results

New live! customers increased 45 per cent on targets set, which had been based on other 3G launches across the global Vodafone network. The experiential marketing campaign represented the best 3G rollout to date.

Measurable results included 40,000 product demonstrations, 100,000 interactions and 8 million gross brand impressions. A senior economist at Macquarie Bank said:

the best thing about the bus was the fact that I was able to spend the entire duration of the journey playing with a Nokia 3G phone and understand the capabilities of Vodafone Live! Very cool and am now seriously thinking of upgrading. So, as a marketing technique, the bus ride was brilliant.

The campaign also won awards:

- Winner 2006 Media Federation of Australia Awards – Technology and Communications category.
- Finalist 2007 Cannes Media Lions.
- Westfield 'Most Outstanding Corporate Branded Display Experience'.
- Qantas 'Best use of promotional space'.
- Featured on Springwise.com.

The agency: Brand Experience Lab www.brandexperiencelab.org

The countries: United States and England
The brands: MSNBC and Volvo

The MSNBC brief

Brand Experience Lab was approached by MSNBC with a very common brand challenge, which was to bring online activities to life offline.

MSNBC Newsbreaker Live was designed to help enrich the MSNBC's consumer experience with compelling, original material. It hoped to reposition its brand and increase awareness of its internet strategy by using the AudienceGames platform.

The MSNBC activity

MSNBC.com liberated movie audiences from the out-of-date trivia, static billboards and impatience of waiting for summer blockbusters to begin with Newsbreakers Live, the first in-cinema, audience participatory game. It was modelled after classic video game favourites including Pong, Break Out and Arkanoid. As bricks broke, real-time headlines from MSNBC. com's RSS newsfeeds fell. The audience then accumulated points and knowledge by using their bodies to control the paddle and capture the headlines, and simultaneously keep the ball moving. Newsbreakers Live premiered at the Bridge: Cinema de Lux in Los Angeles during the opening weekend of 'Spiderman 3'. It continued to travel to the east as the opening act for major blockbusters including 'Harry Potter VII', 'Shrek the Third', 'Pirates of the Caribbean' and 'The Fantastic 4' throughout May, June and July.

The Volvo brief

Volvo commissioned Brand Experience Lab to create an original AudienceGame to emphasize their tagline, 'Life is better lived together'. Volvo wanted to extricate itself from a stuffy brand image and to promote its new XC70 vehicle as a roomy family car. To shift brand perception, Volvo sought out AudienceGames to create a dynamic approach.

The Volvo activity

Volvo took a different approach to the time and place in which audiences could experience the Volvo XC70 AudienceGame. On Saturday 13 October at 8:30 pm in 12 cities across the United Kingdom, cinemas were networked together to play against each other in real time – a world first. The Volvo XC70 is a rugged, all-wheel-drive, family estate car aimed at inspiring shared experiences on and off road. To reach the target market, the AudienceGame was designed to be played by consumers viewing Disney Pixar's new family film 'Ratatouille', which was released that weekend across the United Kingdom. Each cinema was given the ability to drive a virtual Volvo XC70 by working together as a group to control the car. Players scored points along the way by navigating through a challenging off-road course of family-themed obstacles, engaging young and old audiences alike.

The results

Table 16.1   MSBNC and Volvo results

MSNBC.com (United States)	VOLVO (UK)
78% played the game	84% played the game
93% want more games in cinemas	68% want more games in cinemas
86% prefer a game to an ad	74% prefer a game to an ad
71% unaided MSNBC brand recall	21% better image of Volvo
75% more likely to use MSNBC	37% more likely to purchase a Volvo

This innovative technology capitalized on three major global trends: socialization of place, advergaming and edutainment, and cinema advertising growth. The world is moving towards participation. This emerging technology embraces group participation, breaking down barriers and enhancing the experience of the audience.

The agency: Launch Factory

The country: South Africa
The brand: Samsung Mobile

The brief

Samsung approached Launch Factory to launch the new X 820 (the world's thinnest phone). Samsung's new Ultra range of mobile phones are the world's slimmest, and most striking when actually held in the hand. So getting them up close and personal with the core target audience of 25–35-year-old style-conscious males was the challenge.

The activity

A busy, trendy bar. A gorgeous girl stands around anxiously, making fleeting eye-contact with a group of guys (who just happen to fit our target profile). After a minute or two fiddling with her mobile phone, she approaches them to ask how long they've been there. Turns out, she's supposed to meet her sister but she's late and thinks her sister (who's even more gorgeous than her but very scatty!) may already have been and gone. She shows the guys (now very interested) a pic of the 'missing' sister on her new mobile.

She then says she may have got the venues mixed up and her sister's probably at the pub around the corner. She's going to pop over there and check but … what if her sister arrives while she's gone? She gives them her business card and asks them to call should her sister arrive in the interim, before rushing off. Guys discuss her (as guys do!) and notice on her card that she's a Personal Trainer.

Five minutes pass and, lo and behold, her sister arrives. The guys – being guys – call the number to be greeted by her voice-mail, thanking them and offering them an incentive to purchase the ultra-stylish Samsung X820!

The results

After engaging with the target consumers on Friday and Saturday nights, the number of calls to the 'voice-mail' was a phenomenal 56 per cent response! From a client perspective this is what Justine Hume (marketing manager, mobile phones) had to say: 'This campaign was a fresh, innovative way to get prospective consumers to interact with our product. We ultimately managed to not only get people talking into, but also about our phones to others. Well done!'

17 Conclusion

Experiential marketing is revolutionizing marketing and business practice around the world. To survive tough competition, to avoid participating in price wars, and to reap the benefits of loyal customers and target audiences driving word of mouth, experiential marketing is the answer. This book has looked at experiential marketing from both a philosophical and practical perspective, allowing readers to come away with a clear understanding of how to brainstorm, strategize, plan, activate and evaluate integrated experiential marketing campaigns.

The context is marketing communications, so we began by looking at how many long-standing approaches to marketing, such as traditional advertising, are losing effectiveness. We demonstrated how experiential marketing and customer experience management are key differentiators in competitive business environments, paving the way for a new economic playground where brands and consumers enjoy interacting together.

Though experiential marketing is a pioneering approach and has therefore been subject to confusion and scepticism, this book has elaborated on the notable shift in business and marketing towards the new era of communications it represents. This book has positioned the big idea, always in the form of live brand experience, at the core of the experiential marketing programme, inspiring its readers to amplify that real two-way communication using a combination of marketing channels.

The forecast for the future of experiential marketing is that its philosophy will filter through every aspect of brand communication with target audiences and there will eventually be a shift towards a predominance of arranged or requested two-way interactions rather than spontaneous ones that bank on target audiences happening to be at the right place at the right time.

For a successful experiential marketing concept to be born, the right research and brainstorming processes are needed. This book explained how to brainstorm top-line ideas using the BETTER creative brainstorm model, present those top-line ideas for review using the IDEA format, and then refine and structure the plan for best results and effective measurement using SET MESSAGE.

As a reader and an experiential marketer, it is up to you to pass on what you have read and share experiential marketing philosophies with other people throughout your organization. You must participate in this exciting three-dimensional revolution where customers, employees and brands work together as partners, mutually satisfying each other's needs.

Appendix 1
Common experiential marketing jargon explained

Amplification   Live brand experiences do not typically reach as many target consumers as advertising does. However, the reach of the complete experiential marketing campaign can exceed the reach of many adverts by incorporating amplification channels into the experiential marketing campaign. This can be achieved by integrating any of the marketing communications channels into the campaign to amplify the big idea, which is focused on two-way interaction in real-time: the live brand experience. Sometimes with a live brand experience that is exciting and newsworthy, free PR and media coverage can be generated, making it a cost-effective solution with broader reach.

Brand advocacy   When consumers spread positive word-of-mouth to other consumers about a brand, thus perpetuating and increasing brand sales.

Brand ambassador   A person who is used to support and endorse a brand and facilitate an interaction between a brand and its target audience.

Brand loyalty   Considered to be one of the ultimate goals of marketing: a consumer's commitment to consistent repurchasing of a brand.

Brand personality A brand's personality is characterized by human personalities. A company will establish a brand as having certain personality traits in order to market the brand to a specified target audience. Examples of a brand's personality could be, for example, silly, wild, courageous and energetic.

Brand-relevant experience   Creating an experience that is appropriate to the brand's personality, values and target audience that will make it memorable to the consumer, hopefully facilitating brand loyalty and brand advocacy.

Bring the brand personality to life   One of the key objectives of experiential marketing is often to bring the brand personality to life. The brand personality gives the brand an identity, character or association to make it memorable and approachable to the consumer. A brand's personality will be like that of a human (ie, lively, funky, sassy, clean). The goal of experiential marketing often is to create an activity that incorporates the personality traits into the experience. If a clothing brand's personality is 'fashionable and adaptable', an experiential activity could involve a fashion show, where members of the target audience get to create different outfits for every time of day and night.

Change brand perception and/or image   Experiential marketing is an ideal approach to use if the objective is to change a brand's image. By carefully researching the target audience and the brand's new positioning, one can create a live brand experience around the brand that will alter the participants' perception of the brand. Amplification channels can be used to amplify the impact of the live brand experience.

Customer experience management The process of strategically managing a customer's entire experience with a product or a company.

Entertaining Target audiences can be entertained by the brand through having fun and engaging with it during an entertaining live brand experience.

Essence of a brand   A distillation of the brand identity and an encapsulation of the brand values. These values form the core of the brand's identity.

Experiential marketing   Experiential marketing is the process of identifying and satisfying customer needs and aspirations, profitably, engaging them through two-way communications that bring brand personalities to life and add value to the target audience.

Face to face   Face to face means engaging the consumer in the same physical location that they are in via face-to-face communication. During a face-to-face live brand experience, the consumer can interact with the brand, its brand ambassadors, and the product, in order to physically participate in the live brand experience.

Feedback   The measurable response and reaction to an experience with the aim of enabling improvements to be made. Feedback can be obtained through mechanisms such as surveys, which can be given via brand ambassadors, brand micro-sites, or as incentives to participate in a live brand experience or enter a competition.

Field marketing   Field marketing is colloquially deemed 'old news marketing', yet is commonly confused with live brand experiences (a more recent and innovative marketing channel). Field marketing is generally sales promotion support and involves individuals passing out flyers or samples, soliciting and merchandising; field marketing does not usually integrate a two-way interaction, which is the essence of the live brand experience.

Footfall/visitors   The number of people who pass through a specified area or the number of visitors who pass through a website or communication platform.

Generate word-of-mouth   Word-of-mouth is another means of amplifying the reach of an experiential campaign. When a consumer engages in a memorable brand experience, they will tell 17 other people about the activity (Jack Morton Worldwide), and those people will tell other people they know, thus exponentially increasing the reach of the campaign. Generating word-of-mouth is often an objective of experiential marketing.

In-house   Different channels of marketing can all be under one agency's roof. For example, an ATL advertising firm can have an in-house experiential marketing team.

Interactive   A means of engagement between the target audience member and the brand, via a two-way interaction.

Live brand experience   A two-way interaction between a brand and its target audience that can be equally successful across events as well as many interactive technologies and platforms that facilitate communication between consumers and brands in real time.

Media-savvy audience   Because traditional advertising has been used for decades and dominated marketing practice, it is becoming an obvious tactic, especially to younger generations who are privy to the ways in which traditional forms of media try to drive purchasing behaviour. Because audiences are becoming media-savvy, there is a need for another, more innovative form of marketing to inspire consumers to keep buying.

Memorable   One of the key components of an experiential campaign that sets it apart from other forms of media: an unforgettable, wonderful experience for the target audience that will result in brand loyalty and brand advocacy.

One-way-communication approach versus two-way-communication approach   A one-way approach is often utilized in traditional media channels (such as television advertising and billboard advertising). It involves talking *at* the target demographics, rather than *with* the target demographics, thus targeting the left side of their brain (a less pleasant experience). Experiential marketing uses a more innovative approach to marketing, which involves a two-way interaction. The two-way interaction is a live brand experience that allows the consumer to interact with the brand and develop a relationship with the brand, hopefully stimulating brand loyalty and brand advocacy. Two-way interaction also allows the brand to understand what its target audience is thinking about and expecting of the brand.

Paradigm of lateral brain function   Contrary to traditional advertising, experiential marketing affects the right side of the brain in that it aims to fulfil certain human drives, such as comfort and pleasure. The right brain is responsible for generating and affecting emotionally charged feelings and intuition, rather than more rationally inspired thoughts (which is how traditional forms of media target their audience).

Personally relevant marketing   Going beyond standard, static online communications to deliver personalized, targeted messaging that builds customer engagement and lifetime value, while increasing sales opportunities and brand loyalty.

Synergy of all five senses (touch, taste, smell, seeing, hearing)   Live brand experiences, especially when delivered face to face, seek to integrate all of the consumers' five senses into the campaign to make the experience of the brand memorable, two-way and interactive. The senses are targeted during the campaign while continuing to make the experience relevant to the brand's personality and values.

Top-line   An idea in its early stages, which is then developed if agreed upon.

White Papers   Published research in fields such as marketing and politics.

Appendix 2
Further reading

Arussey, L (2005) *Passionate and Profitable: Why customer strategies fail and 10 steps to do them right!*, Wiley, Chichester

Emanuel, R (2002) *The Anatomy of Buzz: How to create word of mouth marketing*, Doubleday, New York

Forrest, E and Mizersk, R (1996) *Interactive Marketing: The future present*, McGraw-Hill, Maidenhead

Gardner, S and Jardin, X (2005) *Buzz Marketing with Blogs for Dummies*, Wiley, Chichester

Gupta, S and Lehmann, D R (2005) *Managing Customers as Investments: The strategic value of customers in the long run*, Wharton School Publishing, Philadelphia, PA

Jones, S K (2005) *Creative Strategy in DIRECT & INTERACTIVE Marketing*, 3rd edn, Racom Communications, Chicago, IL

Kirby, J (2005) *Connected Marketing: The viral, buzz and word of mouth revolution*, Butterworth-Heinemann, Oxford

Lendermann, M (2005) *Experience the Message: How experiential marketing is changing the brand world*, Basic Books, New York

McConnell, B and Huba, J (2002) *Creating Customer Evangelists: How loyal customers become a volunteer sales force*, Kaplan, Wokingham

O'Leary, S and Sheehan, K (2008) *Building Buzz to Beat the Big Boys: Word of mouth marketing for small businesses*, Greenwood, Westport, CT

Peter, J P (1999) *Consumer Behaviour and Marketing Strategy*, McGraw-Hill, Maidenhead

Pine, B J II and Gilmore, J H (1999) *The Experience Economy,* Harvard Business Publishing, Boston, MA

Sargeant, A and West, D (2002) *Direct and Interactive Marketing,* Jossey-Bass, San Francisco, PA

Schmitt, B H (1999) *Experiential Marketing: How to get customers to sense, feel, think, act, relate,* Free Press, Glencoe, IL

Schmitt, B H (2003) *Customer Experience Management: A revolutionary approach to connecting with your customers,* Wiley, Chichester

Shaw, C (2003) *The DNA of Customer Experience,* Palgrave Macmillan, Basingstoke

Shaw, C and Ivens, J (2004) *Building Great Customer Experiences,* Palgrave Macmillan, Basingstoke

Smith, S and Wheeler, J (2002) *Managing the Customer Experience: Turning customers into advocates,* FT Press, London

Index